2017 SQA Past Papers with Answers

Higher ENGLISH

2015, 2016 & 2017 Exams

Hodder Gibson Study Skills Advice – General	– page 3
Hodder Gibson Study Skills Advice – Higher English	– page 5
2015 EXAM	– page 7
2016 EXAM	– page 53
2017 EXAM	– page 93
ANSWERS	– page 143

This book contains the official SQA 2015, 2016 and 2017 Exams for Higher English, with associated SQA-approved answers modified from the official marking instructions that accompany the paper.

In addition the book contains study skills advice. This advice has been specially commissioned by Hodder Gibson, and has been written by experienced senior teachers and examiners in line with the Higher for CfE syllabus and assessment outlines. This is not SQA material but has been devised to provide further guidance for Higher examinations.

Hodder Gibson is grateful to the copyright holders, as credited on the final page of the Answer section, for permission to use their material. Every effort has been made to trace the copyright holders and to obtain their permission for the use of copyright material. Hodder Gibson will be happy to receive information allowing us to rectify any error or omission in future editions.

Hachette UK's policy is to use papers that are natural, renewable and recyclable products and made from wood grown in sustainable forests. The logging and manufacturing processes are expected to conform to the environmental regulations of the country of origin.

Orders: please contact Bookpoint Ltd, 130 Park Drive, Milton Park, Abingdon, Oxon OX14 4SE. Telephone: (44) 01235 827720. Fax: (44) 01235 400454. Lines are open 9.00–5.00, Monday to Saturday, with a 24-hour message answering service. Visit our website at www.hoddereducation.co.uk. Hodder Gibson can be contacted direct on: Tel: 0141 333 4650; Fax: 0141 404 8188; email: hoddergibson@hodder.co.uk

This collection first published in 2017 by
Hodder Gibson, an imprint of Hodder Education,
An Hachette UK Company
211 St Vincent Street
Glasgow G2 5QY

Higher 2015, 2016 and 2017 Exam Papers and Answers © Scottish Qualifications Authority. Study Skills section © Hodder Gibson. All rights reserved. Apart from any use permitted under UK copyright law, no part of this publication may be reproduced or transmitted in any form or by any means, electronic or mechanical, including photocopying and recording, or held within any information storage and retrieval system, without permission in writing from the publisher or under licence from the Copyright Licensing Agency Limited. Further details of such licences (for reprographic reproduction) may be obtained from the Copyright Licensing Agency Limited, www.cla.co.uk.

Typeset by Aptara, Inc.

Printed in the UK

A catalogue record for this title is available from the British Library

ISBN: 978-1-5104-2146-2

2 1

2018 2017

Introduction
Study Skills – what you need to know to pass exams!

Pause for thought

Many students might skip quickly through a page like this. After all, we all know how to revise. Do you really though?

Think about this:

"IF YOU ALWAYS DO WHAT YOU ALWAYS DO, YOU WILL ALWAYS GET WHAT YOU HAVE ALWAYS GOT."

Do you like the grades you get? Do you want to do better? If you get full marks in your assessment, then that's great! Change nothing! This section is just to help you get that little bit better than you already are.

There are two main parts to the advice on offer here. The first part highlights fairly obvious things but which are also very important. The second part makes suggestions about revision that you might not have thought about but which WILL help you.

Part 1

DOH! It's so obvious but …

Start revising in good time

Don't leave it until the last minute – this will make you panic.

Make a revision timetable that sets out work time AND play time.

Sleep and eat!

Obvious really, and very helpful. Avoid arguments or stressful things too – even games that wind you up. You need to be fit, awake and focused!

Know your place!

Make sure you know exactly **WHEN and WHERE** your exams are.

Know your enemy!

Make sure you know what to expect in the exam.

How is the paper structured?

How much time is there for each question?

What types of question are involved?

Which topics seem to come up time and time again?

Which topics are your strongest and which are your weakest?

Are all topics compulsory or are there choices?

Learn by DOING!

There is no substitute for past papers and practice papers – they are simply essential! Tackling this collection of papers and answers is exactly the right thing to be doing as your exams approach.

Part 2

People learn in different ways. Some like low light, some bright. Some like early morning, some like evening / night. Some prefer warm, some prefer cold. But everyone uses their BRAIN and the brain works when it is active. Passive learning – sitting gazing at notes – is the most INEFFICIENT way to learn anything. Below you will find tips and ideas for making your revision more effective and maybe even more enjoyable. What follows gets your brain active, and active learning works!

Activity 1 – Stop and review

Step 1

When you have done no more than 5 minutes of revision reading STOP!

Step 2

Write a heading in your own words which sums up the topic you have been revising.

Step 3

Write a summary of what you have revised in no more than two sentences. Don't fool yourself by saying, "I know it, but I cannot put it into words". That just means you don't know it well enough. If you cannot write your summary, revise that section again, knowing that you must write a summary at the end of it. Many of you will have notebooks full of blue/black ink writing. Many of the pages will not be especially attractive or memorable so try to liven them up a bit with colour as you are reviewing and rewriting. **This is a great memory aid, and memory is the most important thing.**

Activity 2 – Use technology!

Why should everything be written down? Have you thought about "mental" maps, diagrams, cartoons and colour to help you learn? And rather than write down notes, why not record your revision material?

What about having a text message revision session with friends? Keep in touch with them to find out how and what they are revising and share ideas and questions.

Why not make a video diary where you tell the camera what you are doing, what you think you have learned and what you still have to do? No one has to see or hear it, but the process of having to organise your thoughts in a formal way to explain something is a very important learning practice.

Be sure to make use of electronic files. You could begin to summarise your class notes. Your typing might be slow, but it will get faster and the typed notes will be easier to read than the scribbles in your class notes. Try to add different fonts and colours to make your work stand out. You can easily Google relevant pictures, cartoons and diagrams which you can copy and paste to make your work more attractive and **MEMORABLE**.

Activity 3 – This is it. Do this and you will know lots!

Step 1

In this task you must be very honest with yourself! Find the SQA syllabus for your subject (www.sqa.org.uk). Look at how it is broken down into main topics called MANDATORY knowledge. That means stuff you MUST know.

Step 2

BEFORE you do ANY revision on this topic, write a list of everything that you already know about the subject. It might be quite a long list but you only need to write it once. It shows you all the information that is already in your long-term memory so you know what parts you do not need to revise!

Step 3

Pick a chapter or section from your book or revision notes. Choose a fairly large section or a whole chapter to get the most out of this activity.

With a buddy, use Skype, Facetime, Twitter or any other communication you have, to play the game "If this is the answer, what is the question?". For example, if you are revising Geography and the answer you provide is "meander", your buddy would have to make up a question like "What is the word that describes a feature of a river where it flows slowly and bends often from side to side?".

Make up 10 "answers" based on the content of the chapter or section you are using. Give this to your buddy to solve while you solve theirs.

Step 4

Construct a wordsearch of at least 10 × 10 squares. You can make it as big as you like but keep it realistic. Work together with a group of friends. Many apps allow you to make wordsearch puzzles online. The words and phrases can go in any direction and phrases can be split. Your puzzle must only contain facts linked to the topic you are revising. Your task is to find 10 bits of information to hide in your puzzle, but you must not repeat information that you used in Step 3. DO NOT show where the words are. Fill up empty squares with random letters. Remember to keep a note of where your answers are hidden but do not show your friends. When you have a complete puzzle, exchange it with a friend to solve each other's puzzle.

Step 5

Now make up 10 questions (not "answers" this time) based on the same chapter used in the previous two tasks. Again, you must find NEW information that you have not yet used. Now it's getting hard to find that new information! Again, give your questions to a friend to answer.

Step 6

As you have been doing the puzzles, your brain has been actively searching for new information. Now write a NEW LIST that contains only the new information you have discovered when doing the puzzles. Your new list is the one to look at repeatedly for short bursts over the next few days. Try to remember more and more of it without looking at it. After a few days, you should be able to add words from your second list to your first list as you increase the information in your long-term memory.

FINALLY! Be inspired...

Make a list of different revision ideas and beside each one write **THINGS I HAVE** tried, **THINGS I WILL** try and **THINGS I MIGHT** try. Don't be scared of trying something new.

And remember – "FAIL TO PREPARE AND PREPARE TO FAIL!"

Higher English

The course

The Higher English course aims to enable you to develop the ability to:

- listen, talk, read and write, as appropriate to purpose, audience and context
- understand, analyse and evaluate texts, including Scottish texts, as appropriate to purpose and audience in the contexts of literature, language and media
- create and produce texts, as appropriate to purpose, audience and context
- apply knowledge and understanding of language.

The basics

The grade you finally get for Higher English depends on three things:

- The two internal Unit Assessments you do in school or college: "Analysis and Evaluation" and "Creation and Production"; these don't count towards the final grade, but you must have passed them before you can get a final grade.
- Your Portfolio of Writing – this is submitted in April for marking by SQA and counts for 30% of your final grade.
- The two exams you sit in May – that's what this book is all about.

The exams

Reading for Understanding, Analysis and Evaluation

- exam time: 1 hour 30 minutes
- total marks: 30
- weighting in final grade: 30%
- what you have to do: read two passages and answer questions about the ideas and use of language in one of them (25 marks), and then compare the ideas in both passages (5 marks)

Critical Reading

- exam time: 1 hour 30 minutes
- total marks: 40 (20 marks for each Section)
- weighting in final grade: 40%
- what you have to do: Section 1: read an extract from one of the Scottish Texts which are set for Higher and answer questions about it; Section 2: write an essay about a work of literature you have studied during your course.

1 Reading for Understanding, Analysis and Evaluation

Questions which ask for understanding (e.g. questions which say "Identify … " or "Explain what … " etc.)

- Keep your answers fairly short and pay attention to the number of marks available.
- Use your own words as far as possible. This means you mustn't just copy chunks from the passage – you have to show that you understand what it means by rephrasing it in your own words.

Questions about language features (e.g. questions which say "Analyse how … ")

- This type of question will ask you to comment on features such as Word Choice, Imagery, Sentence Structure and Tone.
- You should pick out a relevant language feature and make a valid comment about its impact. Try to make your comments as specific as possible and avoid vague comments (such as "It is a good word to use because it gives me a clear picture of what the writer is saying"). Remember that you will get no marks just for picking out a word, image or feature of a sentence structure – it's the comment that counts.
- Some hints:
  - **Word choice:** Always try to pick a single word and then give its connotations, i.e. what it suggests.
  - **Sentence structure:** Don't just name the feature – try to explain what effect it achieves in that particular sentence.
  - **Imagery:** Try to explain what the image means literally and then go on to explain what the writer is trying to say by using that image.
  - **Tone** This is always difficult – a good tip is to imagine the sentence or paragraph being read out loud and try to spot how the words or the structure give it a particular tone.

The last question

- Make sure you follow the instruction about whether you're looking for agreement or disagreement (or possibly both).
- When you start on Passage 2, you will have already answered several questions on Passage 1, so you should know its key ideas quite well; as you read Passage 2, try to spot important ideas in it which are similar or different (depending on the question).
- Stick to **key ideas** and don't include trivial ones; **three** relevant key ideas will usually be enough – your task is to decide what the most significant ones are.

2 Critical Reading

Section 1 – Scottish Text

The most important thing to remember here is that there are two very different types of question to be answered:

- Three or four questions (for a total of 10 marks) which focus entirely on the extract.
- One question (for 10 marks) which requires knowledge of the whole text (or of another poem or short story by the same writer).

The first type of question will often ask you to use the same type of close textual analysis skills you used in the Reading part of your Analysis and Evaluation Unit. The golden rules are to read each question very carefully and do exactly as instructed, and to remember that (just like the "Analysis" questions in the Reading for Understanding, Analysis and Evaluation paper) there are no marks just for picking out a word or a feature – it's the comment that matters.

The second type of question requires you to discuss common features (of theme and/or technique) in the extract and elsewhere in the writer's work. You can answer this question with a series of bullet points or by writing a mini-essay, so choose the approach you feel most comfortable with.

Finally, a bit of advice for the Scottish Text question: when you see the extract in the exam paper, don't get too confident just because you recognise it (you certainly should recognise it if you've studied properly!). And even if you've answered questions on it before, remember that the questions in the exam are likely to be different, so stay alert.

Section 2 – Critical Essay

A common mistake is to rely too heavily on ideas and whole paragraphs you have used in practice essays and try to use them for the question you have chosen in the exam. The trick is to come to the exam with lots of ideas and thoughts about at least one of the texts you have studied and use these to tackle the question you choose from the exam paper. You mustn't use the exam question as an excuse to trot out an answer you've prepared in advance.

Structure

Every good essay has a structure, but there is no "correct" structure, no magic formula that the examiners are looking for. It's **your** essay, so structure it the way **you** want. As long as you're answering the question all the way through, then you'll be fine.

Relevance

Be relevant to the question **all of the time** – not just in the first and last paragraphs.

Central concerns

Try to make sure your essay shows that you have thought about and understood the central concerns of the text, i.e. what it's "about" – the ideas and themes the writer is exploring in the text.

Quotation

In poetry and drama essays, you're expected to quote from the text, but never fall into the trap of learning a handful of quotations and forcing them all into the essay regardless of the question you're answering. In prose essays, quotation is much less important, and you can show your knowledge more effectively by referring in detail to what happens in key sections of the novel or the short story.

Techniques

You are expected to show understanding of how various literary techniques work within a text, but simply naming them will not get you marks, and structuring your essay around techniques rather than around relevant ideas in the text is not a good idea.

Good luck!

Remember that the rewards for passing Higher English are well worth it! Your pass will help you get the future you want for yourself. In the exam, be confident in your own ability. If you're not sure how to answer a question, trust your instincts and just give it a go anyway – keep calm and don't panic! GOOD LUCK!

HIGHER
2015

National Qualifications 2015

X724/76/11

**English
Reading for Understanding,
Analysis and Evaluation — Text**

FRIDAY, 15 MAY
9:00 AM – 10:30 AM

Total marks — 30

Read the passages carefully and then attempt ALL questions, which are printed on a separate sheet.

HIGHER ENGLISH   **10**   SQA EXAM PAPER 2015

The following two passages consider the negative impact of intensive farming.

Passage 1

Read the passage below and then attempt questions 1 to 8.

In the first passage, Isabel Oakeshott gives a disturbing account of her visit to Central Valley, California, an area where intensive farming is big business.

On a cold, bright November day I stood among a million almond trees and breathed in the sweet air. I was in Central Valley, California, in an orchard stretching over 700,000 acres. Before me was a vision of how the British countryside may look one day. Beyond the almond orchards were fields of pomegranates, pistachios, grapes and apricots. Somewhere in the distance were almost
5   two million dairy cows, producing six billion dollars' worth of milk a year.

It may sound like the Garden of Eden but it is a deeply disturbing place. Among the perfectly aligned rows of trees and cultivated crops are no birds, no butterflies, no beetles or shrubs. There is not a single blade of grass or a hedgerow, and the only bees arrive by lorry, transported across the United States. The bees are hired by the day to fertilise the blossom, part of a
10   multibillion-dollar industry that has sprung up to do a job that nature once did for free.

As for the cows, they last only two or three years, ten-to-fifteen years less than their natural life span. Crammed into barren pens on tiny patches of land, they stand around listlessly waiting to be fed, milked or injected with antibiotics. Through a combination of selective breeding, artificial diets and growth hormones designed to maximise milk production, they are pushed so
15   grotesquely beyond their natural limit that they are soon worn out. In their short lives they never see grass.

Could the British countryside ever look like this? If current trends continue, the answer is yes. Farming in Britain is at a crossroads, threatened by a wave of intensification from America. The first mega-dairies and mega-piggeries are already here. Bees are disappearing, with serious
20   implications for harvests. Hedgerows, vital habitats for wildlife, have halved since the Second World War. The countryside is too sterile to support many native birds. In the past forty years the population of tree sparrows has fallen by 97%.

With an eye to the future, Owen Paterson, the UK environment secretary, has been urging families to buy British food. Choosing to buy fewer imports would reduce the relentless pressure
25   British farmers are under to churn out more for less. Paterson's vision is of a more eco-friendly way of eating, based on locally-produced, seasonal fruit and vegetables and, crucially, British meat.

But, as I discovered when I began looking into the way food is produced, increasingly powerful forces are pulling us in the opposite direction. We have become addicted to cheap meat, fish
30   and dairy products from supply lines that stretch across the globe. On the plus side, it means that supermarkets can sell whole chickens for as little as £3. Things that were once delicacies, such as smoked salmon, are now as cheap as chips. On the downside, cheap chicken and farmed fish are fatty and flaccid. Industrially reared farm animals — 50 billion of them a year worldwide — are kept permanently indoors, treated like machines and pumped with drugs.

35   My journey to expose the truth, to investigate the dirty secret about the way cheap food is produced, took me from the first mega-dairies and piggeries in Britain to factory farms in France, China, Mexico, and North and South America. I talked to people on the front line of the global food industry: treadmill farmers trying to produce more with less. I also talked to their neighbours — people experiencing the side effects of industrial farms. Many had stories about
40   their homes plummeting in value, the desecration of lovely countryside, the disappearance of wildlife and serious health problems linked to pollution.

Page two

SQA EXAM PAPER 2015   **11**   HIGHER ENGLISH

I wanted to challenge the widespread assumption that factory farming is the only way to produce food that everyone can afford. My investigation started in Central Valley, California, because it demonstrates the worst-case scenario — a nightmarish vision of the future for parts of
45 Britain if current practices continue unchecked. It is a five-hour drive south of San Francisco and I knew I was getting close when I saw a strange yellowish-grey smog on the horizon. It looks like the sort of pollution that hangs over big cities, but it comes from the dairies. California's bovine population produces as much sewage as 90 million people, with terrible effects on air quality. The human population is sparse, but the air can be worse than in Los Angeles on a
50 smoggy day.

Exploring the area by car, it was not long before I saw my first mega-dairy, an array of towering, open-sided shelters over muddy pens. The stench of manure was overwhelming — not the faintly sweet, earthy smell of cowpats familiar from the British countryside, but a nauseating reek bearing no relation to digested grass. I saw farms every couple of miles, all with several
55 thousand cows surrounded by mud, corrugated iron and concrete.

It may seem hard to imagine such a scene in Britain but it is not far-fetched. Proposals for an 8,000 cow mega-dairy in Lincolnshire, based on the American model, were thrown out after a public outcry. On local radio the man behind the scheme claimed that "cows do not belong in fields". It will be the first of many similar fights, because dairies are expanding and moving
60 indoors. The creep of industrial agriculture in Britain has taken place largely unnoticed, perhaps because so much of it happens behind closed doors. The British government calls it "sustainable intensification". Without fuss or fanfare, farm animals have slowly disappeared from fields and moved into hangars and barns.

Adapted from an article in The Sunday Times newspaper.

Passage 2

Read the passage below and attempt question 9. While reading, you may wish to make notes on the main ideas and/or highlight key points in the passage.

In the second passage, Audrey Eyton considers the reasons for the introduction of intensive farming and explains why it could be viewed as a mistake.

The founding fathers of intensive farming can claim, "It seemed a good idea at the time!" Indeed it did, in Britain, half a century ago. The post-war government swung into action with zeal, allocating unprecedented funds to agricultural research. The outcome was that the mixed farm, where animals grazed in the fields, was replaced by the huge factories we see today.
5 The aim in confining animals indoors was to cut costs. It succeeded. Indoors, one or two workers can "look after" hundreds of penned or tethered pigs, or a hundred thousand chickens. Great economies were made and thousands of farm workers lost their jobs. This new policy of cheap meat, eggs and cheese for everyone was completely in tune with the national mood, as Britain ripped up its ration books. It was also in tune with nutritional thinking, as nutritionists at
10 that time thought greater consumption of animal protein would remedy all dietary problems.

So factory farming marched on. And became more and more intensive. Where first there were one or two laying hens in a cage, eventually there became five in the same small space. The broiler chicken sheds expanded to cram in vast acres of birds. Many beef cattle were confined in buildings and yards. Until mad cow disease emerged, such animals were fed all kinds of
15 organic matter as cheap food. In the UK dairy cows still spend their summers in the fields, but many of their offspring are reared in the cruelty of intensive veal crate systems.

Page three

The aim of those early advocates of intensive farming was "fast food" — fast from birth to table. Again, they succeeded. Chicken, once an occasional treat, now the most popular meat in Britain, owes its low price largely to the short life of the bird. Today's broiler chicken has
20 become the fastest growing creature on earth: from egg to take-away in seven weeks. Most farm animals now have less than half of their pre-war lifespan. Either they are worn out from overproduction of eggs or milk, or have been bred and fed to reach edible size in a few short weeks or months.

But meat, eggs and dairy products have indeed become cheap, affordable even to the poor. All
25 of which made nutritionists exceedingly happy — until they discovered that their mid-century predecessors had made a mighty blunder. Before intensive farming brought cheap meat and dairy products to our tables, man obtained most of his calories from cereal crops and vegetables. The meat with which he supplemented this diet had a much lower fat content than intensively produced products. Now, however, degenerative diseases like coronary heart disease
30 and several types of cancer have been linked to our increased consumption of fatty foods. War-time Britons, on their measly ration of meat and one ounce of cheese a week, were much healthier.

With this knowledge, the only possible moral justification for intensive farming of animals collapses. The cheap animal production policy doesn't help the poor. It kills them. In addition,
35 the chronic suffering endured by animals in many intensive systems is not just a sentimental concern of the soft-hearted. It is a scientifically proven fact. Cracks are beginning to show in our long-practised animal apartheid system, in which we have convinced ourselves, against all evidence, that the animals we eat are less intelligent, less in need of space and exercise than are those we pat, ride or watch.

40 It is also a scientifically proven fact that intensive farming has caused the loss of hedgerows and wildlife sustained by that habitat, has polluted waterways, decimated rural employment and caused the loss of traditional small farms. We need to act in the interests of human health. We need to show humane concern for animals. We need to preserve what remains of the countryside by condemning the practice of intensive farming. We need to return the animals to
45 the fields, and re-adopt the environmentally friendly, humane and healthy system we had and lost: the small mixed farm.

Adapted from an article in The Observer newspaper.

[END OF TEXT]

National Qualifications 2015

X724/76/21

English
Reading for Understanding, Analysis and Evaluation — Questions

FRIDAY, 15 MAY
9:00 AM – 10:30 AM

Total marks — 30

Attempt ALL questions.

Write your answers clearly in the answer booklet provided. In the answer booklet you must clearly identify the question number you are attempting.

Use **blue** or **black** ink.

Before leaving the examination room you must give your answer booklet to the Invigilator; if you do not, you may lose all the marks for this paper.

HIGHER ENGLISH **14** SQA EXAM PAPER 2015

MARKS

Attempt ALL questions
Total marks — 30

1. Read lines 1—5.

   Identify any **two** positive aspects of Central Valley, California, which are conveyed in these lines. Use your own words in your answer. **2**

2. Read lines 6—10.

   By referring to at least **two** examples, analyse how the writer's use of language creates a negative impression of Central Valley. **4**

3. Read lines 11—16.

   By referring to both word choice **and** sentence structure, analyse how the writer makes clear her disapproval of dairy farming methods used in Central Valley. **4**

4. Read lines 17—19.

   Explain the function of these lines in the development of the writer's argument. You should make close reference to the passage in your answer. **2**

5. Read lines 23—34.

   In your own words, summarise the differences between UK Government food policy and consumer wishes. **4**

6. Read lines 35—41.

   Analyse how both imagery **and** sentence structure are used in these lines to convey the writer's criticism of industrial farming. **4**

7. Read lines 42—55.

   Explain how the writer continues the idea that the Central Valley dairy farming is "nightmarish". Use your own words in your answer. You should make **three** key points. **3**

8. Read lines 56—63.

   Evaluate the effectiveness of the final paragraph as a conclusion to the writer's criticism of industrial farming. **2**

Question on both passages

9. Look at both passages.

   Both writers express their views about intensive farming.

   Identify **three** key areas on which they agree. You should support the points you make by referring to important ideas in both passages.

   You may answer this question in continuous prose or in a series of developed bullet points. **5**

[END OF QUESTION PAPER]

Page two

National Qualifications 2015

X724/76/12

**English
Critical Reading**

FRIDAY, 15 MAY

10:50 AM – 12:20 PM

Total marks — 40

SECTION 1 — Scottish Text — 20 marks

Read an extract from a Scottish text you have previously studied and attempt the questions.

Choose ONE text from either

Part A — Drama   Pages 2–11
or
Part B — Prose   Pages 12–21
or
Part C — Poetry   Pages 22–33

Attempt ALL the questions for your chosen text.

SECTION 2 — Critical Essay — 20 marks

Attempt ONE question from the following genres — Drama, Prose Fiction, Prose Non-fiction, Poetry, Film and Television Drama, or Language.

Your answer must be on a different genre from that chosen in Section 1.

You should spend approximately 45 minutes on each Section.

Write your answers clearly in the answer booklet provided. In the answer booklet you must clearly identify the question number you are attempting.

Use **blue** or **black** ink.

Before leaving the examination room you must give your answer booklet to the Invigilator; if you do not, you may lose all the marks for this paper.

HIGHER ENGLISH **16** SQA EXAM PAPER 2015

SECTION 1 — SCOTTISH TEXT — 20 marks

Choose ONE text from Drama, Prose or Poetry.

Read the text extract carefully and then attempt ALL the questions for your chosen text.

You should spend about 45 minutes on this Section.

PART A — SCOTTISH TEXT — DRAMA

Text 1 — Drama

If you choose this text you may not attempt a question on Drama in Section 2.

Read the extract below and then attempt the following questions.

The Slab Boys by John Byrne

This extract is taken from Act 2 of the play. Phil has been dismissed from his job.

(*Enter PHIL.*)

	SPANKY:	I thought you were away?
	PHIL:	I went along for my wages . . . doll said she gave them to Jack.
	JACK:	The monkey's got them . . .
5	SPANKY:	Catch. (*Flings packet to PHIL.*) 'S that you off, Jack-knife? Not fancy a hot poultice before you go?
	JACK:	If you need a lift home, Alan, let me know . . . I'll try and arrange something . . .
	ALAN:	Thanks.
10	(*Exit JACK.*)	
	SPANKY:	(*To PHIL, who is opening his wage packet*) Your books?
	PHIL:	Yeh . . . P45, the lot . . . (*Reads document:*) "Non-Contributory Pension Scheme" . . . what's that?
	ALAN:	It means you haven't paid directly into . . .
15	PHIL:	Shuttit, you! I'm talking to my friend. Well?
	SPANKY:	How should I know? I've got all these dishes to wash! Can you not give us a hand? There's hundreds of them.
	PHIL:	You're forgetting something, Spanky. I don't work here any more.
	SPANKY:	You never did, Phil.
20	PHIL:	Less of the sarcasm . . . (*Sarcastically*) Slab Boy.
	SPANKY:	At least I still am one.
	PHIL:	Yeh . . . how come? Me and Hector get the heave and you're still here washing dishes safe and secure. How d'you manage it, eh?
	SPANKY:	Going to get out of my road? I've got work to do . . .
25	PHIL:	Work? Has Noddy there been getting to you?
	SPANKY:	Why don't you can it, Phil? Me and the boy wants to get cleared up.

Page two

	PHIL:	Aw . . . it's "me and the boy" now, is it?

PHIL: Aw . . . it's "me and the boy" now, is it?

SPANKY: Yeh . . . what of it?

PHIL: I think I'm going to be sick.

30 SPANKY: Well, don't hang over the shades, there's gum in them already . . .

(*PHIL grabs him. They confront one another. Enter CURRY.*)

CURRY: Still here, McCann? You can go any time, you know.

PHIL: I'm waiting for a phone call.

CURRY: Only urgent personal calls allowed . . .

35 PHIL: This is urgent. I'm waiting for word from the hospital.

CURRY: What's up . . . someone in the family ill?

PHIL: It's my maw.

CURRY: Oh, yes, of course. Were the lacerations severe? It can do a great deal of damage, plate glass . . .

40 PHIL: What?

CURRY: Plate glass . . . the stuff they have in shop windows.

PHIL: What d'you know about shop windows? Who told you about it?

CURRY: There was a bit in today's *Paisley Express* . . . "Ferguslie Park Woman in Store Window Accident" . . .

45 PHIL: It wasn't an accident. She meant to do it.

CURRY: Eh? But the paper said your mother was thrown through the window by a passing car . . .

PHIL: Well, they got it wrong, didn't they? There was a car there but it wasn't passing . . . it was parked. What she done was take a header off the roof . . .
50 straight through the Co. window . . . simple.

CURRY: From the roof of a car? She must've been badly injured.

PHIL: Not a scratch. They say it was the angle she jumped off the roof of the motor.

CURRY: Good God, it must've been a miracle.

55 PHIL: Nope . . . a Ford Prefect.

Page three

HIGHER ENGLISH **18** SQA EXAM PAPER 2015

MARKS

Questions

1. Look at lines 1—15.

   Explain fully the contrast in these lines between the attitude of Jack and Phil towards Alan.   **2**

2. Look at lines 16—31.

   By referring to at least two examples, analyse how the tension between Phil and Spanky is made clear.   **4**

3. Look at lines 32—55.

   By referring to at least two examples, analyse how language is used to convey the feelings of Phil and/or Curry.   **4**

4. In this extract, various aspects of Phil's character are revealed through humour. By referring to this extract and elsewhere in the play, discuss how humour is used to develop Phil's character.   **10**

Page four

SQA EXAM PAPER 2015 **19** HIGHER ENGLISH

Page five

[OPEN OUT FOR QUESTIONS]

DO NOT WRITE ON THIS PAGE

HIGHER ENGLISH **20** SQA EXAM PAPER 2015

OR

Text 2 — Drama

If you choose this text you may not attempt a question on Drama in Section 2.

Read the extract below and then attempt the following questions.

***The Cheviot, the Stag and the Black, Black Oil* by John McGrath**

DUKE: The Queen needs men, and as always, she looks to the North. My Commissioner, Mr Loch, informs me that the response so far has been disappointing.

Enter LOCH, *now an old man.*

5 LOCH: Disappointing? A disgrace. In the whole county of Sutherland, not one man has volunteered.

DUKE: I know you to be loyal subjects of the Queen. I am prepared to reward your loyalty. Every man who enlists today will be given a bounty of six golden sovereigns from my own private purse. Now if you will all step up in an
10 orderly manner, Mr Loch will take your names and give you the money.

The DUKE *sits. Silence. Nobody moves. The* DUKE *stands angrily.*

DUKE: Damn it, do you want the Mongol hordes to come sweeping across Europe, burning your houses, driving you into the sea? (LOCH *fidgets*.) What are you fidgeting for Loch? Have you no pride in this great democracy that we
15 English — er — British have brought to you? Do you want the cruel Tsar of Russia installed in Dunrobin Castle? Step forward.

Silence. Nobody moves.

DUKE: For this disgraceful, cowardly conduct, I demand an explanation.

Short silence. OLD MAN *stands up in audience.*

20 OLD MAN: I am sorry for the response your Grace's proposals are meeting here, but there is a cause for it. It is the opinion of this country that should the Tsar of Russia take possession of Dunrobin Castle, we could not expect worse treatment at his hands than we have experienced at the hands of your family for the last fifty years. We have no country to fight for. You robbed us of our country and
25 gave it to the sheep. Therefore, since you have preferred sheep to men, let sheep now defend you.

ALL: Baa-aa.

The DUKE *and* LOCH *leave.* SOLDIER *beats retreat.*

MC: One man only was enlisted at this meeting. No sooner was he away at Fort
30 George than his house was pulled down, his wife and family turned out, and put in a hut from which an old female pauper was carried a few days before to the churchyard.

Out of thirty-three battalions sent to the Crimea, only three were Highland.

But this was only a small set-back for the recruiters. These parts were still
35 raided for men; almost as fast as they cleared them off the land, they later recruited them into the Army. The old tradition of loyal soldiering was fostered and exploited with careful calculation.

Page six

SQA EXAM PAPER 2015   **21**   HIGHER ENGLISH

MARKS

Questions

5. Look at lines 1—18.

   The Duke uses a variety of tones in his speeches to the people in these lines. By referring to at least two examples, analyse how language is used to create different tones.

   4

6. Look at lines 17—27.

   Analyse how both the stage directions and dialogue convey the local people's defiance of the Duke.

   4

7. Look at lines 29—37.

   Explain how the MC's speech brings this section of the play to an ironic conclusion.

   2

8. Discuss how McGrath develops the theme of change in this extract and elsewhere in the play.

   10

[Turn over

Page seven

HIGHER ENGLISH **22** SQA EXAM PAPER 2015

OR

Text 3 — Drama

If you choose this text you may not attempt a question on Drama in Section 2.

Read the extract below and then attempt the following questions.

Men Should Weep by Ena Lamont Stewart

In this extract from Act 3, Jenny is paying a visit to Maggie and John's tenement home after a period of absence.

	Lily:	Jenny, whit're ye getting at?
	Jenny:	Mammy seems tae think they're letting Bertie hame; but they're no. *No here.* No tae this. Mammy, ye've tae see the Corporation for a Cooncil hoose.
5	Maggie:	A Cooncil house! A Cooncil hoose! Yer daddy's been up tae that lot til he's seek scunnert. Ye've tae wait yer turn in the queue.
	Jenny:	But if they kent aboot Bertie . . .
	Lily:	Is this whit brought ye back, Jenny?
10	Jenny:	It's whit gied me the courage tae come. Least . . . it was ma daddy's face . . . in the water; (*more to herself than the others*) there wis lights shimmerin on the blackness . . . it kind o slinks alang slow, a river, in the night. I was meanin tae let it tak me alang wi it.

Maggie gives a gasp.

	Maggie:	Whit kind o talk is this, Jenny? Did ye no think o us. Yer daddy an me?
15	Jenny:	Think o ye? Oh aye, Mammy, I thought o ye. But thinkin jist made me greet. I was that ashamed o masel . . . Isa and me, we were that rotten tae ye, the things we said.
	Maggie:	That's a bye, Jenny.
20	Jenny:	Naethin's ever *bye*, Mammy; it's a there, like a photy-album in yer heid . . . I kept seein ma daddy, the way he used tae sing tae me when I wis wee; I seen him holdin ma bare feet in his hands tae warm them, an feedin me bread an hot milk oot o a blue cup. (*Pause*) I don't know where you were, Mammy.
	Lily:	Ben the back room wi the midwife, likely. (*Pause*) It's as weel ye came tae yer senses; yon's no the way tae tak oot o yer troubles; a river. But ye're daein fine noo? Ye merriet?
25	Jenny:	No.
	Lily:	Oh. Livin in sin, as they ca it these days, eh?
	Jenny:	(*suddenly flaring up*) Aye, if ye want tae ca it sin! I don't. The man I'm livin wi is kind, an generous.
	Lily:	Oh aye. We can see that. We've had an eye-fu o yer wages o sin.
30	Maggie:	(*mournful*) Aw Jenny. I wisht ye'd earned it.
	Lily:	(*coarse laugh*) Oh, she'll hae earned it, Maggie. On her back.
	Maggie:	*Lily!*
	Lily:	So the Bible's a wrang, is it? The wages o sin's nae deith, it's fancy hair-dos an a swanky coat an pur silk stockins.

Page eight

35	Jenny:	You seem tae ken yer Bible, Auntie Lily. I never pretended tae. But I'm happy, an I'm makin *him* happy. We've a nice wee flat in a clean district, wi trees an wee gardens.
	Lily:	A wee love-nest oot west! Great! Juist great — till yer tired business man gets tired o you an ye're oot on yer ear.
40	Jenny:	Well, ye hevnae changed, Auntie Lily. I've got tae laugh at you.
	Lily:	Laugh awa. I'm no mindin. I've kept ma self-respect.
	Jenny:	Aye. An that's aboot a ye've got.
	Maggie:	Oh, stop it! Stop it! (*Her hands to her head*) I wis that happy . . .
45	Jenny:	Mammy, I'm sorry. We'll sit doon properly an talk. (*She draws a couple of chairs together, deliberately excluding Lily who moves off a little, but keeps within ear-shot and stands, back resting against the table — or the sideboard — watching.*) I've got plans for you.
	Maggie:	Plans?
	Jenny:	Aye. For getting yous a oot o this.
50	Maggie:	Och Jenny, pet; you wis aye fu o dreams.
	Lily:	Aye. Dreams. Fairy-tales. She went awa an impident wee bizzom an she's come back on Christmas Eve, kiddin on she's a fairy wi a magic wand.
55	Jenny:	(*She doesn't even look at Lily*) Listen, Mammy. We canna wait for a hoose frae the cooncil, it'll tak too lang; but mind! Ye've tae get ma daddy tae speak tae them. (*Maggie nods*) So, while ye're waitin, ye're goin tae flit tae a rented hoose.
	Maggie:	Jenny, ye need a lot o money tae flit!
60	Jenny:	I've got that. (*She opens her handbag and produces a roll of notes that makes Maggie's eyes bulge. She gasps.*) There's plenty for the flittin and the key money forbye.

John comes in. He stops at the sight of Jenny and at first his face lights up: then his lips tighten.

Page nine

MARKS

Questions

9. Look at lines 1—21.

   Explain two of Jenny's reasons for visiting the family home.   2

10. Look at lines 22—42.

   Analyse how Lily and Jenny's differing attitudes are shown.   4

11. Look at lines 43—62.

   Analyse the dramatic impact of at least two of the stage directions in these lines.   4

12. By referring to this extract and elsewhere in the play, discuss how Jenny's growing maturity is made clear.   10

Page ten

SQA EXAM PAPER 2015 25 HIGHER ENGLISH

[OPEN OUT FOR QUESTIONS]

DO NOT WRITE ON THIS PAGE

Page eleven

HIGHER ENGLISH   26   SQA EXAM PAPER 2015

SECTION 1 — SCOTTISH TEXT — 20 marks

Choose ONE text from Drama, Prose or Poetry.

Read the text extract carefully and then attempt ALL the questions for your chosen text.

You should spend about 45 minutes on this Section.

PART B — SCOTTISH TEXT — PROSE

Text 1 — Prose

If you choose this text you may not attempt a question on Prose in Section 2.

Read the extract below and then attempt the following questions.

Mother and Son by Iain Crichton Smith

"It isn't my fault I haven't." He spoke wearily. The old interminable argument was beginning again: he always made fresh attacks but as often retired defeated. He stood up suddenly and paced about the room as if he wanted to overawe her with his untidy hair, his thick jersey, and long wellingtons.

5 "You know well enough," he shouted, "why I haven't my day's work. It's because you've been in bed there for ten years now. Do you *want* me to take a job? I'll take a job tomorrow . . . if you'll only say!" He was making the same eternal argument and the same eternal concession: "If you'll only say." And all the time he knew she would never say, and she knew that he would never take any action.

10 "Why, you'd be no good in a job. The manager would always be coming to show you what you had done wrong, and you'd get confused with all those strange faces and they'd laugh at you." Every time she spoke these words the same brutal pain stabbed him. His babyish eyes would be smitten by a hellish despair, would lose all their hope, and cloud over with the pain of the mute, suffering animal. Time and time again he would say to
15 her when she was feeling better and in a relatively humane mood: "I'm going to get a job where the other fellows are!" and time and time again, with the unfathomable and unknowable cunning of the woman, she would strike his confidence dead with her hateful words. Yes, he was timid. He admitted it to himself, he hated himself for it, but his cowardice still lay there waiting for him, particularly in the dark nights of his mind when
20 the shadow lay as if by a road, watching him, tripping behind him, changing its shape, till the sun came to shine on it and bring its plausible explanations. He spoke again, passing his hand wearily over his brow as if he were asking for her pity.

"Why should anybody laugh at me? They don't laugh at the other chaps. Everybody makes mistakes. I could learn as quickly as any of them. Why, I used to do his lessons for
25 Norman Slater." He looked up eagerly at her as if he wanted her to corroborate. But she only looked at him impatiently, that bitter smile still upon her face.

"Lessons aren't everything. You aren't a mechanic. You can't do anything with your hands. Why don't you hurry up with that tea? Look at you. Fat good you'd be at a job."

He still sat despairingly leaning near the fire, his head on his hands. He didn't even hear
30 the last part of her words. True, he wasn't a mechanic. He never could understand how things worked. This ignorance and inaptitude of his puzzled himself. It was not that he wasn't intelligent: it was as if something had gone wrong in his childhood, some lack of interest in lorries and aeroplanes and mechanisms, which hardened into a wall beyond which he could not go through — paradise lay yonder.

Page twelve

SQA EXAM PAPER 2015   27   HIGHER ENGLISH

MARKS

35 He reached up for the tea absent-mindedly and poured hot water into the tea-pot. He watched it for a while with a sad look on his face, watched the fire leaping about it as if it were a soul in hell. The cups were white and undistinguished and he felt a faint nausea as he poured the tea into them. He reached out for the tray, put the tea-cup and a plate with bread and jam on it, and took it over to the bed. His mother sat up and took the
40 tray from him, settling herself laboriously back against the pillows. She looked at it and said:

"Why didn't you wash this tray? Can't you see it's all dirty round the edges?" He stood there stolidly for a moment, not listening, watching her frail, white-clad body, and her spiteful, bitter face. He ate little but drank three cups of tea.

Questions

13. Look at lines 1—22.

By referring to at least two examples, analyse how language reveals the nature of the relationship between mother and son.   **4**

14. Look at lines 27—28.

Identify the tone of the mother's words and analyse how this tone is created.   **3**

15. Look at lines 29—38.

By referring to at least two examples, analyse how language is used to convey the son's reaction to his mother's words.   **3**

16. By referring to this extract and to at least one other story, discuss how Iain Crichton Smith uses contrasting characters to explore theme.   **10**

[Turn over

Page thirteen

HIGHER ENGLISH   28   SQA EXAM PAPER 2015

OR

Text 2 — Prose

If you choose this text you may not attempt a question on Prose in Section 2.

Read the extract below and then attempt the following questions.

The Wireless Set by George Mackay Brown

One afternoon in the late summer of that year the island postman cycled over the hill road to Tronvik with a yellow corner of telegram sticking out of his pocket.

He passed the shop and the manse and the schoolhouse, and went in a wavering line up the track to Hugh's croft. The wireless was playing music inside, Joe Loss and his
5   orchestra.

Betsy had seen him coming and was standing in the door.

"Is there anybody with you?" said the postman.

"What way would there be?" said Betsy. "Hugh's at the lobsters."

"There should be somebody with you," said the postman.

10   "Give me the telegram," said Betsy, and held out her hand. He gave it to her as if he was a miser parting with a twenty-pound note.

She went inside, put on her spectacles, and ripped open the envelope with brisk fingers. Her lips moved a little, silently reading the words.

Then she turned to the dog and said, "Howie's dead." She went to the door. The
15   postman was disappearing on his bike round the corner of the shop and the missionary was hurrying towards her up the path.

She said to him, "It's time the peats were carted."

"This is a great affliction, you poor soul," said Mr. Sinclair the missionary. "This is bad news indeed. Yet he died for his country. He made the great sacrifice. So that we could
20   all live in peace, you understand."

Betsy shook her head. "That isn't it at all," she said. "Howie's sunk with torpedoes. That's all I know."

They saw old Hugh walking up from the shore with a pile of creels on his back and a lobster in each hand. When he came to the croft he looked at Betsy and the missionary
25   standing together in the door. He went into the outhouse and set down the creels and picked up an axe he kept for chopping wood.

Betsy said to him, "How many lobsters did you get?"

He moved past her and the missionary without speaking into the house. Then from inside he said, "I got two lobsters."

30   "I'll break the news to him," said Mr. Sinclair.

From inside the house came the noise of shattering wood and metal.

"He knows already," said Betsy to the missionary. "Hugh knows the truth of a thing generally before a word is uttered."

Hugh moved past them with the axe in his hand.

35   "I got six crabs forby," he said to Betsy, "but I left them in the boat."

He set the axe down carefully inside the door of the outhouse. Then he leaned against the wall and looked out to sea for a long while.

Page fourteen

SQA EXAM PAPER 2015   29   HIGHER ENGLISH

MARKS

"I got thirteen eggs," said Betsy. "One more than yesterday. That old Rhode Islander's laying like mad."

40 The missionary was slowly shaking his head in the doorway. He touched Hugh on the shoulder and said, "My poor man — "

Hugh turned and said to him, "It's time the last peats were down from the hill. I'll go in the morning first thing. You'll be needing a cart-load for the Manse."

The missionary, awed by such callousness, walked down the path between the cabbages
45 and potatoes. Betsy went into the house. The wireless stood, a tangled wreck, on the dresser. She brought from the cupboard a bottle of whisky and glasses. She set the kettle on the hook over the fire and broke the peats into red and yellow flame with a poker. Through the window she could see people moving towards the croft from all over the valley. The news had got round. The mourners were gathering.

50 Old Hugh stood in the door and looked up at the drift of clouds above the cliff. "Yes," he said, "I'm glad I set the creels where I did, off Yesnaby. They'll be sheltered there once the wind gets up."

"That white hen," said Betsy, "has stopped laying. It's time she was in the pot, if you ask me."

Questions

17. Look at lines 1—5.

Explain how Mackay Brown creates both a sense of community life and the role of the wireless set within it.   **2**

18. Look at lines 6—22.

(a) By referring to lines 6—15, analyse how the postman's attitude to Betsy is revealed.   **2**

(b) By referring to lines 16—22, analyse how language is used to convey the different reactions of the missionary and Betsy to the news.   **2**

19. In lines 23—54, Mackay Brown reveals a contrast between the couple's real feelings and the missionary's perception of how they feel.

By referring to at least two examples from these lines, analyse how the contrast is revealed.   **4**

20. In his writing, Mackay Brown explores the relationship between the island/small mainland community and the outside world. By referring to this extract and at least one other story by Mackay Brown, discuss how he does this.   **10**

[Turn over

Page fifteen

HIGHER ENGLISH   **30**   SQA EXAM PAPER 2015

OR

Text 3 — Prose

If you choose this text you may not attempt a question on Prose in Section 2.

Read the extract below and then attempt the following questions.

The Trick Is To Keep Breathing by Janice Galloway

In this extract, Joy is struggling to cope after the death of her partner, Michael.

Look

all I wanted was to be civilised and polite. I wanted to be no trouble. I wanted to be brave and discreet. This had to be the final stage of the endurance test and all I had to do was last out. I thought I was Bunyan's Pilgrim and Dorothy in The Wizard of Oz. But

5 the lasting out was terrible. I made appointments with the doctor and he gave me pills to tide me over when I got anxious. I got anxious when they didn't tide me over into anything different. He gave me more pills. I kept going to work. I was no nearer Kansas or the Celestial City. Then

I started smelling Michael's aftershave in the middle of the night. I would go to bed and

10 there it was, in a cloud all round my head. I thought if I could smell his aftershave he must be around somewhere. I saw him in cars, across the street, in buses, roaring past on strange motorbikes, drifting by the glass panel of my classroom door. I read his horoscope. How could he be having a difficult phase with money if he was dead? Of course he wasn't *dead*: just hiding. At night I sunk my face into his clothes and howled

15 at the cloth. A magazine article said it was fairly common and not as unhealthy as you'd think. Then I would go to bed and wait for the slow seep of aftershave through the ether. I knew he wasn't just a carcass liquefying in a wooden box but an invisible presence hovering in a cloud of Aramis above my bed. I also suspected I was lying. When I found the bottle, tipped on its side and leaking along the rim I knew for sure. I had put it there

20 myself ages ago so I could reach for it and smell his neck when I wanted to feel like hell in the middle of the night. Then I must have knocked it over and been too wilful to admit to what it was later. My own duplicity shocked me. I held onto the bottle for a week or so then threw it out.

My mother was right. I have no common sense. I don't know a damn thing worth

25 knowing.

THE CHURCH	THE MARRIED
THE LAW	WHAT'S WHAT

I haven't a clue.

The clock ticks too loud while I lie still, shrinking.

30 Please god make boulders crash through the roof. In three or four days when the Health Visitor comes she will find only mashed remains, marrowbone jelly oozing between the shards like bitumen. *Well*, she'll say, *We're not doing so well today, are we?* It's too cold. The hairs on my legs are stiff. I shiver and wish the phone would ring.

Needing people yet being afraid of them is wearing me out. I struggle with the paradox

35 all the time and can't resolve it. When people visit I am distraught trying to look as if I can cope. At work I never speak but I want to be spoken to. If anyone does I get anxious and stammer. I'm scared of the phone yet I want it to ring.

Page sixteen

MARKS

Questions

21. Look at lines 1—8.

    Analyse how Galloway makes the reader aware of Joy's efforts to cope with her situation. 2

22. Look at lines 9—23.

    By referring to at least two examples, analyse how the writer conveys Joy's desperation for Michael's presence. 4

23. Look at lines 29—37.

    By referring to at least two examples, analyse how Galloway conveys Joy's feelings of despair. 4

24. By referring to this extract and elsewhere in the novel, discuss how Galloway demonstrates Joy's fear and/or anxiety in relating to other people. 10

[Turn over

Page seventeen

HIGHER ENGLISH   32   SQA EXAM PAPER 2015

OR

Text 4 — Prose

If you choose this text you may not attempt a question on Prose in Section 2.

Read the extract below and then attempt the following questions.

Sunset Song by Lewis Grassic Gibbon

This extract is from the beginning of Part II (Drilling). In this extract Chris reflects on the death of her mother.

Lying down when her climb up the cambered brae was done, panting deep from the rate she'd come at — skirt flying and iron-resolute she'd turn back for nothing that cried or called in all Blawearie — no, not even that whistle of father's! — Chris felt the coarse grass crackle up beneath her into a fine quiet couch. Neck and shoulders and hips and
5   knees she relaxed, her long brown arms quivered by her side as the muscles slacked away, the day drowsed down an aureal light through the long brown lashes that drooped on her cheeks. As the gnomons of a giant dial the shadows of the Standing Stones crept into the east, snipe called and called —

Just as the last time she'd climbed to the loch: and when had that been? She opened her
10   eyes and thought, and tired from that and closed down her eyes again and gave a queer laugh. The June of last year it had been, the day when mother had poisoned herself and the twins.

So long as that and so near as that, you'd thought of the hours and days as a dark, cold pit you'd never escape. But you'd escaped, the black damp went out of the sunshine and
15   the world went on, the white faces and whispering ceased from the pit, you'd never be the same again, but the world went on and you went with it. It was not mother only that died with the twins, something died in your heart and went down with her to lie in Kinraddie kirkyard — the child in your heart died then, the bairn that believed the hills were made for its play, every road set fair with its warning posts, hands ready to snatch
20   you back from the brink of danger when the play grew over-rough. That died, and the Chris of the books and the dreams died with it, or you folded them up in their paper of tissue and laid them away by the dark, quiet corpse that was your childhood.

So Mistress Munro of the Cuddiestoun told her that awful night she came over the rain-soaked parks of Blawearie and laid out the body of mother, the bodies of the twins that
25   had died so quiet in their crib. She nipped round the rooms right quick and pert and uncaring, the black-eyed futret, snapping this order and that, it was her that terrified Dod and Alec from their crying, drove father and Will out tending the beasts. And quick and cool and cold-handed she worked, peeking over at Chris with her rat-like face. *You'll be leaving the College now, I'll warrant, education's dirt and you're better clear of it.*
30   *You'll find little time for dreaming and dirt when you're keeping house at Blawearie.*

And Chris in her pit, dazed and dull-eyed, said nothing, she minded later; and some other than herself went searching and seeking out cloths and clothes. Then Mistress Munro washed down the body that was mother's and put it in a nightgown, her best, the one with blue ribbons on it that she hadn't worn for many a year; and fair she made her and
35   sweet to look at, the tears came at last when you saw her so, hot tears wrung from your eyes like drops of blood. But they ended quick, you would die if you wept like that for long, in place of tears a long wail clamoured endless, unanswered inside your head *Oh mother, mother, why did you do it?*

And not until days later did Chris hear why, for they tried to keep it from her and the
40   boys, but it all came out at the inquest, mother had poisoned herself, her and the twins,

Page eighteen

SQA EXAM PAPER 2015   **33**   HIGHER ENGLISH

MARKS

because she was pregnant again and afraid with a fear dreadful and calm and clear-eyed. So she had killed herself while of unsound mind, had mother, kind-eyed and sweet, remembering those Springs of Kildrummie last of all things remembered, it may be, and the rooks that cried out across the upland parks of Don far down beyond the tunnels of
45   the years.

Questions

25. Look at lines 1—8.

Explain fully how Chris feels in these lines.   **2**

26. Look at lines 9—22.

By referring to at least two examples, analyse how the writer conveys the impact her mother's death has had on Chris.   **4**

27. Look at lines 23—45.

By referring to at least two examples, analyse how the writer conveys the horror of Chris's memory of her mother's death.   **4**

28. Discuss how Grassic Gibbon presents Chris's growing to maturity in this extract and elsewhere in the novel.   **10**

[Turn over

Page nineteen

HIGHER ENGLISH 34 SQA EXAM PAPER 2015

OR

Text 5 — Prose

If you choose this text you may not attempt a question on Prose in Section 2.

Read the extract below and then attempt the following questions.

The Cone-Gatherers by Robin Jenkins

This extract is taken from Chapter Four. Duror has gone to the Big House to see Lady Runcie-Campbell.

Lady Runcie-Campbell was in the office at the front of the house writing letters. When he knocked, she bade him enter in her clear courteous musical voice.

A stranger, hearing her, would have anticipated some kind of loveliness in so charming a speaker; he might not, however, have expected to find such outstanding beauty of face
5 and form married to such earnestness of spirit; and he would assuredly have been both startled and impressed.

Duror, who knew her well, had been afraid that in her presence he might be shamed or inspired into abandoning his scheme against the cone-gatherers. In spite of her clothes, expensive though simple, of her valuable adornments such as earrings, brooches, and
10 rings, and of her sometimes almost mystical sense of responsibility as a representative of the ruling class, she had an ability to exalt people out of their humdrum selves. Indeed, Duror often associated religion not with the smell of pinewood pews or of damp Bibles, but rather with her perfume, so elusive to describe. Her father the judge had bequeathed to her a passion for justice, profound and intelligent; and a determination to
15 see right done, even at the expense of rank or pride. Her husband Sir Colin was orthodox, instinctively preferring the way of a world that for many generations had allowed his family to enjoy position and wealth. Therefore he had grumbled at his wife's conscientiousness, and was fond of pointing out, with affection but without sympathy, the contradiction between her emulation of Christ and her eminence as a baronet's wife.

20 She would have given the cone-gatherers the use of the beach-hut, if Duror had not dissuaded her; and she had not forgotten to ask him afterwards what their hut was like. He had had to lie.

Now, when he was going to lie again, this time knowing it would implicate her in his chosen evil, he felt that he was about to commit before her eyes an obscene gesture,
25 such as he had falsely accused the dwarf of making. In the sunny scented room therefore, where the happy voices of the cricket players on the lawn could be heard, he suddenly saw himself standing up to the neck in a black filth, like a stags' wallowing pool deep in the wood. High above the trees shone the sun and everywhere birds sang; but this filth, as he watched, crept up until it entered his mouth, covered his ears, blinded
30 his eyes, and so annihilated him. So would he perish, he knew; and somewhere in the vision, as a presence, exciting him so that his heart beat fast, but never visible, was a hand outstretched to help him out of that mire, if he wished to be helped.

He saw her hand with its glittering rings held out to invite him to sit down.

"Good morning, Duror," she said, with a smile. "Isn't it just splendid?"

35 "Yes, my lady."

She looked at him frankly and sympathetically: it was obvious she attributed his subdued tone to sorrow over his wife. If at the same time she noticed with surprise that he hadn't shaved, it did not diminish her sympathy, as it would have her husband's.

Page twenty

MARKS

"How is Mrs. Duror?" she asked gently.

40 "Not too well, I'm sorry to say, my lady. This spell of fine weather has upset her. She asked me to thank you for the flowers."

She was so slim, golden-haired, and vital, that her solicitude for Peggy gripped him like a fierce cramp in his belly.

She noticed how pale he had turned, how ill he looked.

45 "I often think of your poor wife, Duror," she said.

She glanced at her husband's portrait in uniform on the desk in front of her.

Duror could not see the photograph from where he sat, but he could see clearly enough in his imagination the original, as gawky as she was beautiful, as glum as she was gay, and as matter-of-fact as she was compassionate.

50 "This war," she went on quickly, "with its dreadful separations has shown me at least what she has missed all these years. Something has come between us and the things we love, the things on which our faith depends: flowers and dogs and trees and friends. She's been cut off so much longer."

Questions

29. Look at lines 1—19.

   By referring to at least two examples, analyse how Jenkins's use of language creates a positive impression of Lady Runcie-Campbell.   4

30. Look at lines 23—43.

   By referring to two examples, analyse how the writer uses language to convey the contrast between Duror and Lady Runcie-Campbell.   4

31. Look at lines 50—53.

   Explain why Lady Runcie-Campbell now feels more able to identify with Peggy's situation.   2

32. In the novel, Duror is presented not just as an evil character, but one who might be worthy of some sympathy.

   With reference to this extract and elsewhere in the novel, explain how both aspects of Duror's character are portrayed.   10

[Turn over

Page twenty-one

HIGHER ENGLISH   36   SQA EXAM PAPER 2015

SECTION 1 — SCOTTISH TEXT — 20 marks

Choose ONE text from Drama, Prose or Poetry.

Read the text extract carefully and then attempt ALL the questions for your chosen text.

You should spend about 45 minutes on this Section.

PART C — SCOTTISH TEXT — POETRY

Text 1 — Poetry

If you choose this text you may not attempt a question on Poetry in Section 2.

Read the poem below and then attempt the following questions.

***To a Mouse, On turning her up in her Nest, with the Plough, November 1785* by Robert Burns**

Wee, sleekit, cowrin, tim'rous beastie,
O, what a panic's in thy breastie!
Thou need na start awa sae hasty,
      Wi' bickering brattle!
5 I wad be laith to rin an' chase thee,
      Wi' murd'ring pattle!

I'm truly sorry Man's dominion
Has broken Nature's social union,
An' justifies that ill opinion,
10   Which makes thee startle,
At me, thy poor, earth-born companion,
      An' fellow-mortal!

I doubt na, whyles, but thou may thieve;
What then? poor beastie, thou maun live!
15 A daimen icker in a thrave
      'S a sma' request:
I'll get a blessin wi' the lave,
      And never miss't!

Thy wee bit housie, too, in ruin!
20 It's silly wa's the win's are strewin!
An' naething, now, to big a new ane,
      O' foggage green!
An' bleak December's winds ensuin,
      Baith snell and keen!

25 Thou saw the fields laid bare an' waste,
An' weary Winter comin fast,
An' cozie here, beneath the blast,
      Thou thought to dwell,
Till crash! the cruel coulter past
30   Out thro' thy cell.

Page twenty-two

MARKS

That wee bit heap o' leaves an' stibble,
Has cost thee monie a weary nibble!
Now thou's turn'd out, for a' thy trouble,
        But house or hald,
35 To thole the Winter's sleety dribble,
        An' cranreuch cauld!

But Mousie, thou art no thy lane,
In proving foresight may be vain:
The best-laid schemes o' Mice an' Men
40   Gang aft agley,
An' lea'e us nought but grief an' pain,
        For promis'd joy!

Still thou are blest, compar'd wi' me!
The present only toucheth thee:
45 But, Och! I backward cast my e'e,
        On prospects drear!
An' forward, tho' I canna see,
        I guess an' fear!

Questions

33. Look at lines 1—18.

Analyse how Burns establishes at least two aspects of the speaker's personality in these lines.   **4**

34. Look at lines 19—36.

By referring to at least two examples, analyse how Burns creates pity for the mouse and its predicament.   **4**

35. Look at lines 37—48.

Explain how the final two verses highlight the contrast between the speaker and the mouse.   **2**

36. Discuss how Burns uses a distinctive narrative voice to convey the central concerns of this poem and at least one of his other poems.   **10**

[**Turn over**

Page twenty-three

OR

Text 2 — Poetry

If you choose this text you may not attempt a question on Poetry in Section 2.

Read the poem below and then attempt the following questions.

War Photographer **by Carol Ann Duffy**

In his dark room he is finally alone
with spools of suffering set out in ordered rows.
The only light is red and softly glows,
as though this were a church and he
5   a priest preparing to intone a Mass.
Belfast. Beirut. Phnom Penh. All flesh is grass.

He has a job to do. Solutions slop in trays
beneath his hands, which did not tremble then
though seem to now. Rural England. Home again
10 to ordinary pain which simple weather can dispel,
to fields which don't explode beneath the feet
of running children in a nightmare heat.

Something is happening. A stranger's features
faintly start to twist before his eyes,
15 a half-formed ghost. He remembers the cries
of this man's wife, how he sought approval
without words to do what someone must
and how the blood stained into foreign dust.

A hundred agonies in black and white
20 from which his editor will pick out five or six
for Sunday's supplement. The reader's eyeballs prick
with tears between the bath and pre-lunch beers.
From the aeroplane he stares impassively at where
he earns his living and they do not care.

Page twenty-four

SQA EXAM PAPER 2015 | 39 | HIGHER ENGLISH

MARKS

Questions

37. Look at lines 1—6.

Analyse how imagery is used to create a serious atmosphere.

2

38. Look at lines 7—12.

Analyse how Duffy conveys the photographer's perception of the difference between life in Britain and life in the war zones abroad.

4

39. Look at lines 13—18.

Analyse the use of poetic technique to convey the distressing nature of the photographer's memories.

2

40. Look at lines 19—24.

Analyse how the use of poetic technique highlights the British public's indifference to the suffering shown in the newspapers they read.

2

41. Referring closely to this poem and to at least one other poem by Duffy, discuss how she explores the link between the past and the present.

10

[Turn over

Page twenty-five

HIGHER ENGLISH   **40**   SQA EXAM PAPER 2015

OR

Text 3 — Poetry

If you choose this text you may not attempt a question on Poetry in Section 2.

Read the poem below and then attempt the following questions.

My Rival's House **by Liz Lochhead**

is peopled with many surfaces.
Ormolu and gilt, slipper satin,
lush velvet couches,
cushions so stiff you can't sink in.
5 Tables polished clear enough to see distortions in.

We take our shoes off at her door,
shuffle stocking-soled, tiptoe — the parquet floor
is beautiful and its surface must
be protected. Dust-
10 cover, drawn shade,
won't let the surface colour fade.

Silver sugar-tongs and silver salver,
my rival serves us tea.
She glosses over him and me.
15 I am all edges, a surface, a shell
and yet my rival thinks she means me well.
But what squirms beneath her surface I can tell.
Soon, my rival
capped tooth, polished nail
20 will fight, fight foul for her survival.
Deferential, daughterly, I sip
and thank her nicely for each bitter cup.

And I have much to thank her for.
This son she bore —
25 first blood to her —
never, never can escape scot free
the sour potluck of family.
And oh how close
this family that furnishes my rival's place.

30 Lady of the house.
Queen bee.
She is far more unconscious,
far more dangerous than me.
Listen, I was always my own worst enemy.
35 She has taken even this from me.

She dishes up her dreams for breakfast.
Dinner, and her salt tears pepper our soup.
She won't
give up.

Page twenty-six

MARKS

Questions

42. Look at lines 1—11.

Explain why the speaker feels uncomfortable in her rival's house.   **2**

43. Look at lines 12—22.

By referring to at least two examples, analyse how the poet creates a tense atmosphere in these lines.   **4**

44. Look at lines 23—39.

By referring to at least two examples, discuss how the speaker's resentment of her rival is made clear.   **4**

45. Discuss how Lochhead uses descriptive detail to explore personality in this and at least one other poem.   **10**

[Turn over

HIGHER ENGLISH 42 SQA EXAM PAPER 2015

OR

Text 4 — Poetry

If you choose this text you may not attempt a question on Poetry in Section 2.

Read the poem below and then attempt the following questions.

Visiting Hour **by Norman MacCaig**

The hospital smell
combs my nostrils
as they go bobbing along
green and yellow corridors.

5   What seems a corpse
is trundled into a lift and vanishes
heavenward.

I will not feel, I will not
feel, until
10 I have to.

Nurses walk lightly, swiftly,
here and up and down and there,
their slender waists miraculously
carrying their burden
15 of so much pain, so
many deaths, their eyes
still clear after
so many farewells.

Ward 7. She lies
20 in a white cave of forgetfulness.
A withered hand
trembles on its stalk. Eyes move
behind eyelids too heavy
to raise. Into an arm wasted
25 of colour a glass fang is fixed,
not guzzling but giving.
And between her and me
distance shrinks till there is none left
but the distance of pain that neither she nor I
30 can cross.

She smiles a little at this
black figure in her white cave
who clumsily rises
in the round swimming waves of a bell
35 and dizzily goes off, growing fainter,
not smaller, leaving behind only
books that will not be read
and fruitless fruits.

Page twenty-eight

SQA EXAM PAPER 2015   43   HIGHER ENGLISH

MARKS

Questions

46. Look at lines 1—7.

    Analyse how the poet's use of language conveys his response to his surroundings.   **2**

47. Look at lines 8—18.

    Analyse how MacCaig uses language to highlight his own sense of inadequacy.   **4**

48. Look at lines 19—38.

    Analyse how the poet's use of language emphasises the painful nature of the situation for both patient and visitor.   **4**

49. By referring to this poem, and at least one other by MacCaig, discuss how he explores the theme of loss in his work.   **10**

[Turn over

Page twenty-nine

OR

Text 5 — Poetry

If you choose this text you may not attempt a question on Poetry in Section 2.

Read the poem below and then attempt the following questions.

An Autumn Day **by Sorley MacLean**

On that slope
on an autumn day,
the shells soughing about my ears
and six dead men at my shoulder,
5 dead and stiff — and frozen were it not for the heat —
as if they were waiting for a message.

When the screech came
out of the sun,
out of an invisible throbbing,
10 the flame leaped and the smoke climbed
and surged every way:
blinding of eyes, splitting of hearing.

And after it, the six men dead
the whole day:
15 among the shells snoring
in the morning,
and again at midday
and in the evening.

In the sun, which was so indifferent,
20 so white and painful;
on the sand which was so comfortable,
easy and kindly;
and under the stars of Africa,
jewelled and beautiful.

25 One Election took them
and did not take me,
without asking us
which was better or worse:
it seemed as devilishly indifferent
30 as the shells.

Six men dead at my shoulder
on an Autumn day.

Page thirty

MARKS

Questions

50. Look at lines 1—12.

By referring to at least two examples, analyse how the poet's use of language emphasises the impact of this experience.　　　4

51. Look at lines 13—24.

By referring to at least two examples, analyse how the poet uses language to highlight how meaningless the men's deaths were.　　　4

52. Look at lines 25—32.

Explain what the speaker finds puzzling when he reflects on the men's deaths.　　　2

53. Nature is a significant aspect in MacLean's poetry. Discuss how he uses nature to convey the central concern(s) of this poem and those of at least one other poem.　　　10

[Turn over

Page thirty-one

OR

Text 6 — Poetry

If you choose this text you may not attempt a question on Poetry in Section 2.

Read the poem below and then attempt the following questions.

Two Trees **by Don Paterson**

One morning, Don Miguel got out of bed
with one idea rooted in his head:
to graft his orange to his lemon tree.
It took him the whole day to work them free,
5 lay open their sides, and lash them tight.
For twelve months, from the shame or from the fright
they put forth nothing; but one day there appeared
two lights in the dark leaves. Over the years
the limbs would get themselves so tangled up
10 each bough looked like it gave a double crop,
and not one kid in the village didn't know
the magic tree in Miguel's patio.

The man who bought the house had had no dream
so who can say what dark malicious whim
15 led him to take his axe and split the bole
along its fused seam, and then dig two holes.
And no, they did not die from solitude;
nor did their branches bear a sterile fruit;
nor did their unhealed flanks weep every spring
20 for those four yards that lost them everything
as each strained on its shackled root to face
the other's empty, intricate embrace.
They were trees, and trees don't weep or ache or shout.
And trees are all this poem is about.

Page thirty-two

MARKS

Questions

54. Look at lines 1—12.

    By referring to at least two examples, analyse how the poet's use of poetic technique emphasises the importance of the story of the trees.   **4**

55. Look at lines 13—16.

    By referring to at least two examples, analyse how the poet's use of language creates an impression of "the man".   **4**

56. Explain the irony of the final two lines.   **2**

57. Discuss how Paterson develops the theme of relationships in this and at least one other poem.   **10**

[END OF SECTION 1]

[Turn over

Page thirty-three

HIGHER ENGLISH 48 SQA EXAM PAPER 2015

SECTION 2 — CRITICAL ESSAY — 20 marks

Attempt ONE question from the following genres — Drama, Prose Fiction, Prose Non-fiction, Poetry, Film and Television Drama, or Language.

Your answer must be on a different genre from that chosen in Section 1.

You should spend approximately 45 minutes on this Section.

PART A — DRAMA

Answers to questions on Drama should refer to the text and to such relevant features as characterisation, key scene(s), structure, climax, theme, plot, conflict, setting . . .

1. Choose a play in which a major character's actions influence the emotions of others.

   Briefly explain how the dramatist presents these emotions and actions and discuss how this contributes to your understanding of the play as a whole.

2. Choose a play in which there is a scene involving a moment of conflict or of resolution to conflict.

   By referring to details of the scene, explain how the dramatist presents this moment and discuss how this contributes to your appreciation of the play as a whole.

3. Choose a play which explores an important issue or issues within society.

   Briefly explain the nature of the issue(s) and discuss how the dramatist's presentation of the issue(s) contributed to your appreciation of the play as a whole.

Page thirty-four

PART B — PROSE FICTION

> *Answers to questions on Prose Fiction should refer to the text and to such relevant features as characterisation, setting, language, key incident(s), climax, turning point, plot, structure, narrative technique, theme, ideas, description . . .*

4. Choose a novel **or** short story in which the method of narration is important.

   Outline briefly the writer's method of narration and explain why you feel this method makes such a major contribution to your understanding of the text as a whole.

5. Choose a novel **or** short story in which there is a moment of significance for one of the characters.

   Explain briefly what the significant moment is and discuss, with reference to appropriate techniques, its significance to the text as a whole.

6. Choose a novel **or** short story which has a satisfying ending.

   Discuss to what extent the ending provides a successful conclusion to the text as a whole.

PART C — PROSE NON-FICTION

> *Answers to questions on Prose Non-fiction should refer to the text and to such relevant features as ideas, use of evidence, stance, style, selection of material, narrative voice . . .*
>
> *Non-fiction texts can include travel writing, journalism, autobiography, biography, essays . . .*

7. Choose a non-fiction text which recreates a moment in time.

   Discuss how the description effectively recreates this moment and show how important this is to your appreciation of the text as a whole.

8. Choose a non-fiction text which is structured in a particularly effective way.

   Explain how the structure enhances the impact of the writer's message.

9. Choose a non-fiction text which made you consider your views about a social or political or ethical issue.

   Explain what the issue is and how the writer uses language effectively to engage you.

[Turn over

Page thirty-five

HIGHER ENGLISH · 50 · SQA EXAM PAPER 2015

PART D — POETRY

Answers to questions on Poetry should refer to the text and to such relevant features as word choice, tone, imagery, structure, content, rhythm, rhyme, theme, sounds, ideas . . .

10. Choose a poem which takes as its starting point a memorable experience.

    Discuss how the poet's presentation of the experience helps you to appreciate its significance.

11. Choose a poem which encourages you to think differently or to understand something in a new way.

    Discuss how the poet's ideas and techniques led you to change your thinking or understanding.

12. Choose a poem which is written in a particular poetic form or which has a particularly effective structure.

    Discuss how the poet's use of form or structure contributes to the impact of the poem's central concern(s).

PART E — FILM AND TELEVISION DRAMA

Answers to questions on Film and Television Drama* should refer to the text and to such relevant features as use of camera, key sequence, characterisation, mise-en-scène, editing, music/sound, special effects, plot, dialogue . . .

13. Choose a film **or** television drama in which the setting in time or place is important.

    Explain how the film or programme makers use media techniques effectively to create this setting.

14. Choose a film **or** television drama where the hero is not completely good and/or the villain is not completely bad.

    Explain how the film or programme makers use media techniques to develop the hero and/or villain.

15. Choose a film **or** television drama in which lighting and/or sound makes an important contribution to the impact of a particular sequence.

    Explain how the film or programme makers use lighting and/or sound to enhance your appreciation of the sequence.

* "television drama" includes a single play, a series or a serial.

Page thirty-six

SQA EXAM PAPER 2015   51   HIGHER ENGLISH

PART F — LANGUAGE

Answers to questions on Language should refer to the text and to such relevant features as register, accent, dialect, slang, jargon, vocabulary, tone, abbreviation . . .

16. Choose the language associated with a particular vocational or interest group.

    Identify some examples of the language used within the group and discuss to what extent this shared language contributes to the effectiveness of the group's activities.

17. Choose the language of radio or television reporting on a topic such as sport, films, nature, science . . .

    Identify some of the features of this language and discuss to what extent they are effective in communicating with the target audience.

18. Choose a commercial advertising campaign which makes use of persuasive language.

    By examining specific examples, evaluate their effectiveness in achieving the purpose of the campaign.

[END OF SECTION 2]

[END OF QUESTION PAPER]

Page thirty-seven

[BLANK PAGE]

DO NOT WRITE ON THIS PAGE

HIGHER
2016

National Qualifications 2016

X724/76/11

English
Reading for Understanding,
Analysis and Evaluation — Text

THURSDAY, 5 MAY
9:00 AM – 10:30 AM

Total marks — 30

Read the passages carefully and then attempt ALL questions, which are printed on a separate sheet.

The following two passages consider whether or not 16-year-olds should be allowed to vote.

Passage 1

Read the passage below and then attempt questions 1 to 7.

In the first passage, Catherine Bennett puts forward the case for allowing 16-year-olds to vote.

Rude, impulsive, sulky . . . still, let our 16-year-olds vote.

There are hugely important questions to address before 16-year-olds can be invited into the complicated UK electoral process. Are they sufficiently mature? Can they tell one party from another? Are they too preoccupied by a combination of exams and hectic social lives to be bothered? Even worrying about their appearance has been cited as a reason why under-18s might
5 struggle to give adequate thought to the political and economic issues facing Britain today.

There was a long period, between being sixteen myself and then, decades later, getting to know some present-day teenagers, including the one in my own house, when I would have agreed with champions of the status quo. I presumed — without knowing any — that these 16-year-olds were as clueless as my younger self, but with an increased obsession with their peer group, a result of
10 unpatrolled access to social media, greater affluence, and being subject to a constant barrage of entertainment.

If these factors were not enough to guarantee extreme teen disengagement with the political process, scientists have supplied biological reasons to question the efficiency of teenagers' smartphone-fixated brains. The last time there was a significant move to reduce the voting age,
15 the biologist Richard Dawkins set out the potential risks posed by the undeveloped teenage brain to our current epistocracy. An epistocracy — as of course all older voters will know — is government by wise people, that is, those with fully developed grey matter. In the article, Dawkins cited evidence from neuroscientists that "the brain undergoes major reconstruction from the onset of puberty which continues until 20 or beyond". Crucial, if I understand them
20 correctly, is the importance of this continuing development to the frontal lobes. This is the area at the front of the brain which "enables us to think in the abstract, weigh moral dilemmas and control our impulses". It was not even clear, the author said, that teenagers are developed enough to "be making life-changing decisions for themselves".

If we simply accept this argument, what does it mean in practice? It means that a grown-up who
25 believes in wizardry or unicorns or vampires can become a Member of Parliament, but a school pupil the age of, say, Malala Yousafzai, has yet to acquire the intellectual credentials to vote. Malala had been the victim of a terrorist attack in Pakistan as a result of her blog advocating education for girls, had recovered and continued to campaign tirelessly for equal educational opportunities for all children. This led to her becoming, in 2014, at the age of seventeen, the
30 youngest recipient of the Nobel Peace Prize.

Of course, it would be naïve to suggest that all teenagers can be as accomplished as Malala. However, there is, in fact, considerable evidence that the "unfinished" brain can be pretty good at sport, music, creating computer software and raising thousands of pounds for charity. True, 16-year-olds can be rude, sulky, reckless and unreliable. But the adult world is scarcely exempt
35 from these characteristics. Perhaps — as politicians must hope — most teenagers know too little about politics to make self-congratulatory comparisons between themselves and the at times limited brain power on show during parliamentary debates. The evidence of their own eyes confirms that, when considering normal behaviour, 16-year-olds barely compete in terms of incivility, tantrums, profanity, impulsivity, prejudice, time-wasting and an unedifying
40 dependency on tabloid websites, when compared to millions of fully enfranchised grown-ups. If law-makers ever think of restricting voting by the inadequately brained, illiterate, non-taxpaying or ignorant, the consequences for some adults would be chilling.

Page two

SQA EXAM PAPER 2016   **57**   HIGHER ENGLISH

Indeed, recent research suggests that those who have been emphasising the negative effects of social media and modern technology on the developing brain may have got it all wrong. Sixteen
45 and seventeen-year-olds are part of the iGeneration, the first generation who have grown up with the digital innovations of the 21st century. They are flexible enough mentally to develop their political worldview from the wide range of sources to be found on the Internet, too media aware to be taken in by spin doctors and manipulative politicians.

Our teenagers do have their flaws. No, they don't always evince much money sense, although
50 they do, as consumers, pay sales tax. Yes, if voting booths were bedrooms they would probably leave wet towels all over them. But having now witnessed some of the more loveable teenage qualities — idealism, energy, a sense of injustice, open-mindedness — these seem to be exactly the ones of which modern politics is starved. Even a limited turnout by young voters, minus all the ones who are supposedly too apathetic or too busy insulting police officers or attending
55 Ibiza-themed foam parties, might inject some life into the next election.

Naturally, engaged teenagers would want answers on stuff that directly affects them such as unpaid internships, exams, student debt, the minimum wage, benefits and perhaps any military engagements in which they might be invited to serve. However, it might lead to a fresh look at policies that affect future generations, by voters who will actually be around to experience the
60 consequences. If voting has to be rationed, maybe it should be elderly citizens — who may not see the impact of, say, political inaction on climate change or carelessness about fuel sustainability — who should give way to 16-year-olds.

We could compromise: make it seventeen. Then 16-year-olds would only have a year to wait — after they have already married, donated an organ, bought fireworks, and signed up to fight for
65 their country — before they would be allowed to choose, alone in an exposed voting booth, between competing political visions. Judging by the current resistance of adults who believe they know so much better, you'd think we were doing our young people a great big favour.

Passage 2

Read the passage below and attempt question 8. While reading, you may wish to make notes on the main ideas and/or highlight key points in the passage.

In the second passage, Julia Hartley-Brewer puts forward her arguments for not allowing 16-year-olds to vote.

Letting 16-year-olds vote would be a disaster.

I have decided that it is only right and fair that my 8-year-old daughter should be allowed to vote. She knows her politics and can name the party leaders on sight, which is more than can be said for a large proportion of voters — and she pays tax. Every time she saves up her pocket money to buy a new toy or game, it comes with a price tag that includes a hefty 20 per cent of
5 VAT. On all these grounds, she has just as much of a claim to have her say about Britain's future as do the   16 and 17-year-olds of this country. And yet no one is demanding that she is given the vote because, well, she's an 8-year-old. She's a child; she doesn't have the intellectual and emotional development of an adult so she doesn't get to have the rights of adults.

So why is it that so many people — including prominent politicians — believe that we should be
10 giving 16 and 17-year-olds the right to vote? The call for the voting age to be lowered to sixteen is as absurd an idea as you'll hear.

Page three

Yes, 16 and 17-year-olds were allowed to vote in the Scottish referendum. And what did they achieve? The turn-out for that tiny age group was a lot higher than among most other younger voters (largely, it is thought, because they were encouraged to turn out to vote by their parents) but it did not enthuse the 18 to 20 age bracket, which as per usual largely didn't bother at all. Wouldn't our democracy be better served if we spent more time, effort and resources on engaging the people who already have the right to vote, rather than just adding on a few million voters who will never vote again after their first trip to the polling station?

Ah, but that's not the point, the protagonists claim. We should allow 16 and 17-year-olds to vote because they are legally allowed to do other, far more important, life-changing or life-risking things than put a cross on a ballot paper, so why not let them vote as well? And that would be a really good argument, if it were true. Because, in actual fact, we don't allow our 16 and 17-year-olds to do very much. They can't legally drink alcohol or smoke, for starters. We don't trust them to be sensible with a pint of lager so why trust them with a stubby pencil in a polling booth?

Okay, but they can get a job and pay income tax and that's not fair if they don't have a say in the government that sets those taxes, right? But income tax isn't the only tax we pay so why should that be the crucial decider? We all pay VAT on many of the goods we purchase from a very young age so, on that argument, my 8-year-old should be eligible to vote too.

Allowing 16 and 17-year-olds to vote would be a disaster. Voting is, after all, not a privilege like receiving pocket money or being permitted to stay out past your usual curfew on a Saturday night. It's a right. And a hard-won right at that.

When politicians say they want 16 and 17-year-olds to vote, what they really mean is that they want 16 and 17-year-olds to vote for them. This is not about empowering young people or shifting the focus of debate to issues more relevant to 16 and 17-year-olds. Mainstream politics will continue to focus on issues important to adults, such as the economy and the state of the health service. It is simply calculated electioneering on the part of cynical politicians to retain power.

Don't believe the nonsense being spouted in the name of democracy. There is absolutely nothing wrong with making people wait until they are eighteen to vote.

[END OF TEXT]

Page four

H National Qualifications 2016

X724/76/21

English
Reading for Understanding, Analysis and Evaluation — Questions

THURSDAY, 5 MAY
9:00 AM – 10:30 AM

Total marks — 30

Attempt ALL questions.

Write your answers clearly in the answer booklet provided. In the answer booklet, you must clearly identify the question number you are attempting.

Use **blue** or **black** ink.

Before leaving the examination room you must give your answer booklet to the Invigilator; if you do not, you may lose all the marks for this paper.

HIGHER ENGLISH **60** SQA EXAM PAPER 2016

MARKS

Attempt ALL questions

Total marks — 30

1. Read lines 1—5.

   Analyse **two** ways in which the writer attempts to engage the reader's interest in the opening paragraph.

   2

2. Read lines 6—23.

   (a) By referring to **either** the writer's viewpoint **or** to scientific research, explain why some people think teenagers should not be allowed to vote. Use your own words as far as possible in your answer.

   2

   (b) By referring to **at least two** examples, analyse how language is used to suggest that young people are not capable of voting.

   4

3. Read lines 24—30.

   Explain how the writer uses the example of Malala Yousafzai to develop her argument.

   2

4. Read lines 31—42.

   By referring to both word choice **and** sentence structure, analyse how the writer creates a negative impression of adults.

   4

5. Read lines 43—48.

   Explain why those who emphasise "the negative effects of social media and modern technology . . . may have got it all wrong". Use your own words in your answer.

   3

6. Read lines 49—55.

   By referring to **at least two** examples, analyse how the writer uses language to emphasise the positive contribution which teenage voters could make.

   4

7. Read lines 56—67.

   By referring to both tone **and** use of contrast, analyse how the writer emphasises her support of teenagers being allowed to vote.

   4

Question on both passages

8. Look at both passages.

   The writers disagree about whether or not 16 and 17-year-olds should be allowed to vote.

   Identify **three** key areas on which they disagree. You should support the points by referring to important ideas in both passages.

   You may answer this question in continuous prose or in a series of developed bullet points.

   5

[END OF QUESTION PAPER]

Page two

National Qualifications 2016

X724/76/12

**English
Critical Reading**

THURSDAY, 5 MAY
10:50 AM – 12:20 PM

Total marks — 40

SECTION 1 — Scottish Text — 20 marks

Read an extract from a Scottish text you have previously studied and attempt the questions.

Choose ONE text from either

Part A — Drama   Pages 02–07
or
Part B — Prose   Pages 08–17
or
Part C — Poetry   Pages 18–28

Attempt ALL the questions for your chosen text.

SECTION 2 — Critical Essay — 20 marks

Attempt ONE question from the following genres — Drama, Prose Fiction, Prose Non-Fiction, Poetry, Film and Television Drama, or Language.

Your answer must be on a different genre from that chosen in Section 1.

You should spend approximately 45 minutes on each Section.

Write your answers clearly in the answer booklet provided. In the answer booklet you must clearly identify the question number you are attempting.

Use **blue** or **black** ink.

Before leaving the examination room you must give your answer booklet to the Invigilator; if you do not, you may lose all the marks for this paper.

HIGHER ENGLISH   **62**   SQA EXAM PAPER 2016

SECTION 1 — SCOTTISH TEXT — 20 marks

Choose ONE text from Drama, Prose or Poetry.

Read the text extract carefully and then attempt ALL the questions for your chosen text.

You should spend about 45 minutes on this Section.

PART A — SCOTTISH TEXT — DRAMA

Text 1 — Drama

If you choose this text you may not attempt a question on Drama in Section 2.

Read the extract below and then attempt the following questions.

The Slab Boys by John Byrne

In this extract, from Act 2 of the play, Jack Hogg is looking for Phil, who has received a phone call.

	JACK:	I'm looking for your chum.
	SPANKY:	What're you wanting him for?
	JACK:	There's a phone call in Mr Barton's office . . . sounded rather urgent. Girl said it was the hospital.
5	SPANKY:	That's all right, I'll take it.
	JACK:	No, no . . . she was most insistent she speak to McCann himself . . .
	SPANKY:	I'll take it, I said . . .
	JACK:	No, I don't think . . .
	SPANKY:	I'm authorised! (*Exits.*)
10	JACK:	Hey . . . (*Exits.*)

(*Pause. Enter SADIE.*)

| | SADIE: | Too bloody soft, that's my trouble . . . He's not getting off with it, this time. Fifteen shillings? Not on your nelly . . . (*Sits down. Eases shoes off.*) Oooooooohhhhh . . . I should trade these in for a set of casters . . . |

15   (*Enter LUCILLE. Crosses to sink.*)

Any Epsom salts, hen?

	LUCILLE:	Waaahh! God, it's you! What're you playing at, Sadie?
	SADIE:	Have you seen that shy boy McCann on your travels?
	LUCILLE:	Shy?
20	SADIE:	Aye . . . fifteen bob shy. He still owes us for that dance ticket he got.
	LUCILLE:	Not again? When're you going to wise up? You'll just need to wait and grab him at the Town Hall . . .
	SADIE:	Oh, no . . . I'll not be seeing any Town Hall the night, sweetheart. If I thought these had to burl me round a dance floor . . . (*Cradles feet.*)

Page two

SQA EXAM PAPER 2016   63   HIGHER ENGLISH

MARKS

25   LUCILLE: Are you not going? Aw, Sadie, it was a right scream last year.

      SADIE: I know, flower . . .

      LUCILLE: That man of yours was a howl.

      SADIE: Aye . . . hysterical. Who else would sprint the length of the hall with a pint of Younger's in their fist and try leapfrogging over the top of Miss Walkinshaw
30   with that beehive hairdo of hers . . . eh? Only that stupid scunner I've got . . .

      LUCILLE: How long was he off his work with the leg?

      SADIE: Too long, sweetheart. He had my heart roasted, so he did. Sitting there with the bloody leg up on the fender shouting at me to put his line on at the bookie's for him. "See that?" I says. "If you're not up and back at your work
35   tomorrow I'll draw this across your back!" I had the poker in my hand . . . and I would've done it and all. Had me up to high doh. Couldn't get the stookie down the dungarees quick enough. Men? I wouldn't waste my time, hen.

      LUCILLE: Come off it, Sadie . . .

      SADIE: I'd to take the first one that came along. I'd've been better off with a lucky bag.

40   LUCILLE: They're not all like that, for God's sake.

      SADIE: You'll learn, flower . . . you're young yet. You can afford to sift through the dross . . . till you come to the real rubbish at the bottom.

      LUCILLE: Not this cookie. Lucille Bentley . . . Woman of the World . . . Fling Out Your Men!

45   SADIE: Wait till you get to my age and all you've got to show's bad feet and a display cabinet . . .

      LUCILLE: Who wants to get to your age?

Questions

1.   Look at lines 1–10.

   Explain how dialogue and/or stage directions are used to convey Spanky's attitude to Jack.   **2**

2.   Look at lines 12–31.

   By referring to at least **two** examples in these lines, analyse how humour is created.   **4**

3.   Look at lines 32–47.

   By referring to at least **two** examples, analyse how language is used to convey the different attitudes of Sadie and Lucille towards men.   **4**

4.   By referring to this extract and to elsewhere in the play, discuss the role played by women.   **10**

Page three   **[Turn over**

OR

Text 2 — Drama

If you choose this text you may not attempt a question on Drama in Section 2.

Read the passage below and then attempt the following questions.

The Cheviot, the Stag and the Black, Black Oil by John McGrath

In this extract, Patrick Sellar is standing trial for murder.

MC: Of all the many evictors, Mr Patrick Sellar was the only one who did not escape the full majesty of the law. He was charged with the murder of three people and numerous crimes at — Inverness High Court.

         The Company become a murmuring JURY.

5   *Enter the JUDGE. They stand, then sit silently.*

         Enter PATRICK SELLAR.

SELLAR: Re the charge of culpable homicide, my Lord — can you believe, my good sir, that I, a person not yet cognosed or escaped from a madhouse, should deliberately, in open day, by means of an officer who has a wife and family,

10   burn a house with a woman in it? Or that the officer should do so, instead of ejecting the tenant? The said tenant and woman being persons of whom we have no felonious intent, no malice, no ill-will.

JUDGE: Therefore, I would ask you (the jury) to ignore all the charges except two. One of these concerns the destruction of barns. In this case, Mr Sellar has

15   ignored a custom of the country, although he has not infringed the laws of Scotland. And the second case concerns the burning of the house of Chisholm. And here we are reminded of the contradictory nature of the testimony. Now if the jury are at all at a loss on this part of the case, I would ask them to take into consideration the character of the accused, for this is always of value in

20   balancing contradictory testimony. For here there is, in the first place, real evidence as regards Mr Sellar's conduct towards the sick — which in all cases has been proved to be most humane. And secondly, there are the letters of Sir George Abercrombie, Mr Fenton and Mr Brodie — which, although not evidence, must have some weight with the jury. And there are the testimonies

25   of Mr Gilzean, and Sir Archibald Dunbar — (*Sees him in the audience, waves.*) — hello, Archie. All of them testifying to Mr Sellar's humanity of disposition. How say you?

JURY: Oh, not guilty, no, no, no, etc.

JUDGE: My opinion completely concurs with that of the jury.

30   *JURY applaud PATRICK SELLAR.*

SELLAR: Every reformer of mankind has been abused by the established errors, frauds and quackery. But where the reformers have been right at bottom, they have, by patience, and by their unabating zeal and enthusiasm, got forward, in spite of every opposition. And so, I trust, will Lord and Lady Stafford, in their

35   generous exertions to better the people in this country.

Page four

SQA EXAM PAPER 2016 65 HIGHER ENGLISH

MARKS

More applause. Distant humming of "Land of Hope and Glory".

SELLAR: *(pointing to the mountains, from behind which a giant statue slowly emerges — eventually dwarfing the entire hall.)*

40 In lasting memorial of George Granville, Duke of Sutherland, Marquess of Stafford, K.G., an upright and patriotic nobleman, a judicious, kind and liberal landlord; who identified the improvement of his vast estates with the prosperity of all who cultivated them; a public yet unostentatious benefactor, who, while he provided useful employment for the active labourer, opened wide his hands to the distresses of the widow, the sick and the traveller: a
45 mourning and grateful tenantry, uniting with the inhabitants of the neighbourhood, erected *this pillar* . . .

Questions

5. Look at lines 7–12.

   Identify **one** tone used by Sellar in these lines and analyse how language is used to create this tone.   2

6. Look at lines 13–27.

   By referring to at least **two** examples, analyse how the language of the speech suggests the Judge's bias in favour of Sellar.   4

7. Look at lines 31–46.

   By referring to at least **two** examples, analyse how Sellar attempts to present "the reformers" and/or the Duke of Sutherland in a positive light.   4

8. Discuss how McGrath presents authority in this scene and elsewhere in the play.   10

[Turn over

Page five

HIGHER ENGLISH 66 SQA EXAM PAPER 2016

OR

Text 3 — Drama

If you choose this text you may not attempt a question on Drama in Section 2.

Read the extract below and then attempt the following questions.

Men Should Weep **by Ena Lamont Stewart**

In this extract from Act 1, scene 1, John comes in to find Maggie talking to her sister, Lily.
John comes in carrying books under his arm. He is a big, handsome man. He puts down his books, gives Maggie a pat: they exchange warm smiles. He goes to sink and has a glass of water.

5	Maggie:	Ye dry, John? I'll pit the kettle on. I've jist minded I promised yer auld lady a cup in her bed.
	John:	She a right?
	Maggie:	Oh aye. Jist as usual . . . greetin an eatin.
	John:	(*turning to Lily with as much of a smile as he can muster*) An how's Lil?
	Lily:	I wish you'd leave aff cryin me Lil. Ma name's Lily.
10	John:	An it couldna suit ye better.
	Lily:	Whit d'ye mean by that, eh?
	Maggie:	Don't you two stert up! I've had enough the day. (*To Lily*) He didna mean onythin.
	Lily:	Well if he didna mean onythin he shouldna say onythin!
15	John:	Goad help us!
	Lily:	(*to Maggie*) Whit aboot yon ironin?
	Maggie:	Och, never heed. I'm that tired it wad kill me tae watch ye.
	Lily:	It'll be steamie day again afore ye've got that lot done.
	Maggie:	Well, I canna help it.
20	John:	Yous women! Ye've nae system!
	Lily:	Oh, I suppose if *you* was a wumman you'd hae everythin jist perfect! The weans a washed and pit tae bed at six, an everythin a spick an span. Naethin tae dae till bedtime but twiddle yer thumbs. Huh!
	John:	I'd hae a system . . .
25	Lily and Maggie:	(*together*) He'd hae a system!
	John:	Aye, I'd hae a *system*. Ony man wull tell ye, ye can dae naethin properly wi'oot ye hae a *system*.
	Lily:	And ony wumman'll tell ye that there's nae system ever inventit that disnae go tae Hell when ye've a hoose-fu o weans and a done aul granny tae look efter.
30	Maggie:	Never heed him, Lily. Ye should see him tryin tae mak the breakfast on a Sunday; ye'd get yer kill! If he's fryin bacon, he's fryin bacon, see? He's no keepin an eye on the toast an on the kettle, an breakin the eggs intae the pan a at the same time.

Page six

SQA EXAM PAPER 2016   **67**   HIGHER ENGLISH

MARKS

	John:	Well, it's no ma job. If it *wis* ma job . . .
35	Maggie:	We ken: ye'd hae a system.
	Lily:	Well, if you're sure there's naethin I can dae, Maggie, I'll awa.
	Maggie:	Och no, wait and hae a wee cup wi us.
	Lily:	Naw . . . I'll mak yin at hame and hae something tasty tae it. A rarebit, mebbe.
	John:	(*winking at Maggie*) Aye, you dae that Lily; nae use hintin for ony rarebits here.
40	Lily:	(*not having seen the wink*) I like that! Hint! The cheek! It was me brung yon tin o baked beans that's sittin up on your dresser this minute, John Morrison!
	Maggie:	Och, he's only pullin yer leg, Lily.
	Lily:	If that's a sense o humour I'm glad I hevna got one. Yous men! I wouldna see one o you in ma road.
45	John:	Oh ho! If a man jist crep ontae your horizon, ye'd be efter him like a cock at a grosset.
	Lily:	(*hauling on her coat*) I'm no stayin here tae be insultit. Ye can keep the beans, Maggie, but that's the last ye're getting frae me till ye learn some folks their manners. Aye. And ye can tell yon precious Alec o yours that the next time he
50		maks enough at the dugs, tae get fleein drunk in the middle o Argyle Street, he can pay me back ma ten shillingy note.
		She stamps out of the room, slamming the door
	Maggie:	Ye shouldna tease Lily, John. Yin o they days she'll tak the huff and no come back, and whaur'll I be then?

Questions

9. Look at lines 1–15.

Analyse how dialogue and/or stage directions are used to convey John's relationship with Maggie, **and** John's relationship with Lily in these lines.   **4**

10. Look at lines 20–35.

By referring to at least **two** examples, analyse how both Maggie and Lily try to undermine John's opinion that women have "nae system".   **4**

11. Look at lines 39–52.

Explain any **two** reasons for Lily's negative feelings when she leaves.   **2**

12. By referring to this extract and to elsewhere in the play, discuss John's role within the family.   **10**

[Turn over

Page seven

HIGHER ENGLISH   **68**   SQA EXAM PAPER 2016

SECTION 1 — SCOTTISH TEXT — 20 marks

Choose ONE text from Drama, Prose or Poetry.

Read the text extract carefully and then attempt ALL the questions for your chosen text.

You should spend about 45 minutes on this Section.

PART B — SCOTTISH TEXT — PROSE

Text 1 — Prose

If you choose this text you may not attempt a question on Prose (Fiction or Non-Fiction) in Section 2.

Read the extract below and then attempt the following questions.

The Crater by Iain Crichton Smith

"All present and correct, sir," said Sergeant Smith.

"All right, let's go then," said Lieutenant Mackinnon.

Down the trench they went, teeth and eyes grinning, clattering over the duckboards with their Mills bombs and their bayonets and their guns. "What am I doing here?" thought
5 Robert, and "Who the hell is making that noise?" and "Is the damned wire cut or not?" and "We are like a bunch of actors," and "I'm leading these men, I'm an officer."

And he thought again, "I hope the guns have cut that barbed wire."

Then he and they inched across No Man's Land following the line of lime which had been laid to guide them. Up above were the stars and the air was cool on their faces. But there
10 were only a few stars, the night was mostly dark, and clouds covered the moon. Momentarily he had an idea of a huge mind breeding thought after thought, star after star, a mind which hid in daylight in modesty or hauteur but which at night worked out staggering problems, pouring its undifferentiated power over the earth.

On hands and knees he squirmed forward, the others behind him. This was his first raid
15 and he thought, "I am frightened." But it was different from being out in the open on a battlefield. It was an older fear, the fear of being buried in the earth, the fear of wandering through eternal passageways and meeting grey figures like weasels and fighting with them in the darkness. He tested the wire. Thank God it had been cut. And then he thought, "Will we need the ladders?" The sides of the trenches were so deep sometimes
20 that ladders were necessary to get out again. And as he crawled towards the German trenches he had a vision of Germans crawling beneath British trenches undermining them. A transparent imagined web hung below him in the darkness quivering with grey spiders.

He looked at his illuminated watch. The time was right. Then they were in the German trenches. The rest was a series of thrustings and flashes. Once he thought he saw or
25 imagined he saw from outside a dugout a man sitting inside reading a book. It was like looking through a train window into a house before the house disappears. There were Mills bombs, hackings of bayonets, scurryings and breathings as of rats.

Page eight

SQA EXAM PAPER 2016   **69**   HIGHER ENGLISH

MARKS

A white face towered above him, his pistol exploded and the face disappeared. There was
a terrible stink all around him, and the flowing of blood. Then there was a long silence.
30 Back. They must get back. He passed the order along. And then they wriggled back again
avoiding the craters which lay around them, created by shells, and which were full of
slimy water. If they fell into one of these they would be drowned. As he looked, shells
began to fall into them sending up huge spouts of water. Over the parapet. They were
over the parapet. Crouched they had run and scrambled and were over. Two of them were
35 carrying a third. They stumbled down the trench. There were more wounded than he had
thought. Wright . . . one arm seemed to have been shot off. Sergeant Smith was bending
over him. "You'll get sent home all right," he was saying. Some of the men were tugging
at their equipment and talking feverishly. Young Ellis was lying down, blood pouring from
his mouth. Harris said, "Morrison's in the crater."

40 He and Sergeant Smith looked at each other. They were both thinking the same: there is
no po   it. They could see each other's eyes glaring whitely through the black,
but c   essions on the faces. The shells were still falling, drumming and
shak   out there, these dead moons.

ey Robert's state of mind.   **2**

amples, analyse how language is used to create a

     4

15.   Look at lines 23–43.

By referring to at least **two** examples, analyse how language is used to highlight the
tense nature of the soldiers' situation.   **4**

16.   By referring to this and to at least one other short story by Iain Crichton Smith,
discuss the impact of extreme situations on his characters.   **10**

[Turn over

Page nine

HIGHER ENGLISH **70** SQA EXAM PAPER 2016

OR

Text 2 — Prose

If you choose this text you may not attempt a question on Prose (Fiction or Non-Fiction) in Section 2.

Read the extract below and then attempt the following questions.

The Whaler's Return by George Mackay Brown

He put his head through the door and saw a few farmers sitting round the fire drinking. The barmaid was standing at a mirror twisting her yellow hair at the back of her head. At last she got a fine burnished knot on it and drove a pin through to hold it in place.

Flaws hadn't seen a woman for six months. He went in and asked for a mug of ale.

5   "We only sell whisky here," said the girl, "threepence a glass."

"A glass of whisky then," said Flaws.

He thought it might be the last chance he would ever have to speak to a pretty girl. Peterina was good and hard-working, but rather ugly.

Flaws stood at the bar and drank his whisky. The four farmers sat round the fire saying
10   little. It was Wednesday in Hamnavoe, the day they drove in their beasts to sell at the mart.

"Do you do much trade in the White Horse?" said Flaws to the barmaid.

"We welcome only the better sort of person here," said the girl, "the quiet country men, not the ruffians and tramps from the herring boats and the whalers. And of course the office workers too, and business people. We're always very busy in the evening after the
15   shops and offices close. No fighting scum from the boats ever cross the threshold of the White Horse." Out of her pretty mouth she spat on the stone floor.

Flaws was glad he was wearing his decent suit of broadcloth, the one his old mother always packed in mothballs at the bottom of his chest for departures and home-comings.

He ordered two glasses of whisky, one for the barmaid. She smiled at him sweetly. They
20   touched rims till the glasses made a small music and the whisky trembled into yellow circles. Flaws was transported. He longed to touch her burnished head. Given time, solitude, and another dram or two, he could well imagine himself kissing her across the bar.

"I haven't seen you in the White Horse before," said the barmaid. "What is your occupation,
25   sir?"

"God forgive me for telling a lie," said Flaws to himself. Then he squared his shoulders and said, "I only visit the islands now and then. I'm a commercial traveller. I travel for earthenware and china."

The barmaid glittered at him with eyes, teeth, hair, rings.

30   The door opened and Small the lawyer's clerk tiptoed in, his drunken nose (Flaws thought) redder than ever. He went up to the bar slowly, eyeing Flaws the way a hunter eyes his quarry. "If it isn't Flaws!" he cried at last. "If it isn't my old friend! And did you catch many whales at Greenland, eh? I can smell the blubber and the oil with you. I warrant you have a fine pile of sovereigns in your pocket. You're the first seaman ever to get into the White
35   Horse."

Flaws could have killed the little drunken clerk at that moment. The barmaid was suddenly looking at him with eyes as cold as stones.

Page ten

SQA EXAM PAPER 2016   **71**   HIGHER ENGLISH

MARKS

Flaws hoisted his box on his shoulder and made for the door without a word. His pocket was heavy with more silver and copper; he had broken another sovereign in the White
40 Horse. He stood, hot with shame and resentment, on the road outside.

"A commercial traveller!" cried Small the lawyer's clerk at the bar. Suddenly the interior of the White Horse was loud with merriment, the deep bass laughter of the farmers mingling with the falsetto mirth of the lawyer's clerk and the merry tinkle of the barmaid.

Flaws walked on towards Birsay, red in the face.

Questions

17. Look at lines 1–16.

By referring to at least **two** examples, analyse how language is used to create a striking impression of the barmaid.   4

18. Look at lines 17–29.`

By referring to at least **two** examples, analyse how language is used to indicate the significance of this moment for Flaws.   4

19. "He stood, hot with shame and resentment . . ." (line 40)

From your reading of the whole extract, explain why Flaws felt "shame" and "resentment" at this point.   2

20. By referring to this extract and to at least one other short story, discuss the use of literal and metaphorical journeys in Mackay Brown's stories.   10

[Turn over

Page eleven

HIGHER ENGLISH   72   SQA EXAM PAPER 2016

OR

Text 3 — Prose

If you choose this text you may not attempt a question on Prose (Fiction or Non-Fiction) in Section 2.

Read the extract below and then attempt the following questions.

The Trick Is To Keep Breathing by Janice Galloway

In this extract, Joy describes her home and the early days of her relationship with Michael.

The cottage was tiny but cheap. There was a bus stop right outside the door and people with no sense used to look in while they were waiting for the bus, as though I was TV. But it also meant travel: buses stopping and starting right outside my door for whenever I needed to go somewhere. It made me feel free. I papered every wall myself and built shelves,
5   wired my own plugs and painted the place fresh. A kind of damp smell hung on in the kitchen but it was my own place, my home now. Paul helped move my things. The parting wasn't bitter. We wanted to be civilised and polite. Unexplained bouts of weeping disturbed the quiet some evenings but I figured they were good signs. Everybody needs to cry now and then. I was there less than six months when Michael phoned his two word call.

10   *She knows.*

He moved in the same night with three carrier bags. There was nowhere else for him to go. He missed the kids but we were OK. Some nights we'd stay awake right through on the pleasure of holding the other warm body in the dark we never expected would be there. We got up red-eyed for work to go to the same place in the same car, came home together
15   at night. When we washed the dishes, we'd watch our reflections in the night-blacked window, kissing.

One night, he got out of bed and didn't come back for a while. It was 2am. I got uneasy about it. I found him in the kitchenette, right at the back of the cottage, turning lilac in the cold. He was kneeling on the concrete looking at something. I kneeled down too and tried
20   to see what it was. There was a mushroom growing out of the skirting. **LOOK** he said, **LOOK**. We didn't know what to think. I poked it with a fork and it broke off. We went back to bed and tried to forget about it.

We were in the kitchen cooking: I was throwing spaghetti onto the roughcast to see if it was ready while he was stirring sauce. The spaghetti landed awkwardly and I saw another
25   mushroom right next to where it had settled on the wall. **LOOK** I said and we both looked again. This one was more securely attached. It didn't break first time so Michael got a knife and cut it away from the side of the window. It left a little pink trail like anaemic blood where it had been growing. After a month there were little shoots all along the hallway. Mould drew lines round the tops of walls and baby mushrooms appeared overnight. I
30   wouldn't let him touch them because I thought they were dangerous or something. I didn't know where they were coming from and preferred just to let them alone in case. In case. Maybe I thought they would go away if we pretended hard enough. Every so often, I would find him in the hall or the kitchen, peering down and scratching with a penknife, then trying to hide it when he saw me coming. I would hear him in the bathroom, running the
35   taps and washing his hands. He got a book from the library and read up about mushrooms.

Page twelve

SQA EXAM PAPER 2016   73   HIGHER ENGLISH

MARKS

Dry rot, he said, matter-of-factly.

Dry rot. He gave me the book so I could read about it too. It was more sinister than the name. The house was being eaten from the inside by this thing. The spores could pass through concrete and plaster and multiply by the thousand thousand as we slept. They
40 could take over the whole structure if they wanted. I lay awake at night wondering what was going on out there in the hall while we were in our beds. The estimates for fixing it were unbelievable. I started having trouble sleeping. I avoided looking at the walls or skirting during the day.

Meantime Michael's council application paid off. The place was too big but he took it. It
45 was cheerful, bright, full of windows. Yellow walls and white woodwork. It was important he had his own place so he needn't feel dependent. Besides I didn't want anyone staying with me out of necessity. People gave us bits of things to fill it with. We shipped in the clothes from the cottage during the night, away from the silent spores, the creeping red clouds.

Questions

21. Look at lines 1–9.

    By referring to at least examples, analyse how the writer's use of language conveys Joy's attempts to be optimistic about her new life.   **3**

22. Look at lines 17–35.

    By referring to at least examples, analyse how the writer's use of language conveys Joy's growing sense of anxiety.   **3**

23. Look at lines 36–49.

    Analyse how the writer's use of language highlights the contrast between the cottage and Michael's council house. You should refer to both sides of the contrast in your answer.   **4**

24. By referring to this extract, and to elsewhere in the novel, discuss how Galloway conveys the impact of Joy's relationship with Michael.   **10**

[Turn over

Page thirteen

OR

Text 4 — Prose

If you choose this text you may not attempt a question on Prose (Fiction or Non-Fiction) in Section 2.

Read the extract below and then attempt the following questions.

Sunset Song by Lewis Grassic Gibbon

In this extract, which is from Part III (Seed-Time), Chris's father has just died.

And out she went, though it wasn't near kye-time yet, and wandered away over the fields; it was a cold and louring day, the sound of the sea came plain to her, as though heard in a shell, Kinraddie wilted under the greyness. In the ley field Old Bob stood with his tail to the wind, his hair ruffled up by the wind, his head bent away from the smore of it. He heard
5   her pass and gave a bit neigh, but he didn't try to follow her, poor brute, he'd soon be over old for work. The wet fields squelched below her feet, oozing up their smell of red clay from under the sodden grasses, and up in the hills she saw the trail of the mist, great sailing shapes of it, going south on the wind into Forfar, past Laurencekirk they would sail, down the wide Howe with its sheltered glens and its late, drenched harvests, past Brechin
10 smoking against its hill, with its ancient tower that the Pictish folk had reared, out of the Mearns, sailing and passing, sailing and passing, she minded Greek words of forgotten lessons, Παντα ρεί, *Nothing endures.* And then a queer thought came to her there in the drookèd fields, that nothing endured at all, nothing but the land she passed across, tossed and turned and perpetually changed below the hands of the crofter folk since the oldest of
15 them had set the Standing Stones by the loch of Blawearie and climbed there on their holy days and saw their terraced crops ride brave in the wind and sun. Sea and sky and the folk who wrote and fought and were learnéd, teaching and saying and praying, they lasted but as a breath, a mist of fog in the hills, but the land was forever, it moved and changed below you, but was forever, you were close to it and it to you, not at a bleak remove it held
20 you and hurted you. And she had thought to leave it all!

She walked weeping then, stricken and frightened because of that knowledge that had come on her, she could never leave it, this life of toiling days and the needs of beasts and the smoke of wood fires and the air that stung your throat so acrid, Autumn and Spring, she was bound and held as though they had prisoned her here. And her fine bit plannings!
25 — they'd been just the dreamings of a child over toys it lacked, toys that would never content it when it heard the smore of a storm or the cry of sheep on the moors or smelt the pringling smell of a new-ploughed park under the drive of a coulter. She could no more teach a school than fly, night and day she'd want to be back, for all the fine clothes and gear she might get and hold, the books and the light and learning.

30 The kye were in sight then, they stood in the lithe of the freestone dyke that ebbed and flowed over the shoulder of the long ley field, and they hugged to it close from the drive of the wind, not heeding her as she came among them, the smell of their bodies foul in her face — foul and known and enduring as the land itself. Oh, she hated and loved in a breath! Even her love might hardly endure, but beside it the hate was no more than the
35 whimpering and fear of a child that cowered from the wind in the lithe of its mother's skirts.

Page fourteen

SQA EXAM PAPER 2016 — 75 — HIGHER ENGLISH

MARKS

And again that night she hardly slept, thinking and thinking till her head ached, the house quiet enough now without fairlies treading the stairs, she felt cool and calm, if only she could sleep. But by morning she knew she couldn't go on with Uncle and Auntie beside her,
40 they smothered her over with their years and their canny supposings. Quick after breakfast she dressed and came down and Auntie cried out, real sharplike, *Mighty be here, Chris, where are you going?* as though she owned Blawearie stick and stone, hoof and hide. And Chris looked at her coolly, *I'm away to Stonehaven to see Mr Semple, can I bring you anything?* Uncle Tam rose up from the table then, goggling, with his medals clinking, *Away*
45 *to Stonehive? What are you jaunting there for? I'll transact any business you have.* Their faces reddened up with rage, she saw plain as daylight how near it lay, dependence on them, she felt herself go white as she looked at them.

Questions

25. Look at lines 1–20.

By referring to at least **two** examples, analyse how the writer creates a sense of Chris's physical surroundings **and/or** her awareness of Scotland's past. **4**

26. Look at lines 21–36.

By referring to at least **two** examples, analyse how the writer reveals Chris's feelings about staying on the land **and/or** her previous plans to leave. **4**

27. Look at lines 37–47.

Analyse how dialogue is used to convey the attitude of at least **one** of the characters. **2**

28. By referring to this extract and to elsewhere in the novel, discuss how Grassic Gibbon develops the idea that *"Nothing endures"*. **10**

[Turn over

Page fifteen

HIGHER ENGLISH | **76** | **SQA EXAM PAPER 2016**

OR

Text 5 — Prose

If you choose this text you may not attempt a question on Prose (Fiction or Non-Fiction) in Section 2.

Read the extract below and then attempt the following questions.

***The Cone-Gatherers* by Robin Jenkins**

In this extract, Roderick is on his way to visit the cone-gatherers in their hut.

By the time the hut came in sight he was exhausted, in body and spirit; sweat of exertion and of fear drenched him. Near some yew trees whose branches reached the ground, forming dark caverns, he halted, to look into his bag to make sure that the cake, the symbol of reconciliation, had not been made to vanish by the evil presences he had just
5 defied. Reassured, he stood breathing in the woodsmoke drifting up so peacefully out of the rusted chimney.

If his senses had not been so preternaturally alert, and if from the dirty hut had not irradiated a light illuminating every leaf on all the trees about it, he would never have noticed the lurker under the cypress, entangled in the thin green bony arms that curled
10 out like an octopus's. No sunshine struck there, and even the luminance from the hut seemed to fail. At first he could not tell who it was, although he was sure it was not one of the cone-gatherers. He felt cold, and frightened, and sick at heart. Here at the very hut was the most evil presence of all, and it was visible.

When he realised that the motionless figure under the cypress was Duror, he crept in
15 dismay into a cave of yew. It was his first retreat, and it was cowardly. Yet he could not force himself to complete the pilgrimage and knock on the door. Duror was a barrier he could not pass.

As he crouched in the earthy darkness like an animal, he wondered what Duror's purpose could be in lurking there. The gamekeeper hated the men in the hut and wished to have
20 them expelled from the wood. Was he now spying on them in the hope that he would find them engaged in some wrong-doing, such as working today, which was Sunday? By their agreement with his mother they were not to work on Sundays. But Duror himself shot deer on Sundays; he did not often go to church, and when he did he sat with his arms folded and a smile of misery on his lips. Why then did he hate the cone-gatherers and wish to
25 drive them away? Was it because they represented goodness, and himself evil? Coached by his grandfather, Roderick knew that the struggle between good and evil never rested: in the world, and in every human being, it went on. The war was an enormous example. Good did not always win. So many times had Christian been overcome and humiliated; so long had Sir Galahad searched and suffered. In the end, aye, in the bitter end, the old judge
30 had said, with a chuckle, good would remain alone in the field, victorious.

The minutes passed. Nothing had changed. The blue smoke still rose from the chimney. Duror had not moved. In his den of yew Roderick grew cramped; and in an even darker, narrower den of disillusionment his mind whimpered.

Half an hour, at insect's pace, crept by. Only a leaf or two had fallen from a tree, as a
35 breeze stirred. Far away, over the loch, a gull had screamed.

Page sixteen

MARKS

Had Duror gone mad? Was this the change his mother had asked Mrs. Morton about? Again Roderick recalled the scene at the deer drive with Duror embracing as if in love the screaming deer and hacking at its throat with a knife. Mrs. Morton, who was Duror's friend, had talked about the perils of the wood; she had mentioned the cone-gatherers, but
40 perhaps in her heart she had been meaning Duror. If he was mad, then, was he now waiting with a gun to commit murder?

Peeping through the yew needles, Roderick saw in imagination the door of the hut open, and the cone-gatherers come out, the tall one who slightly limped and always frowned, and the small one who stooped and smiled. Then in the cypress the gun cracked, and the
45 two men lay dead on the grass.

Questions

29. Look at lines 1–13.

    By referring to at least **two** examples, analyse how the writer uses language effectively to create a sinister atmosphere. **4**

30. Look at lines 18–45.

    By referring to at least **two** examples, analyse how Roderick is presented as a mature character despite his youth. **4**

31. Duror is important in this extract, although he actually does very little. With reference to the extract as a whole, explain why he is important. **2**

32. With reference to this extract, and to elsewhere in the novel, discuss how the writer develops the theme of conflict between good and evil. **10**

[Turn over

Page seventeen

HIGHER ENGLISH   78   SQA EXAM PAPER 2016

SECTION 1 — SCOTTISH TEXT — 20 marks

Choose ONE text from Drama, Prose or Poetry.

Read the text extract carefully and then attempt ALL the questions for your chosen text.

You should spend about 45 minutes on this Section.

PART C — SCOTTISH TEXT — POETRY

Text 1 — Poetry

If you choose this text you may not attempt a question on Poetry in Section 2.

Read the poem below and then attempt the following questions.

A Poet's Welcome to His Love-Begotten Daughter; The First Instance that entitled him to the Venerable Appellation of Father **by Robert Burns**

        Thou's welcome, wean, mishanter fa' me,
        If thought of thee, or of thy mammy,
        Shall ever daunton me or awe me,
                My sweet wee lady!
    5   Or if I blush when thou shalt ca' me
                Ti-ta or daddy.

        Tho' now they ca' me fornicator,
        An' tease my name in kintry clatter,
        The mair they talk, I'm kent the better,
    10   E'en let them clash;
        An auld wife's tongue's a feckless matter
                To gie ane fash.

        Welcome! my bonnie, sweet, wee dochter,
        Tho' ye come here a wee unsought for,
    15 And tho' your comin' I hae fought for,
                Baith kirk and queir;
        Yet, by my faith, ye're no unwrought for
                That I shall swear!

        Sweet fruit o' monie a merry dint,
    20 My funny toil is now a' tint,
        Sin' thou came to the warl' asklent,
                Which fools may scoff at;
        In my last plack thy part's be in 't
                The better ha'f o't.

    25 Tho' I should be the waur bestead,
        Thou's be as braw and bienly clad,
        And thy young years as nicely bred
                Wi' education,
        As onie brat o' wedlock's bed,
    30   In a' thy station.

Page eighteen

SQA EXAM PAPER 2016   79   **HIGHER ENGLISH**

MARKS

Wee image o' my bonnie Betty,
I, fatherly, will kiss and daut thee,
As dear, an' near my heart I set thee
       Wi' as guid will
35 As a' the priests had seen me get thee
       That's out o' hell.

Lord grant that thou may ay inherit
Thy mither's person, grace an' merit,
An' thy poor, worthless daddy's spirit,
40   Without his failins,
'Twill please me mair to see thee heir it,
       Than stockit mailens.

For if thou be what I wad hae thee,
And tak the counsel I shall gie thee,
45 I'll never rue my trouble wi' thee,
       The cost nor shame o't,
But be a loving father to thee,
       And brag the name o't.

Questions

33. Look at lines 1–6.

Analyse how the speaker conveys his feelings about his newly born child.   **2**

34. Look at lines 7–18.

By referring to at least **two** examples, analyse how the poet's language makes clear the speaker's response to his critics.   **4**

35. Look at lines 25–48.

By referring to at least **two** examples, analyse how the poet's language effectively reveals aspects of the speaker's personality.   **4**

36. Discuss Burns' treatment of the religious **and/or** moral concerns of his time in this, and at least one other, poem.   **10**

[Turn over

Page nineteen

HIGHER ENGLISH 80 SQA EXAM PAPER 2016

OR

Text 2 — Poetry

If you choose this text you may not attempt a question on Poetry in Section 2.

Read the extract below and then attempt the following questions.

Mrs Midas **by Carol Ann Duffy**

It was late September. I'd just poured a glass of wine, begun
to unwind, while the vegetables cooked. The kitchen
filled with the smell of itself, relaxed, its steamy breath
gently blanching the windows. So I opened one,
5   then with my fingers wiped the other's glass like a brow.
He was standing under the pear tree snapping a twig.

Now the garden was long and the visibility poor, the way
the dark of the ground seems to drink the light of the sky,
but that twig in his hand was gold. And then he plucked
10   a pear from a branch — we grew Fondante d'Automne —
and it sat in his palm like a light bulb. On.
I thought to myself, Is he putting fairy lights in the tree?

He came into the house. The doorknobs gleamed.
He drew the blinds. You know the mind; I thought of
15   the Field of the Cloth of Gold and of Miss Macready.
He sat in that chair like a king on a burnished throne.
The look on his face was strange, wild, vain. I said,
What in the name of God is going on? He started to laugh.

I served up the meal. For starters, corn on the cob.
20   Within seconds he was spitting out the teeth of the rich.
He toyed with his spoon, then mine, then with the knives, the forks.
He asked where was the wine. I poured with shaking hand,
a fragrant, bone-dry white from Italy, then watched
as he picked up the glass, goblet, golden chalice, drank.

25   It was then that I started to scream. He sank to his knees.
After we had both calmed down, I finished the wine
on my own, hearing him out. I made him sit
on the other side of the room and keep his hands to himself.
I locked the cat in the cellar. I moved the phone.
30   The toilet I didn't mind. I couldn't believe my ears:

how he'd had a wish. Look, we all have wishes; granted.
But who has wishes granted? Him. Do you know about gold?
It feeds no one; aurum, soft, untarnishable; slakes
no thirst. He tried to light a cigarette; I gazed, entranced,
35   as the blue flame played on its luteous stem. At least,
I said, you'll be able to give up smoking for good.

Page twenty

SQA EXAM PAPER 2016   81   HIGHER ENGLISH

MARKS

Questions

37. Look at lines 1–12.

By referring to at least **two** examples, analyse how the poet's language conveys the contrast in atmosphere between stanza 1 and stanza 2.   **4**

38. Look at lines 13–24.

Analyse how the poet's language in these lines creates an unsettling mood.   **2**

39. Look at lines 25–36.

By referring to at least **two** examples, analyse how the poet's language presents the character of Mrs Midas.   **4**

40. By referring closely to this poem, and to at least one other poem by Duffy, discuss how the poet explores the attempts of characters to cope with life-changing situations.   **10**

[Turn over

Page twenty-one

HIGHER ENGLISH   82   SQA EXAM PAPER 2016

OR

Text 3 — Poetry

If you choose this text you may not attempt a question on Poetry in Section 2.

Read the extract below and then attempt the following questions.

The Bargain **by Liz Lochhead**

The river in January is fast and high.
You and I
are off to the Barrows.
Gathering police-horses twitch and fret
5 at the Tron end of London Road and Gallowgate.
The early kick-off we forgot
has us, three thirty, rubbing the wrong way
against all the ugly losers
getting ready to let fly
10 where the two rivers meet.

January, and we're
looking back, looking forward,
don't know which way

but the boy
15 with three beautiful Bakelite
Bush radios for sale in Meadow's Minimarket is
buttonpopping stationhopping he
doesn't miss a beat sings along it's easy
to every changing tune

20 Yes today we're in love aren't we?
with the whole splintering city
its big quick river wintry bridges
its brazen black Victorian heart.
So what if every other tenement
25 wears its hearth on its gable end?
All I want
is my glad eye to catch
a glint in your flinty Northern face again
just once. Oh I know it's cold
30 and coming down
and no we never lingered long among
the Shipbank traders.
Paddy's Market underneath the arches
stank too much today
35 the usual wetdog reek rising
from piles of old damp clothes.

Page twenty-two

SQA EXAM PAPER 2016 · **83** · **HIGHER ENGLISH**

MARKS

Questions

41. Look at lines 1–13.

By referring to at least **two** examples, analyse how the language in these lines introduces the deterioration of the speaker's relationship.

4

42. Look at lines 14–19.

Analyse how the poet's language creates a change of mood.

2

43. Look at lines 20–36.

By referring to at least **two** examples, analyse how the poet uses setting to reflect the current state of the speaker's relationship.

4

44. By referring to this poem, and at least one other poem by Lochhead, discuss how she explores the theme of difficult relationships.

10

[Turn over

Page twenty-three

OR

Text 4 — Poetry

If you choose this text you may not attempt a question on Poetry in Section 2.

Read the poem below and then attempt the following questions.

Memorial by Norman MacCaig

Everywhere she dies. Everywhere I go she dies.
No sunrise, no city square, no lurking beautiful mountain
but has her death in it.
The silence of her dying sounds through
5 the carousel of language, it's a web
on which laughter stitches itself. How can my hand
clasp another's when between them
is that thick death, that intolerable distance?

She grieves for my grief. Dying, she tells me
10 that bird dives from the sun, that fish
leaps into it. No crocus is carved more gently
than the way her dying
shapes my mind. — But I hear, too,
the other words,
15 black words that make the sound
of soundlessness, that name the nowhere
she is continuously going into.

Ever since she died
she can't stop dying. She makes me
20 her elegy. I am a walking masterpiece,
a true fiction
of the ugliness of death.
I am her sad music.

Page twenty-four

SQA EXAM PAPER 2016   **85**   HIGHER ENGLISH

MARKS

Questions

45. Look at lines 1–8.

By referring to at least **two** examples, analyse how the language emphasises the devastating impact of the loved one's death on the speaker's life.   **3**

46. Look at lines 9–17.

By referring to at least **two** examples, analyse how the language conveys the close bond between the loved one and the speaker.   **4**

47. Look at lines 18–23.

By referring to at least **two** examples, analyse how the language emphasises the fact that the subject's death remains ever present in the speaker's mind.   **3**

48. Discuss how reaction to suffering is explored in this, and at least one other, poem by MacCaig.   **10**

[Turn over

Page twenty-five

OR

Text 5 — Poetry

If you choose this text you may not attempt a question on Poetry in Section 2.

Read the poem below and then attempt the following questions.

Shores **by Sorley MacLean**

If we were in Talisker on the shore
where the great white mouth
opens between two hard jaws,
Rubha nan Clach and the Bioda Ruadh,
5   I would stand beside the sea
renewing love in my spirit
while the ocean was filling
Talisker bay forever:
I would stand on the bareness of the shore
10 until Prishal bowed his stallion head.

And if we were together
on Calgary shore in Mull,
between Scotland and Tiree,
between the world and eternity,
15 I would stay there till doom
measuring sand, grain by grain,
and in Uist, on the shore of Homhsta
in presence of that wide solitude,
I would wait there forever
20 for the sea draining drop by drop.

And if I were on the shore of Moidart
with you, for whom my care is new,
I would put up in a synthesis of love for you
The ocean and the sand, drop and grain.
25 And if we were on Mol Stenscholl Staffin
when the unhappy surging sea dragged
the boulders and threw them over us,
I would build the rampart wall
against an alien eternity grinding (its teeth).

Page twenty-six

SQA EXAM PAPER 2016   **87**   HIGHER ENGLISH

MARKS

Questions

49. Look at lines 1–14.

By referring to at least **two** examples, analyse how language is used to convey the powerful impact of the landscape on the speaker.   4

50. Look at lines 15–24.

By referring to at least **two** examples, analyse how language is used effectively to convey the intensity of the speaker's love.   4

51. Look at lines 25–29.

By referring to ideas **and/or** language, evaluate the effectiveness of these lines as a conclusion to the poem.   2

52. Referring closely to this and to at least one other poem, discuss how MacLean explores the impact of time on human experience.   10

[Turn over

Page twenty-seven

HIGHER ENGLISH **88** SQA EXAM PAPER 2016

MARKS

OR

Text 6 — Poetry

If you choose this text you may not attempt a question on Poetry in Section 2.

Read the poem below and then attempt the following questions.

***The Thread* by Don Paterson**

Jamie made his landing in the world
so hard he ploughed straight back into the earth.
They caught him by the thread of his one breath
and pulled him up. They don't know how it held.
5   And so today I thank what higher will
brought us to here, to you and me and Russ,
the great twin-engined swaying wingspan of us
roaring down the back of Kirrie Hill

and your two-year-old lungs somehow out-revving
10 every engine in the universe.
All that trouble just to turn up dead
was all I thought that long week. Now the thread
is holding all of us: look at our tiny house,
son, the white dot of your mother waving.

Questions

53. Look at lines 1–4.

   By referring to at least **two** examples, analyse how the poet's use of language suggests the difficulties surrounding Jamie's birth.   **4**

54. Look at lines 5–10.

   Analyse how the poet's use of language conveys the present circumstances of the family.   **2**

55. Look at lines 11–14.

   By referring to at least **two** examples, evaluate the effectiveness of these lines as a conclusion to the poem.   **4**

56. Discuss how the poet explores the fragility of human life in this, and at least one other, poem.   **10**

[END OF SECTION 1]

Page twenty-eight

SQA EXAM PAPER 2016   89   HIGHER ENGLISH

SECTION 2 — CRITICAL ESSAY — 20 marks

Attempt ONE question from the following genres — Drama, Prose Fiction, Prose Non-fiction, Poetry, Film and Television Drama, or Language.

Your answer must be on a different genre from that chosen in Section 1.

You should spend approximately 45 minutes on this Section.

PART A — DRAMA

Answers to questions on Drama should refer to the text and to such relevant features as characterisation, key scene(s), structure, climax, theme, plot, conflict, setting . . .

1. Choose a play in which a central character is in conflict with **or** rejects another character.

    Briefly explain the circumstances of the conflict or rejection and go on to discuss the consequences of this conflict or rejection for the play as a whole.

2. Choose a play in which the historical **and/or** geographical **and/or** social setting is important to your understanding of the play.

    Explain how the dramatist presents the setting and discuss why it is important to your understanding of the play as a whole.

3. Choose a play which has an effective opening scene **or** concluding scene.

    By briefly referring to details of the scene, explain how the dramatist made it effective and discuss how it contributes to your appreciation of the text as a whole.

[Turn over

Page twenty-nine

HIGHER ENGLISH　　90　　SQA EXAM PAPER 2016

PART B — PROSE FICTION

> *Answers to questions on Prose Fiction should refer to the text and to such relevant features as characterisation, setting, language, key incident(s), climax, turning point, plot, structure, narrative technique, theme, ideas, description . . .*

4. Choose a novel **or** short story in which there is a central character to whom you react with mixed feelings.

   With reference to appropriate techniques, briefly explain why you react to the character in this way and discuss how this reaction adds to your understanding of the text as a whole.

5. Choose a novel **or** short story that deals with a theme of moral **or** social significance.

   With reference to appropriate techniques, explain how the writer develops this theme and discuss why its development adds to your appreciation of the text as a whole.

6. Choose a novel **or** short story in which the choice of setting is central to your appreciation of the text.

   Briefly explain how the writer effectively creates setting and, with reference to appropriate techniques, discuss how the writer's presentation of the setting is central to your appreciation of the text as a whole.

PART C — PROSE NON-FICTION

> *Answers to questions on Prose Non-Fiction should refer to the text and to such relevant features as ideas, use of evidence, stance, style, selection of material, narrative voice . . .*
>
> *Non-fiction texts can include travel writing, journalism, autobiography, biography, essays . . .*

7. Choose a non-fiction text in which the writer engages your interest in a place **or** culture.

   Discuss, with reference to appropriate techniques, how the writer successfully engages your interest in this place or culture.

8. Choose a non-fiction text in which the writer describes a traumatic **or** rewarding experience.

   Discuss, with reference to appropriate techniques, how the writer conveys the traumatic or rewarding nature of the experience.

9. Choose a non-fiction text in which the writer attempts to influence the reader's opinion on a person **or** an issue.

   Discuss, with reference to appropriate techniques, how the writer attempts to influence the reader's opinion on the person or the issue.

Page thirty

PART D — POETRY

Answers to questions on Poetry should refer to the text and to such relevant features as word choice, tone, imagery, structure, content, rhythm, rhyme, theme, sounds, ideas . . .

10. Choose a poem in which the poet creates a vivid sense of a particular time **or** a particular place.

    Discuss how the poet's vivid depiction of time or place adds to your appreciation of the central concern(s) of the poem.

11. Choose a poem with a moral **or** social **or** political theme.

    Discuss, with reference to appropriate techniques, how the poet's presentation of the theme deepens your understanding of the poem as a whole.

12. Choose a poem in which the poet effectively creates a character **or** persona.

    Discuss, with reference to appropriate techniques, how the poet's effective creation of the character or persona enhances your appreciation of the poem as a whole.

[Turn over for next question

Page thirty-one

HIGHER ENGLISH **92** SQA EXAM PAPER 2016

PART E — FILM AND TELEVISION DRAMA

Answers to questions on Film and Television Drama* should refer to the text and to such relevant features as use of camera, key sequence, characterisation, mise-en-scène, editing, music/sound, special effects, plot, dialogue . . .

13. Choose a film **or** television drama in which there is a particularly tense or dramatic sequence.

    Explain how the film or programme makers use media techniques to achieve this effect.

14. Choose a film **or** television drama which concerns an individual **or** a group of characters facing a significant challenge.

    Explain how the film or programme makers use media techniques to convey the significance of this challenge.

15. Choose a film **or** television drama which is targeted at a specific audience.

    Explain how the film or programme makers use media techniques to target this audience.

* "television drama" includes a single play, a series or a serial.

PART F — LANGUAGE

Answers to questions on Language should refer to the text and to such relevant features as register, accent, dialect, slang, jargon, vocabulary, tone, abbreviation . . .

16. Choose a particular area of language associated with mass communication, eg advertising, broadcasting, technology.

    Identify specific examples and discuss to what extent they are effective.

17. Choose language used in a specific work setting such as hospital, courtroom, garage, school, parliament . . .

    Identify specific examples of the language used and evaluate their effectiveness within the work setting.

18. Choose the language associated with pressure groups (multi-cultural organisations, environmental agencies, faith groups, campaigners for equality . . .)

    By referring to specific examples, discuss what makes the language of one such group successful in achieving its purpose to persuade.

[END OF SECTION 2]

[END OF QUESTION PAPER]

Page thirty-two

HIGHER
2017

H National Qualifications 2017

X724/76/11

English
Reading for Understanding,
Analysis and Evaluation — Text

THURSDAY, 11 MAY
9:00 AM – 10:30 AM

Total marks — 30

Read the passages carefully and then attempt ALL questions, which are printed on a separate sheet.

HIGHER ENGLISH 96 SQA EXAM PAPER 2017

This Question Paper replaces the original SQA 2017 Past Paper, which cannot be reproduced for copyright reasons. As such, it should be stressed that it is not an official SQA-verified section, although every care has been taken by the Publishers to ensure that it offers appropriate practice material for Higher English.

The following two passages focus on video games.

Passage 1

Read the passage below and then attempt questions 1 to 5.

In the first passage, Steven Johnson, writing in The Times newspaper, considers whether video games are as bad for young people as is often claimed.

Reading books enriches the mind; playing video games deadens it — you can't get much more conventional than the conventional wisdom that kids today would be better off spending more time reading books, and less time zoning out in front of their video games.

5   For the record, I think that the virtues of reading books are great. We should all encourage our kids to read more. But even the most avid reader is inevitably going to spend his or her time with other media — games, television, movies, the internet. Yet the question is whether these other forms of culture have intellectual virtues in their own right — different from, but comparable to, reading. Where most critics allege a dumbing down, I see a progressive story: popular culture steadily, but almost imperceptibly, making our brains sharper as we soak in

10   entertainment usually dismissed as so much lowbrow fluff. I hope to persuade you that increasingly the non-literary popular culture is honing different mental skills that are just as important as the ones exercised by reading books.

The most powerful example of this trend is found in the world of video games. And the first and last thing that should be said about the experience of playing today's video games, the thing

15   you almost never hear, is that games are fiendishly, sometimes maddeningly, hard. The dirty little secret of gaming is how much time you spend not having fun. You may be frustrated; you may be confused or disorientated; you may be stuck. But when you put the game down and move back into the real world, you may find yourself mentally working through the problem you have been wrestling with, as though you were worrying a loose tooth.

20   So why does anyone bother playing these things? And why does a seven-year-old soak up, for instance, the intricacies of industrial economics in the game form of SimCity 2000, when the same subject would send him screaming for the exits in a classroom? To date, there has been little direct research into the question of how games get children to learn without realising that they are learning. But I believe a strong case can be made that the power of games to captivate

25   largely involves their ability to tap into the brain's natural reward circuitry. If you create a system in which rewards are both clearly defined and achieved by exploring an environment, you will find human brains drawn to those systems, even if they are made up of virtual characters and simulated sidewalks. In the game world, reward is everywhere. The gaming universe is literally teeming with objects that deliver very clearly articulated rewards: more life, access to

30   new levels, new equipment, new spells. Most of the crucial work in game design focuses on keeping players notified of potential rewards available to them, and how much these rewards are currently needed. Most games offer a fictional world where rewards are larger, and more vivid, and more clearly defined than life.

Page two

SQA EXAM PAPER 2017   **97**   HIGHER ENGLISH

You may just want to win the game, of course, or perhaps you want to see the game's narrative
35 completed, or in the initial stages of play, you may just be dazzled by the game's graphics. But
most of the time, when you're hooked on a game, what draws you in is an elemental form of
desire: the desire to see the Next Thing. After all, with the occasional exception, the actual
content of the game is often childish or gratuitously menacing. Much of the role play inside
the gaming world alternates between drive-by shooting and princess-rescuing. It is not the
40 subject matter that attracts; it is the reward system that draws those players in, and keeps their
famously short attention spans locked on the screen.

Playing down the content of video games shouldn't be seen as a cop-out. We ignore the
content of many other activities that are widely considered to be good for the brain. No one
complains about the simplistic, militaristic plot of chess games. We teach algebra to children
45 knowing full well that the day they leave the classroom 99 per cent of those kids will never
again directly employ their algebraic skills. Learning algebra isn't about acquiring a specific
tool; it's about building up a mental muscle that will come in handy elsewhere.

So it is with games. It's not what you're thinking about when you're playing a game, it's the way
you're thinking that matters. Novels may activate our imagination and may conjure up powerful
50 emotions, but games force you to analyse, to choose, to prioritise, to decide. From the outside,
the primary activity of a gamer looks like a fury of clicking and shooting. But if
you peer inside the gamer's mind, the primary activity turns out to be another creature
altogether: making decisions, some of them snap judgements, some of them long-term
strategies.

Adapted from an article in The Times newspaper, May 2005

Passage 2

**Read the passage below and attempt question 6. While reading, you may wish to make notes on
the main ideas and/or highlight key points in the passage.**

*In the second passage, the politician and journalist Boris Johnson, writing on his own website,
takes a different view about video games.*

It's the snarl that gives the game away. It's the sobbing and the shrieking and the horrible
pleading — that's how you know your children are undergoing a sudden narcotic withdrawal. As
the strobing colours die away and the screen goes black, you listen to the wail of protest from
the offspring and you know that you have just turned off their drug, and you know that they are,
5 to a greater or lesser extent, addicts.

Millions of seven-to-fifteen-year olds are hooked, especially boys, and it is time someone had
the guts to stand up, cross the room and just say no to Nintendo. It is time to garrotte the Game
Boy and paralyse the PlayStation, and it is about time, as a society, that we admitted the
catastrophic effect these blasted gizmos are having on the literacy and the prospects of young
10 males.

We demand that teachers provide our children with reading skills; we expect the schools to fill
them with a love of books; and yet at home we let them slump in front of the consoles. We get on
with our hedonistic 21st-century lives while in some other room the nippers are bleeping and
zapping in speechless rapture, their passive faces washed in explosions and gore. They sit for so
15 long that their souls seem to have been sucked down the cathode ray tube.

Page three

They become like blinking lizards, motionless, absorbed, only the twitching of their hands showing that they are still conscious. These machines teach them nothing. They stimulate no ratiocination, discovery or feat of memory — though some of them may cunningly pretend to be educational. I have just watched an eleven-year-old play a game that looked fairly historical, on
20 the packet. Your average guilt-ridden parent might assume that it taught the child something about the Vikings and medieval siege warfare. Phooey! The red soldiers robotically slaughtered the white soldiers, and then they did it again, that was it. Everything was programmed, spoon-fed, immediate — and endlessly showering the player with undeserved praise, richly congratulating him for his bogus massacres.

25 The more addictive these games are to the male mind, the more difficult it is to persuade boys to read books. It's not that these young people lack the brains; the raw circuitry is better than ever. It's the software that's the problem. They have not been properly programmed, because they have not read enough. The only way to learn to write is to be forced time and again to articulate your own thoughts in your own words, and you haven't a hope of doing this if you haven't read enough
30 to absorb the basic elements of vocabulary, grammar, rhythm, style and structure; and young males in particular won't read enough if we continually capitulate and let them fritter their lives away in front of these drivelling machines.

So I say now: go to where your children are sitting in auto-lobotomy in front of the console. Summon up all your strength, all your courage. Steel yourself for the screams and yank out that
35 plug. And if they still kick up a fuss, then get out the sledgehammer and strike a blow for literacy.

Adapted from an article published on Boris Johnson's website in June 2006

[END OF QUESTION PAPER]

Page four

SQA EXAM PAPER 2017 99 HIGHER ENGLISH

[OPEN OUT]

DO NOT WRITE ON THIS PAGE

[BLANK PAGE]

DO NOT WRITE ON THIS PAGE

National Qualifications 2017

X724/76/21

English
Reading for Understanding, Analysis and Evaluation — Questions

THURSDAY, 11 MAY
9:00 AM – 10:30 AM

Total marks — 30

Attempt ALL questions.

Write your answers clearly in the answer booklet provided. In the answer booklet you must clearly identify the question number you are attempting.

Use **blue** or **black** ink.

Before leaving the examination room you must give your answer booklet to the Invigilator; if you do not, you may lose all the marks for this paper.

HIGHER ENGLISH **102** SQA EXAM PAPER 2017

MARKS

Attempt ALL questions
Total marks — 30

1. Read lines 1–12.

   (a) Analyse how the writer's word choice in lines 1–3 emphasises the "conventional wisdom" that reading books is better than playing video games. **2**

   (b) Explain in your own words "the question" the writer asks in line 6 about "other forms of culture". **2**

   (c) **By referring to at least two features of language in lines 8–12** ("Where ... books"), analyse how the writer emphasises the contrast between his positive view of "other forms of culture" and the negative view held by "most critics". **4**

2. By referring to lines 13–19, analyse how the writer uses both sentence structure and imagery to convey the difficulty of playing video games **4**

3. Read lines 20–33.

   Identify **three** reasons why "reward" is so important to the learning process involved in playing video games. Use your own words as far as possible. **3**

4. Read lines 34–47.

   Identify **two** criticisms and **two** defences the writer makes of video games. **4**

5. Read lines 48–54.

   (a) Explain in your own words the key distinction the writer makes between reading a novel and playing a video game. **2**

   (b) Analyse how the writer's use of language in lines 50–54 ("From ... strategies") conveys the contrast between what a gamer looks like from "the outside" and what is happening "inside the gamer's mind". **4**

Question on both passages

6. Look at both passages.

   The writers disagree about video games.

   Identify three key areas on which they disagree.

   You should support the points by referring to important ideas in both passages.

   You may answer this question in continuous prose or in a series of developed bullet points. **5**

[END OF QUESTION PAPER]

Page two

National Qualifications 2017

X724/76/12

English Critical Reading

THURSDAY, 11 MAY
10:50 AM – 12:20 PM

Total marks — 40

SECTION 1 — Scottish Text — 20 marks

Read an extract from a Scottish text you have previously studied and attempt the questions.

Choose ONE text from either

Part A — Drama   Pages 02–13
or
Part B — Prose   Pages 14–23
or
Part C — Poetry   Pages 24–35

Attempt ALL the questions for your chosen text.

SECTION 2 — Critical Essay — 20 marks

Attempt ONE question from the following genres — Drama, Prose Fiction, Prose Non-Fiction, Poetry, Film and Television Drama, or Language.

Your answer must be on a different genre from that chosen in Section 1.

You should spend approximately 45 minutes on each Section.

Write your answers clearly in the answer booklet provided. In the answer booklet, you must clearly identify the question number you are attempting.

Use **blue** or **black** ink.

Before leaving the examination room you must give your answer booklet to the Invigilator; if you do not, you may lose all the marks for this paper.

HIGHER ENGLISH 104 SQA EXAM PAPER 2017

SECTION 1 — SCOTTISH TEXT — 20 marks

Choose ONE text from Drama, Prose or Poetry.

Read the text extract carefully and then attempt ALL the questions for your chosen text.

You should spend about 45 minutes on this Section.

PART A — SCOTTISH TEXT — DRAMA

Text 1 — Drama

If you choose this text you may not attempt a question on Drama in Section 2.

Read the extract below and then attempt the following questions.

The Slab Boys by John Byrne

In this extract, from Act 2 of the play, Spanky and Phil believe that Hector has just lost his job.

	SPANKY:	We'd like to present this little . . . er . . . this token of . . . er . . .
	HECTOR:	There was five of them . . . plus a squared-off fitch with my name on it . . .
	SPANKY:	Are you going to shut your face and listen, Shorty? Me and Phil's trying to make a presentation here.
5	PHIL:	It's a quid.
	SPANKY:	Shut up.
	HECTOR:	Sorry, what were you saying?
	SPANKY:	We know it's come as a bit of a surprise to you, Hector . . . you having to leave the Slab Room . . .
10	HECTOR:	It's a bombshell . . . no kidding . . .
	SPANKY:	(*to Phil*) Doesn't make it easy, does he? Er . . . so what me and Phil's done is . . . er . . . well, we put round the hat and . . . er . . .
	PHIL:	Carry on, you're doing fine.
	SPANKY:	It's not a lot, you understand . . .
15	PHIL:	It's a quid, son.
	SPANKY:	Shut up, will you!
	PHIL:	Give us it. (*Snatches 'presentation'.*) What Spanky was trying to say, Hector, is . . . er . . . och, here.
	SPANKY:	It's a quid.
20		*They clap.*
	HECTOR:	What's this for?
	PHIL:	Not even a "Thank you, boys, I'm really touched." You are leaving the Slab Room, right?
	HECTOR:	Yeh, but . . .
25	SPANKY:	Then that'll tide you over . . . you and your maw . . .

Page two

PHIL:	Till you get another job.
HECTOR:	Eh?
SPANKY:	He said, till you get another job.
HECTOR:	Eh?

30 SPANKY *and* PHIL (*together*): Till you get another job!

HECTOR:	I've already got another job.
PHIL:	Christ, that was quick. Is there a mobile Broo outside?
HECTOR:	That's what I was along seeing Willie about . . . my new job . . . I start on a desk on Monday.

35 SPANKY *and* PHIL (*together*): What????

HECTOR:	I'm a Designer now. Seven quid a week back-dated a fortnight, rising in annual increments to twelve pounds fifteen and eleven after tax at the end of four years. God, I don't think I feel too well . . .
SPANKY:	Me too . . .

40 HECTOR: It's the excitement.

(*Enter* Alan.)

ALAN:	Hey . . . guess what? Since two of you guys are vacating the Slab, Curry thought I should step in and fill the breach . . . how about that? Where are the gum crystals kept again? (*Hunts around.*) Oh . . . there was a phone call came

45

	through to Willie's office . . . I said I'd pass the message on . . .
PHIL:	Eh? Is my maw safe??
ALAN:	You didn't get in.
PHIL:	What?
ALAN:	Exceptionally high number of applicants this year . . . something like that . . .

Page three

MARKS

Questions

1. Look at lines 1—20.

   By referring to **at least two** examples, analyse how dialogue is used to reveal the attitudes of the slab boys (Phil and Spanky) to Hector's situation at this point.

   3

2. Look at lines 21—40.

   By referring to **at least two** examples, analyse how humour is used in relation to Hector's announcement.

   4

3. Look at lines 42—49.

   By referring to **at least two** examples, analyse how language is used to convey Alan's character **and/or** attitudes.

   3

4. By referring to this extract and to elsewhere in the play, discuss how Byrne develops the theme of opportunity.

   10

Page four

SQA EXAM PAPER 2017   **107**   HIGHER ENGLISH

[OPEN OUT FOR QUESTIONS]

DO NOT WRITE ON THIS PAGE

Page five

OR

Text 2 — Drama

If you choose this text you may not attempt a question on Drama in Section 2.

Read the extract below and then attempt the following questions.

***The Cheviot, the Stag and the Black, Black Oil* by John McGrath**

This extract focuses on a shooting party in the Highlands.

Enter shooting party with large armoury. GHILLIE, LORD CRASK, *and* LADY PHOSPHATE OF RUNCORN.

    LADY PH: Her Royal Majesty the Queen is so right about the charm of this divine part of the world, what? Your estates, Lord Crask, abound in brown trout and
5   grouse — what? —

    LORD CRASK: Has your Ladyship sampled the salmon?

    LADY PH: The rugged beauty hereabouts puts one in mind of the poetic fancies of dear Lord Tennyson — what?

    LORD CRASK: Lady Phosphate of Runcorn you are too kind.

10 LADY PH: Oh listen for the vale profound is overflowing with the sound.

    Blast of gunfire.

GHILLIE (*tries to stop them*): No no no no — the beaters are just having their tea.

    LADY PH: As one does. What?

    LORD CRASK: What?

15   *Goes to fire;* GHILLIE *restrains him.*

GHILLIE (*to audience*): That's nothing, you should see him when he's fishing.

    LADY PH: How far do your domains extend over this beauteous countryside, Lord Crask?

    LORD CRASK: I have about 120,000 acres down that way, but most of it's over that way.

20 LADY PH: Oh Archie . . . Capital, capital, capital . . .

    LORD CRASK: Oh yes I've got bags of that too — 200,000 shares in Argentine Beef, half a million tied up in shipping, and a mile or two of docks in Wapping.

    LADY PH: Topping —

    LORD CRASK: No Wapping —

25 LADY PH: What?

    LORD CRASK *goes to shoot —* GHILLIE *restrains him.*

    GHILLIE: No no no no no.

    LADY PH: Your highland air is very bracing — I quite fancy a small port . . .

    LORD CRASK: Oh — how would you like Lochinver?

30 LADY PH: No no no, I mean I'd like to wet my whistle —

    LORD CRASK (*waving hand*): We've left a bush over there for that sort of thing . . .

Page six

GHILLIE *whistles up the beaters.*

GHILLIE: Any moment now sir . . .

LORD CRASK: Here come the grouse, Lady Phosphate —

35 LADY PH: What?

LORD CRASK: The grouse —

LADY PH: Oh, how lovely. (*She gets out a sten gun.*) I find it so moving that all over the north of North Britain, healthy, vigorous people are deriving so much innocent pleasure at so little cost to their fellow human beings.

40 *Barrage.* GHILLIE *aims* LORD CRASK's *gun up higher, struggles with him.* LADY PHOSPHATE *fires her sten from the hip. Bombs, shells, etc. Barrage ends.*

GHILLIE: Oh no — Thon was a nice wee boy.

Music — guitar and mandolin begins. LORD CRASK *and* LADY PHOSPHATE *sing a duet.*

BOTH: Oh it's awfully, frightfully, ni-i-ice,
45 Shooting stags, my dear, and grice —
And there's nothing quite so righ-it-it
As a fortnight catching trite:

And if the locals should complain,
Well we can clear them off again.

50 LADY PH: We'll clear the straths

LORD CRASK: We'll clear the paths

LADY PH: We'll clear the bens

LORD CRASK: We'll clear the glens

BOTH: We'll show them we're the ruling class.

Page seven

HIGHER ENGLISH 110 SQA EXAM PAPER 2017

MARKS

Questions

5. Look at lines 1—19.

   By referring to **at least two** examples, analyse how language is used to convey the characters of **both** Lady Phosphate and Lord Crask.

   4

6. Look at lines 20—42.

   By referring to **at least two** examples, analyse how humour is used to reveal central concerns.

   4

7. Look at lines 44—54.

   Explain how the singers' attitudes to **both** the local people and environment are made clear.

   2

8. By referring to this extract and to elsewhere in the play, discuss how McGrath explores the effects of social class.

   10

Page eight

SQA EXAM PAPER 2017 111 HIGHER ENGLISH

[OPEN OUT FOR QUESTIONS]

DO NOT WRITE ON THIS PAGE

Page nine

HIGHER ENGLISH 112 SQA EXAM PAPER 2017

OR

Text 3 — Drama

If you choose this text you may not attempt a question on Drama in Section 2.

Read the extract below and then attempt the following questions.

Men Should Weep by Ena Lamont Stewart

In this extract from Act 2, scene 1, Granny is waiting to be collected by her daughter-in-law, Lizzie.

Mrs Harris opens the door to Lizzie, a hard-faced harridan about fifty

Lizzie:	(*ignoring the others*) Well? Ye ready?
Mrs Bone:	Ready? She's been sittin here waitin on ye for the last hauf-oor.
Lizzie:	Got a yer claes packed? An yer pension book?
5 Granny:	Aye, Lizzie; it's here.
Lizzie:	See's a look at it. (*Granny starts to fumble with her bag. Mrs Bone goes to help her*) Hev they men no been for the bed yet?
Mrs Harris:	If they'd hae been for the bed it wouldna be staunin up against yon wa, would it?
10 Lizzie:	(*taking the pension book from Mrs Bone*) Here! Ye've drawn this week's. Ye got the money?
Granny:	Naw, Lizzie . . . I gied it tae Maggie.
Lizzie:	Well, it's no Maggie's, it's mines. If ye're comin tae bide wi me, ye're no comin tae bide *aff* me.
15 Granny:	She got some things aff the grocer she'd tae pay for, an she wis needin a vest an socks for Bertie gaun up tae the hospital.
Lizzie:	Oh? So Bertie gets new socks at ma expense, does he? And whit does she think you're gonna live on for the next week? Air?
Mrs Harris: 20	Ach, leave the puir aul wife alane. Shairly ye can scrape up a bit tae eat for her; it's no as if ye wis takin in a big hulkin brute o a man tae feed.
Lizzie:	I'm no takin in naebody tae feed. Folks that canna pay for their meat'll find nae room in ma hoose.
Mrs Bone:	Oo! An her yer puir dead husband's mither. Oo! I'm surprised at ye, Lizzie Morrison.
25 Mrs Harris:	I thought you said you wis never surprised — at anythin human.
Mrs Bone:	That's jist whit I said: *anythin human.*

They both stare hard at Lizzie, then shake their heads at each other

Lizzie:	I've tae earn every penny that comes intae ma hoose.
Mrs Harris: 30	Aye, we ken that. An you don't dae sae bad either, ye aul miser. Buyin up aul claes for a copper or twa and sellin them at sixpence a week . . .
Mrs Bone:	Or she'll loan ye the dough tae buy them outright — at fifty percent.

Page ten

Mrs Harris:	Aye, she's got a right kind heart, she wouldae see ye stuck; no if she could mak a guid thing oot o it.
35	Lizzie:	Ye're jealous! Ye hevna the brains tae mak a bit yersels. But ye're no above tradin wi me when it suits ye. Aye, an gettin a bargain.

Mrs Harris ⎫
Mrs Bone: ⎬ (*together*) A bargain? Frae *you*?
⎭

They look at each other and shake their heads

Mrs Harris: I canna mind ony bargain.

Lizzie: Whit aboot yon veloory hat ye bought aff me?

40 Mrs Harris: Veloory hat? Veloory hat . . . ? Oh, ye mean yon scabby aul felt bunnet wi the moultin bird on tap? Oh aye, I mind! If yon wis veloory, I'm a wally dug.

Lizzie: It wis veloory. It belanged tae a lady in Kelvinside whaur I did a bit on a Saturday.

Mrs Bone: A bit whit? Pinchin?

45 Lizzie: Here! I could pit ye tae the Polis for that.

Mrs Harris: No roon aboot here ye couldnae. They a ken ye.

Granny: Oh, I'm nae wantin tae leave here! I wisht I could bide wi Maggie till I dee!

Lizzie: Bide then!

Granny: Ye ken I cannae bide. Alec and Isa's needin the room.

50 Mrs Harris: Some folks is right selfish. You've naebody but yersel tae think aboot, an ye'll no tak the aul wife aff Maggie's hauns wi'oot kickin up a fuss.

Lizzie sits down and loosens her coat

Mrs Bone: I thought you wis in a hurry tae get aff?

Lizzie: I'm sittin right here till Maggie comes hame wi whit's left o Granny's pension.

55 Mrs Bone: Huh! Whit a hope you've got. Whit d'ye think'll be left?

Lizzie: Aye . . . mebbe y're right . . . In that case, I'll jist hae tae tak whit she bought.

She gets up and goes to open food cupboard. Mrs Harris grabs her

Mrs Harris: Here! Mrs Bone and me's in chairge o this hoose till Lily comes; you keep yer dirty aul neb oot of the cupboards or we'll shout for the Polis.

Page eleven

HIGHER ENGLISH 114 SQA EXAM PAPER 2017

MARKS

Questions

9. Look at lines 1—27.

   By referring to **at least two** examples, analyse how **both** stage directions and dialogue are used to create a clear impression of Lizzie in these lines.   4

10. Look at lines 28—46.

    By referring to **at least two** examples, analyse how language is used to convey the feelings of the neighbours (Mrs Harris and Mrs Bone) towards Lizzie.   4

11. Although Granny says very little in these lines, she is important in highlighting central concerns. By considering the extract as a whole, explain why she is important.   2

12. By referring to this extract and to elsewhere in the play, discuss how Lamont Stewart develops the theme of community.   10

Page twelve

SQA EXAM PAPER 2017   115   HIGHER ENGLISH

[OPEN OUT FOR QUESTIONS]

DO NOT WRITE ON THIS PAGE

HIGHER ENGLISH 116 SQA EXAM PAPER 2017

SECTION 1 — SCOTTISH TEXT — 20 marks

Choose ONE text from Drama, Prose or Poetry.

Read the text extract carefully and then attempt ALL the questions for your chosen text.

You should spend about 45 minutes on this Section.

PART B — SCOTTISH TEXT — PROSE

Text 1 — Prose

If you choose this text you may not attempt a question on Prose (Fiction or Non-Fiction) in Section 2.

Read the extract below and then attempt the following questions.

The Red Door by Iain Crichton Smith

As he stared at the door he felt strange flutterings within him. First of all the door had been painted very lovingly so that it shone with a deep inward shine such as one might find in pictures. And indeed it looked like a picture against the rest of the house which wasn't at all modern but on the contrary was old and intertwined with all sorts of rusty
5 pipes like snakes.

He went back from the door and looked at it from a distance as people in art galleries have to do when studying an oil painting. The more he regarded it the more he liked it. It certainly stood out against the drab landscape as if it were a work of art. On the other hand the more he looked at it the more it seemed to express something in himself which
10 had been deeply buried for years. After a while there was something boring about green and as for blue it wouldn't have suited the door at all. Blue would have been too blatant in a cold way. And anyway the sky was already blue.

But mixed with his satisfaction he felt what could only be described as puzzlement, a slight deviation from the normal as if his head were spinning and he were going round in circles.
15 What would the neighbours say about it, he wondered. Never in the history of the village had there been a red door before. For that matter he couldn't remember seeing even a blue door himself, though he had heard of the existence of one.

The morning was breaking all over the village as he looked. Blue smoke was ascending from chimneys, a cock was crowing, belligerent and heraldic, its red claws sunk into the
20 earth, its metallic breast oriental and strange. There was a dew all about him and lying on the fences ahead of him. He recognised that the village would wake to a new morning, for the red door would gather attention to itself.

And he thought to himself, "I have always sought to hide among other people. I agree to whatever anybody tells me to do. If they think I should go to church, I go to church. If they
25 want me to cut peats for them, I do. I have never," he thought with wonder, "been myself." He looked down at his grey fisherman's jersey and his wellingtons and he thought, "I have always worn these things because everybody else does. I have never had the courage to wear what I wanted to wear, for example a coloured waistcoat and a coloured jacket."

The red door stood out against the whiteness of the frost and the glimmerings of snow. It
30 seemed to be saying something to him, to be asking him a question. Perhaps it was pleading with him not to destroy it. Perhaps it was saying, "I don't want to be green. There must be a place somewhere for me as myself. I wish to be red. What is wrong with red anyway?" The door seemed to him to have its own courage.

Page fourteen

MARKS

Wine of course was red and so was blood. He drank none of the former and only saw the
35 latter when he cut himself while repairing a fence or working with wood when a nail would
prick his finger.

But really was he happy? That was the question. When he considered it carefully he knew
that he wasn't. He didn't like eating alone, he didn't like sitting in the house alone, he
didn't like having none who belonged to him, to whom he could tell his secret thoughts,
40 for example that such and such was a mean devil and that that other one was an
ungrateful rat.

He had to keep a perpetually smiling face to the world, that was his trouble. But the red
door didn't do that. It was foreign and confident. It seemed to be saying what it was, not
what it thought others expected it to say. On the other hand, he didn't like wellingtons and
45 a fisherman's jersey. He hated them in fact: they had no elegance.

Now Mary had elegance. Though she was a bit odd, she had elegance. It was true that the
villagers didn't understand her but that was because she read many books, her father
having been a teacher. And on the other hand she made no concessions to anybody. She
seemed to be saying, "You can take me or leave me." She never gossiped. She was proud
50 and distant. She had a world of her own.

Questions

13. Look at lines 1—12.

   By referring to **at least two** examples, analyse how the language emphasises the
   differences between the red door and the existing surroundings.   4

14. Look at lines 18—33.

   By referring to **at least two** examples, analyse how language is used to highlight the
   significance of the red door at this moment in Murdo's life.   4

15. Look at lines 37—45.

   Analyse how the language reveals Murdo's deep-rooted unhappiness.   2

16. By referring to this extract and to at least one other short story, discuss how Crichton
   Smith explores the conflict between individuality and conformity.   10

[Turn over

Page fifteen

HIGHER ENGLISH   118   SQA EXAM PAPER 2017

OR

Text 2 — Prose

If you choose this text you may not attempt a question on Prose (Fiction or Non-Fiction) in Section 2.

Read the extract below and then attempt the following questions.

Tartan **by George Mackay Brown**

They crossed a field to the third house, a hovel. From the door they heard muttering and sighing inside. "There's breath in this house," said Kol. He leapt into the middle of the floor with a loud beserk yell, but it might have been a fly buzzing in the window for all the attention the old woman paid to him. "Ah," she was singing over the sheeted dead child on
5   the bed, "I thought to see you a shepherd on Morven, or maybe a fisherman poaching salmon at the mouth of the Naver. Or maybe you would be a man with lucky acres and the people would come from far and near to buy your corn. Or you might have been a holy priest at the seven altars of the west."

There was a candle burning at the child's head and a cross lay on his breast, tangled in his
10 cold fingers.

Arnor, Havard, and Sven crossed themselves in the door. Kol slunk out like an old dog.

They took nothing from that house but trudged uphill to a neat grey house built into the sheer brae.

At the cairn across the valley, a mile away, a group of plaided men stood watching them.

15 At the fourth door a voice called to them to come in. A thin man was standing beside a loom with a half-made web in it. "Strangers from the sea," he said, "you are welcome. You have the salt in your throats and I ask you to accept ale from Malcolm the weaver."

They stood round the door and Malcolm the weaver poured horns of ale for each of them.

"This is passable ale," said Havard. "If it had been sour, Malcolm the weaver, we would
20 have stretched you alive on your loom. We would have woven the thread of eternity through you."

Malcolm the weaver laughed.

"What is the name of this place?" said Arnor.

"It is called Durness," said Malcolm the weaver. "They are good people here, except for the
25 man who lives in the tall house beyond the cairn. His name is Duncan, and he will not pay me for the cloth I wove for him last winter, so that he and his wife and his snovelly-nosed children could have coats when the snow came."

"On account of the average quality of your ale, we will settle matters with this Duncan," said Arnor. "Now we need our cups filled again."

30 They stayed at Malcolm the weaver's house for an hour and more, and when they got up to go Kol staggered against the door. "Doubtless somebody will pay for this," he said thickly.

They took with them a web of cloth without asking leave of Malcolm. It was a gray cloth of fine quality and it had a thick green stripe and a thin brown stripe running up and down and a very thick black stripe cutting across it horizontally. It was the kind of Celtic weave
35 they call tartan.

Page sixteen

SQA EXAM PAPER 2017 119 HIGHER ENGLISH

MARKS

"Take it, take it by all means," said Malcolm the weaver.

"We were going to take it in any case," said Sven.

"Tell us," said Havard from the door, "who is the girl in Durness with black hair and black eyes and a cleft chin?"

40 "Her name is Morag," said Malcolm the weaver, "and she is the wife of John the shepherd. John has been on the hill all week with the new lambs. I think she is lonely."

Questions

17. Look at lines 1—13.

   By referring to **at least two** examples, analyse how the writer uses language to convey the emotional impact of the child's death.   4

18. Look at lines 15—41.

   By referring to **at least two** examples, analyse how the writer uses language to reveal the character **and/or** attitudes of Malcolm the weaver.   4

19. Look at the whole extract.

   By referring closely to the extract, analyse how the characters of **two** of the Vikings are conveyed.   2

20. By referring to this extract and to at least one other short story, discuss how Mackay Brown explores the relationship between the individual and the community.   10

[Turn over

Page seventeen

HIGHER ENGLISH 120 SQA EXAM PAPER 2017

OR

Text 3 — Prose

If you choose this text you may not attempt a question on Prose (Fiction or Non-Fiction) in Section 2.

Read the extract below and then attempt the following questions.

The Trick Is To Keep Breathing **by Janice Galloway**

On the map, it's called Bourtreehill, after the elder tree, the bourtree, Judas tree; protection against witches. The people who live here call it Boot Hill. Boot Hill is a new estate well outside the town it claims to be part of. There was a rumour when they started building the place that it was meant for undesirables: difficult tenants from other places,
5   shunters, overspill from Glasgow. That's why it's so far away from everything. Like most rumours, it's partly true. Boot Hill is full of tiny, twisty roads, wild currant bushes to represent the great outdoors, pubs with plastic beer glasses and kids. The twisty roads are there to prevent the kids being run over. The roads are meant to make drivers slow down so they get the chance to see and stop in time. This is a dual misfunction. Hardly anyone
10 has a car. If one does appear on the horizon, the kids use the bends to play chicken, deliberately lying low and leaping out at the last minute for fun. The roads end up more conducive to child death than if they had been straight. What they do achieve is to make the buses go slow. Buses are infrequent so the shelters are covered in graffiti and kids hanging from the roofs. Nobody waits in these shelters even when it's raining. It rains a lot.
15 The buses take a long time.

When I was small I always wanted a red front door. This front door is bottle green. The key never surrenders first time. I have to rummage through my bag and every pocket while I stand at the door as though I'm begging to be mugged. The first time we came, there were two sets of numbers on the door; one large and black; the other brass and much smaller.
20 Like this:

13 ₁₃

We laughed and left them on, wondering if the previous tenants had been amnesiacs or phobics. When I came back alone, I took both sets off. There are four little holes on the door where they used to be

    •

        •

   •   •   and a
25
different colour of paint underneath. I wondered what had moved away the previous tenants with their amnesia or their phobia. I wondered where they were now. Anyway, I didn't want those numbers on the door: it was a signal I could do without. I was angry I hadn't done it before. The nameplate was something he had bought, so I left it on. It says
30 his name. Not mine.

Page eighteen

SQA EXAM PAPER 2017 121 HIGHER ENGLISH

MARKS

Grit wells up when I open the door. There are always withered leaves in the porch. It seems to sit at the end of a natural tunnel of wind and makes itself difficult even on mild days. Litter accumulates on either side of the porch step: the porch is full of curled, brown leaves. Slaters run frantic in the sudden emptiness overhead while I fight my way inside.
35 This makes me shiver. Every time. I notice a little shell of something dead that's been there for weeks now because I can't pick it up, not even through paper. I hate the feel of them, gritty little packets. Insects make me sick. They have their skeletons outside, too many eyes, unpredictable legs and you can never tell where their mouths are. Spiders are worse. But today there are only the slaters. They disgust me but I'm not afraid of them. I push the
40 letters with my foot till they are well clear of the dead one and pick them up with the tips of my fingers.

A bill from the lawyer, a note from the Health Visitor and a postcard from Marianne.

I've been Whitewater Rafting

The postcard has a picture of a butterfly and a gushing torrent of water in the background.
45 The words on the back are smudged as though some of the water from the front of the card has splashed over and made the ink run. This makes it hard to read but I get the general drift.

Camping better than anticipated. Leaving for the
Canadian border tomorrow. Scenery wonderful.
50 You would hate it. Love   Mxx

I forget about the slaters and try to feel the other continent through the card. It doesn't work. I make tea and check out the livingroom. The spill on the rug is almost dry. I find the bottle open from last night but not the lid. I put an envelope over the neck, sitting the bottle aside so I don't kick it later, then reshape cushions trying to keep my feet on the rug
55 because my shoes make a terrible noise on the floorboards. But things have to be set in place. A lot depends on stillness later and I have to get a lot of moving around out of my system now. Stillness helps when I'm alone. It keeps me contained.

Questions

21. Look at lines 1—15.

    By referring to **at least two** examples, analyse how the writer uses language to convey a negative impression of Bourtreehill.

    4

22. Look at lines 16—41.

    By referring to **at least two** examples, analyse how the writer's use of language reveals Joy's anxiety.

    4

23. Look at lines 42—57.

    Analyse how the writer's use of language emphasises Joy's attempts to cope with her situation.

    2

24. By referring to this extract and to elsewhere in the novel, discuss how Galloway explores the impact of loneliness.

    10

Page nineteen   **[Turn over**

HIGHER ENGLISH **122** SQA EXAM PAPER 2017

OR

Text 4 — Prose

If you choose this text you may not attempt a question on Prose (Fiction or Non-Fiction) in Section 2.

Read the extract below and then attempt the following questions.

Sunset Song by Lewis Grassic Gibbon

In this extract, which is from Part II (Drilling), it is threshing time at Chae Strachan's farm.

Not that they'd much to shout for that winter themselves, the Strachans; folk said it was easy to see why Chae was so strong on Rich and Poor being Equal: he was sore in need of the sharing out to start ere he went clean broke himself. Maybe old Sinclair or the wife were tight with the silver that year, but early as December Chae had to sell his corn, he
5 brought the first threshing of the season down in Kinraddie. John Guthrie and Will were off at the keek of dawn when they saw the smoke rise from the engines, Chris followed an hour later to help Chae's wife with the dinner and things. And faith! broke he might be but he wasn't mean, Chae, when the folk came trampling in to eat there was broth and beef and chicken and oat-cakes, champion cakes they made at the Knapp; and loaf and jelly
10 and dumpling with sugar and milk; and if any soul were that gutsy he wanted more he could hold to the turnip-field, said Chae.

The first three men to come in Chris hardly saw, so busied she was pouring their broth for them. Syne, setting the plates, she saw Alec Mutch, his great lugs like red clouts hung out to dry: and he cried *Ay, Chris!* and began to sup as though he hadn't seen food for a
15 fortnight. Beside him was Munro of the Cuddiestoun, he was eating like a colie ta'en off its chain, Chae's thresh was a spree to the pair of them. Then more trampling and scraping came from the door, folk came drifting in two-three at a time, Chris over-busied to notice their faces, but some watched her and gave a bit smile and Cuddiestoun cried to father, *Losh, man, she's fair an expert getting, the daughter. The kitchen's more her style than the*
20 *College.*

Some folk at the tables laughed out at that, the ill-nature grinned from the faces of them, and suddenly Chris hated the lot, the English Chris came back in her skin a minute, she saw them the yokels and clowns everlasting, dull-brained and crude. Alec Mutch took up the card from Cuddiestoun then and began on education and the speak ran round the tables.
25 Most said it was a coarse thing, learning, just teaching your children a lot of damned nonsense that put them above themselves, they'd turn round and give you their lip as soon as look at you. But Chae was sitting down himself by then and he wouldn't have that. *Damn't man, you're clean wrong to think that. Education's the thing the working man wants to put him up level with the Rich.* And Long Rob of the Mill said *I'd have thought a bit*
30 *balance in the bank would do that.* But for once he seemed right in agreement with Chae — *the more education the more of sense and the less of kirks and ministers.* Cuddiestoun and Mutch were fair shocked at that, Cuddiestoun cried out *Well, well, we'll hear nothing coarse of religion,* as though he didn't want to hear anything more about it and was giving out orders. But Long Rob wasn't a bit took aback, the long rangy childe, he just cocked an
35 eye at Cuddiestoun and cried *Well, well, Munro, we'll turn to the mentally afflicted in general, not just in particular. How's that foreman of yours getting on, Tony? Is he still keeping up with his shorthand?* There was a snicker at that, you may well be sure, and Cuddiestoun closed up quick enough, here and there folk had another bit laugh and said Long Rob was an ill hand to counter. And Chris thought of her clowns and yokels, and was
40 shamed as she thought — Chae and Long Rob they were, the poorest folk in Kinraddie!

Page twenty

SQA EXAM PAPER 2017   123   HIGHER ENGLISH

MARKS

Questions

25. Look at lines 1—11.

    By referring to **at least two** examples, explain how important aspects of Chae's character are revealed.   3

26. Look at lines 12—20.

    By referring to **at least two** examples, analyse how humour is created.   3

27. Look at lines 21—40.

    By referring to **at least two** examples, analyse how the writer conveys the differing attitudes of those present.   4

28. By referring to this extract and to elsewhere in the novel, discuss how Grassic Gibbon conveys Chris's conflicting emotions towards the community of Kinraddie.   10

[Turn over

Page twenty-one

HIGHER ENGLISH   **124**   SQA EXAM PAPER 2017

OR

Text 5 — Prose

If you choose this text you may not attempt a question on Prose (Fiction or Non-Fiction) in Section 2.

Read the extract below and then attempt the following questions.

The Cone-Gatherers by Robin Jenkins

In this extract, a storm is brewing.

In the tip of the tall larch they were in a good position to watch the approach of the storm. At the sea end of the loch for the past half hour indigo clouds had been mustering, with rumbles of thunder still distant and half-hearted. More ominous was the river of radiance pouring straight down into the orange mass of the tree. After long excited consultations,
5 the finches had whisked away. The two men were the only living creatures left in the tree tops.

At the very crest, Calum was frightened and exhilarated. He chattered involuntarily, making no sense. Instead of dropping the golden cones safely into his bag he let them dribble out of his hands so that, in the expectancy before the violence of the storm, the
10 tiny stots from one transfigured branch to another could be clearly heard. Several times he reached up and raised his hand, so that it was higher than the tree.

Neil, a little lower down, was fastened by a safety belt. His rheumatism had heralded the rain, so that the climb to the top had been for him a long slow agony which he did not wish to repeat. That was why he did not give the order to go down; he hoped the storm
15 would pass over without striking them. He too was agitated, finding the cones exasperatingly small and his bag insatiable. The belt chafed his waist, and his arms and legs ached. Above all, Calum's meaningless chatters distressed him. He shouted to him several times to stop. Calum only screamed back, not in defiance, but in uncontrollable excitement.

20 Then that cascade of light streaming into the larch ceased, leaving it dark and cold. Black clouds were now overhead. Thunder snarled. Colour faded from the wood. A sough of wind shook the gloomy host of trees. Over the sea flashed lightning. Yet, far to the east, islands of peace and brightness persisted in the sky.

The first few drops of rain fell, as large as cones.

25 "We'd better get down," shouted Neil, and he tugged frantically at the buckle of his belt with his stiff sticky blackened fingers.

Calum slithered down and helped to loose him. He was giggling.

"Whether we go down or not," said Neil, "we'll get soaked to the skin. But up here the lightning might be dangerous."

30 "I don't like the lightning, Neil."

"Nobody does. What's been the matter with you? You're not a child. You've been in a storm before."

Page twenty-two

MARKS

"Did you see the light, Neil?"

"How could I miss seeing it? It was in my eyes, blinding me."

35 "Was it from heaven, Neil?"

"Heaven?" Neil's shout was astonished and angry. "What are you talking about?"

Calum pressed close to him eagerly.

"Do you mind what you said yon time, Neil? We were in the shed together, with the horse. You said it was always as bright as that in heaven."

40 "In the shed, with the horse? What shed and what horse?"

"It was called Peggy, Neil."

Neil remembered. "But that was more than twenty years ago," he cried.

"Aye, but you said it, Neil. You said heaven was always as bright as that."

His face wet with rain and tears, Neil clung to the tree and shut his eyes.

45 "Maybe I did, Calum," he said.

"And mind what else you said, Neil? You said that was where our mither was. You said that, Neil, in the shed."

"Maybe I did."

Questions

29. Look at lines 1—6.

    Analyse how the writer effectively describes the impending storm.

    2

30. Look at lines 7—19.

    By referring to **at least two** examples, analyse how the writer's use of language conveys Calum's reaction to the storm.

    4

31. Look at lines 25—48.

    By referring to **at least two** examples, analyse how dialogue is used to convey aspects of the relationship between Calum and Neil.

    4

32. By referring to this extract and to elsewhere in the novel, discuss how Jenkins uses symbolism to develop the central concerns of the text.

    10

[Turn over

Page twenty-three

HIGHER ENGLISH   SQA EXAM PAPER 2017

SECTION 1 — SCOTTISH TEXT — 20 marks

Choose ONE text from Drama, Prose or Poetry.

Read the text extract carefully and then attempt ALL the questions for your chosen text.

You should spend about 45 minutes on this Section.

PART C — SCOTTISH TEXT — POETRY

Text 1 — Poetry

If you choose this text you may not attempt a question on Poetry in Section 2.

Read the extract below and then attempt the following questions.

Address To The Deil by Robert Burns

'O Prince! O chief of many thronéd Pow'rs
That led th' embattl'd Seraphim to war—'— Milton.

O Thou! whatever title suit thee—
Auld Hornie, Satan, Nick, or Clootie,
Wha in yon cavern grim an' sootie,
        Clos'd under hatches,
5 Spairges about the brunstane cootie,
        To scaud poor wretches!

Hear me, auld Hangie, for a wee,
An' let poor damnéd bodies be;
I'm sure sma' pleasure it can gie,
10   Ev'n to a deil,
To skelp an' scaud poor dogs like me,
        An' hear us squeel!

Great is thy pow'r, an' great thy fame;
Far kenm'd an' noted is thy name;
15 An' tho' yon lowin' heuch's thy hame,
        Thou travels far;
An' faith! thou's neither lag nor lame,
        Nor blate, nor scaur.

Whyles, ranging like a roarin' lion,
20 For prey, a' holes and corners tryin';
Whyles, on the strong-wind'd tempest flyin',
        Tirlin' the kirks;
Whyles, in the human bosom pryin',
        Unseen thou lurks.

25 I've heard my rev'rend graunie say,
In lanely glens ye like to stray;
Or where auld ruin'd castles grey
        Nod to the moon,
Ye fright the nightly wand'rer's way,
30   Wi' eldritch croon.

Page twenty-four

SQA EXAM PAPER 2017 127 HIGHER ENGLISH

MARKS

When twilight did my graunie summon,
To say her pray'rs, douse, honest woman!
Aft 'yont the dyke she's heard you bummin',
       Wi' eerie drone;
35 Or, rustlin', thro' the boortrees comin',
       Wi' heavy groan.

Ae dreary, windy, winter night,
The stars shot down wi' sklentin light,
Wi' you, mysel, I gat a fright,
40   Ayont the lough;
Ye, like a rash-buss, stood in sight,
       Wi' wavin' sough.

The cudgel in my nieve did shake,
Each brist'ld hair stood like a stake,
45 When wi' an eldritch, stoor 'quaick, quaick',
       Amang the springs,
Awa ye squatter'd like a drake,
       On whistlin' wings.

Questions

33. Look at lines 1—12.

By referring to **at least two** examples, analyse how the poet's use of language presents a light-hearted depiction of the Deil.

4

34. Look at lines 13—24.

Analyse how the poet's use of language portrays the Deil as a powerful being.

2

35. Look at lines 25—48

By referring to **at least two** examples, analyse how Burns mocks superstitious beliefs.

4

36. By referring to this extract and to at least one other poem by Burns, discuss the poet's use of humour in his exploration of serious issues.

10

[Turn over

Page twenty-five

HIGHER ENGLISH   128   SQA EXAM PAPER 2017

OR

Text 2 — Poetry

If you choose this text you may not attempt a question on Poetry in Section 2.

Read the poem below and then attempt the following questions.

Valentine **by Carol Ann Duffy**

Not a red rose or a satin heart.

    I give you an onion.
It is a moon wrapped in brown paper.
It promises light
5   like the careful undressing of love.

    Here.
It will blind you with tears
like a lover.
It will make your reflection
10 a wobbling photo of grief.

I am trying to be truthful.

Not a cute card or a kissogram.

    I give you an onion.
Its fierce kiss will stay on your lips,
15 possessive and faithful
as we are,
for as long as we are.

    Take it.
Its platinum loops shrink to a wedding ring,
20 if you like.
Lethal.
Its scent will cling to your fingers,
cling to your knife.

Page twenty-six

MARKS

Questions

37. Look at lines 1—5.

By referring to **at least two** examples, analyse how the poet uses language to challenge **and/or** reinforce traditional stereotypes associated with romantic love.

4

38. Look at lines 6—17.

By referring to **at least two** examples, analyse how the poet uses language to suggest a "truthful" view of love.

4

39. Look at lines 18—23.

By referring to the poet's use of language, evaluate the effectiveness of these lines as a conclusion to the poem.

2

40. By referring to this poem and to at least one other poem by Duffy, discuss how the poet explores emotional conflict within an individual.

10

[Turn over

Page twenty-seven

OR

Text 3 — Poetry

If you choose this text you may not attempt a question on Poetry in Section 2.

Read the poem below and then attempt the following questions.

For my Grandmother Knitting **by Liz Lochhead**

There is no need they say
but the needles still move
their rhythms in the working of your hands
as easily
5   as if your hands
were once again those sure and skilful hands
of the fisher-girl.

You are old now
and your grasp of things is not so good
10   but master of your moments then
deft and swift
you slit the still-ticking quick silver fish.
Hard work it was too
of necessity.

15   But now they say there is no need
as the needles move
in the working of your hands
once the hands of the bride
with the hand-span waist
20   once the hands of the miner's wife
who scrubbed his back
in a tin bath by the coal fire
once the hands of the mother
of six who made do and mended
25   scraped and slaved slapped sometimes
when necessary.

But now they say there is no need
the kids they say grandma
have too much already
30   more than they can wear
too many scarves and cardigans —
gran you do too much
there's no necessity . . .

Page twenty-eight

SQA EXAM PAPER 2017 **131** HIGHER ENGLISH

MARKS

At your window you wave
35 them goodbye Sunday.
With your painful hands
big on shrunken wrists.
Swollen-jointed. Red. Arthritic. Old.
But the needles still move
40 their rhythms in the working of your hands
easily
as if your hands remembered
of their own accord the pattern
as if your hands had forgotten
45 how to stop.

Questions

41. Look at lines 1—14.

    By referring to **at least two** examples, analyse how the poet's use of language conveys a sense of **both** the past and the present. 4

42. Look at lines 15—26.

    Analyse how the poet uses the idea of "hands" to convey **two** different stages in the grandmother's past life. 2

43. Look at lines 27—45.

    By referring to **at least two** examples, analyse how the poet's use of language creates a bleak mood or atmosphere. 4

44. By referring to this poem and to at least one other poem by Lochhead, discuss how she explores the theme of personal **and/or** social change. 10

[Turn over

Page twenty-nine

OR

Text 4 — Poetry

If you choose this text you may not attempt a question on Poetry in Section 2.

Read the poem below and then attempt the following questions.

Basking Shark by Norman MacCaig

To stub an oar on a rock where none should be,
To have it rise with a slounge out of the sea
Is a thing that happened once (too often) to me.

But not too often — though enough. I count as gain
5 That once I met, on a sea tin-tacked with rain,
That roomsized monster with a matchbox brain.

He displaced more than water. He shoggled me
Centuries back — this decadent townee
Shook on a wrong branch of his family tree.

10 Swish up the dirt and, when it settles, a spring
Is all the clearer. I saw me, in one fling,
Emerging from the slime of everything.

So who's the monster? The thought made me grow pale
For twenty seconds while, sail after sail,
15 The tall fin slid away and then the tail.

Page thirty

MARKS

Questions

45. Look at lines 1—3.

Analyse how the poet's use of language conveys the nature of the encounter.　　2

46. Look at lines 4—9.

By referring to **at least two** examples, analyse how language is used to suggest the impact of the experience on the speaker.　　4

47. Look at lines 10—15.

By referring to **at least two** examples, analyse how the poet's language reveals a sense of new understanding.　　4

48. By referring to this poem and to at least one other poem by MacCaig, discuss how the poet uses symbolism to develop central ideas in his poetry.　　10

[Turn over

Page thirty-one

OR

Text 5 — Poetry

If you choose this text you may not attempt a question on Poetry in Section 2.

Read the poem below and then attempt the following questions.

Heroes **by Sorley MacLean**

I did not see Lannes at Ratisbon
nor MacLennan at Auldearn
nor Gillies MacBain at Culloden,
but I saw an Englishman in Egypt.

5   A poor little chap with chubby cheeks
and knees grinding each other,
pimply unattractive face —
garment of the bravest spirit.

He was not a hit "in the pub
10 in the time of the fists being closed,"
but a lion against the breast of battle,
in the morose wounding showers.

His hour came with the shells,
with the notched iron splinters,
15 in the smoke and flame,
in the shaking and terror of the battlefield.

Word came to him in the bullet shower
that he should be a hero briskly,
and he was that while he lasted,
20 but it wasn't much time he got.

He kept his guns to the tanks,
bucking with tearing crashing screech,
until he himself got, about the stomach,
that biff that put him to the ground,
25 mouth down in sand and gravel,
without a chirp from his ugly high-pitched voice.

No cross or medal was put to his
chest or to his name or to his family;
there were not many of his troop alive,
30 and if there were their word would not be strong.
And at any rate, if a battle post stands,
many are knocked down because of him,
not expecting fame, not wanting a medal
or any froth from the mouth of the field of slaughter.

35 I saw a great warrior of England,
a poor manikin on whom no eye would rest;
no Alasdair of Glen Garry;
and he took a little weeping to my eyes.

Page thirty-two

MARKS

Questions

49. Look at lines 1—8.

Analyse how the poet's use of language makes it clear that the soldier was not a conventional hero.　　2

50. Look at lines 13—26.

By referring to **at least two** examples, analyse how the poet's use of language conveys the hardships suffered by the soldier in battle.　　4

51. Look at lines 27—38.

By referring to **at least two** examples, analyse how the poet uses language to create a sense of pity.　　4

52. By referring to this poem and to at least one other poem by MacLean, discuss how the poet explores the theme of destruction.　　10

[Turn over

HIGHER ENGLISH 136 SQA EXAM PAPER 2017

OR

Text 6 — Poetry

If you choose this text you may not attempt a question on Poetry in Section 2.

Read the extract below and then attempt the following questions.

Nil Nil **by Don Paterson**

From the top, then, the zenith, the silent footage:
McGrandle, majestic in ankle-length shorts,
his golden hair shorn to an open book, sprinting
the length of the park for the long hoick forward,
5   his balletic toe-poke nearly bursting the roof
of the net; a shaky pan to the Erskine St End
where a plague of grey bonnets falls out of the clouds.
But ours is a game of two halves, and this game
the semi they went on to lose; from here
10 it's all down, from the First to the foot of the Second,
McGrandle, Visocchi and Spankie detaching
like bubbles to speed the descent into pitch-sharing,
pay-cuts, pawned silver, the Highland Division,
the absolute sitters ballooned over open goals,
15 the dismal nutmegs, the scores so obscene
no respectable journal will print them; though one day
Farquhar's spectacular bicycle-kick
will earn him a name-check in Monday's obituaries.
Besides the one setback — the spell of giant-killing
20 in the Cup (Lochee Violet, then Aberdeen Bon Accord,
the deadlock with Lochee Harp finally broken
by Farquhar's own-goal in the replay)
nothing inhibits the fifty-year slide
into Sunday League, big tartan flasks,
25 open hatchbacks parked squint behind goal-nets,
the half-time satsuma, the dog on the pitch,
then the Boys' Club, sponsored by Skelly Assurance,
then Skelly Dry Cleaners, then nobody;
stud-harrowed pitches with one-in-five inclines,
30 grim fathers and perverts with Old English Sheepdogs
lining the touch, moaning softly.
Now the unrefereed thirty-a-sides,
terrified fat boys with callipers minding
four jackets on infinite, notional fields;
35 ten years of dwindling, half-hearted kickabouts
leaves two little boys — Alastair Watt,
who answers to "Forty", and wee Horace Madden,
so smelly the air seems to quiver above him —
playing desperate two-touch with a bald tennis ball

Page thirty-four

SQA EXAM PAPER 2017   **137**   HIGHER ENGLISH

MARKS

40 in the hour before lighting-up time.
    Alastair cheats, and goes off with the ball
    leaving wee Horace to hack up a stone
    and dribble it home in the rain;
    past the stopped swings, the dead shanty-town
45 of allotments, the black shell of Skelly Dry Cleaners
    and into his cul-de-sac, where, accidentally,
    he neatly back-heels it straight into the gutter
    then tries to swank off like he meant it.

    Unknown to him, it is all that remains
50 of a lone fighter-pilot, who, returning at dawn
    to find Leuchars was not where he'd left it,
    took time out to watch the Sidlaws unsheathed
    from their great black tarpaulin, the haar burn off Tayport
    and Venus melt into Carnoustie, igniting
55 the shoreline; no wind, not a cloud in the sky
    and no one around to admire the discretion
    of his unscheduled exit

Questions

53. Look at lines 1—6 ("From . . . the net;).

    Analyse how the poet's language creates a celebratory mood.   **2**

54. Look at lines 9—29 ("from here . . . inclines").

    By referring to **at least two** examples, analyse how the poet's use of language creates an atmosphere of decline.   **4**

55. Look at lines 41—57.

    By referring to **at least two** examples, analyse how the poet's use of language conveys the tragic situation of **both** the community and the pilot.   **4**

56. By referring to this extract and to at least one other poem by Paterson, discuss how the poet explores the impact of loss.   **10**

[END OF SECTION 1]

[Turn over

Page thirty-five

HIGHER ENGLISH   138   SQA EXAM PAPER 2017

SECTION 2 — CRITICAL ESSAY — 20 marks

Attempt ONE question from the following genres — Drama, Prose Fiction, Prose Non-Fiction, Poetry, Film and Television Drama, or Language.

Your answer must be on a different genre from that chosen in Section 1.

You should spend approximately 45 minutes on this Section.

PART A — DRAMA

> *Answers to questions on Drama should refer to the text and to such relevant features as characterisation, key scene(s), structure, climax, theme, plot, conflict, setting . . .*

1. Choose a play in which a major character behaves in an impulsive **or** calculating **or** emotional manner.

    With reference to appropriate techniques, briefly explain the circumstances surrounding this behaviour and discuss how this behaviour adds to your understanding of the play as a whole.

2. Choose a play in which there is a scene which influences the course of future events.

    With reference to appropriate techniques, explain how the scene influences the course of events and discuss how it contributes to your appreciation of the text as a whole.

3. Choose a play which deals with the theme of honour **or** shame **or** betrayal.

    With reference to appropriate techniques, explain how the dramatist presents the theme and discuss why it is important to your understanding of the play as a whole.

Page thirty-six

PART B — PROSE FICTION

> *Answers to questions on Prose Fiction should refer to the text and to such relevant features as characterisation, setting, language, key incident(s), climax, turning point, plot, structure, narrative technique, theme, ideas, description . . .*

4. Choose a novel **or** short story in which there is a character who experiences rejection **or** isolation.

   With reference to appropriate techniques, explain the rejection **or** isolation, and discuss how this aspect adds to your appreciation of the text as a whole.

5. Choose a novel **or** short story which has an effective opening **or** conclusion.

   With reference to appropriate techniques, explain why the opening **or** conclusion is effective and discuss how it adds to your appreciation of the text as a whole.

6. Choose a novel **or** short story which deals with the theme of love **or** loss **or** redemption.

   With reference to appropriate techniques, explain how the writer develops this theme, and discuss how it adds to your understanding of the text as a whole.

PART C — PROSE NON-FICTION

> *Answers to questions on Prose Non-Fiction should refer to the text and to such relevant features as ideas, use of evidence, stance, style, selection of material, narrative voice . . .*
>
> *Non-fiction texts can include travel writing, journalism, autobiography, biography, essays . . .*

7. Choose a non-fiction text in which the writer reports on aspects of war **or** injustice **or** human suffering.

   With reference to appropriate techniques, discuss how the writer engages your interest in these aspects of war **or** injustice **or** human suffering.

8. Choose a non-fiction text which gives you a detailed insight into a place **or** a person's life.

   With reference to appropriate techniques, discuss how the writer successfully engages your interest in the place **or** the person's life.

9. Choose a non-fiction text which makes effective use of humour to make a significant point.

   With reference to appropriate techniques, discuss how the writer uses humour to make the significant point.

Page thirty-seven

[Turn over

HIGHER ENGLISH   140   SQA EXAM PAPER 2017

PART D — POETRY

> *Answers to questions on Poetry should refer to the text and to such relevant features as word choice, tone, imagery, structure, content, rhythm, rhyme, theme, sounds, ideas . . .*

10. Choose a poem in which the poet challenges accepted beliefs **or** attitudes **or** conventions.

    With reference to appropriate techniques, discuss how the poet's challenge of these accepted beliefs **or** attitudes **or** conventions enhances your appreciation of the poem as a whole.

11. Choose a poem which deals with a powerful emotion.

    With reference to appropriate techniques, discuss how the poet's presentation of this powerful emotion enhances your appreciation of the poem as a whole.

12. Choose a poem which makes effective use of imagery **and/or** sound to convey central concern(s).

    With reference to appropriate techniques, discuss how the poet's use of imagery **and/or** sound contributes to the presentation of the poem's central concern(s).

PART E — FILM AND TELEVISION DRAMA

> *Answers to questions on Film and Television Drama* should refer to the text and to such relevant features as use of camera, key sequence, characterisation, mise-en-scène, editing, music/sound, special effects, plot, dialogue . . .*

13. Choose a film **or** television drama in which the opening sequence is particularly effective in engaging the audience's interest.

    With reference to appropriate techniques, discuss how the film or programme makers succeed in engaging the audience's interest.

14. Choose a film **or** television drama in which the main character faces a significant moment of change.

    With reference to appropriate techniques, discuss how the film or programme makers convey the significance of this change.

15. Choose a film **or** television drama in which special effects make an important contribution to the impact of the film **or** television drama as a whole.

    With reference to appropriate techniques, discuss how the special effects are used to enhance your appreciation of the film **or** television drama as a whole.

* "television drama" includes a single play, a series or a serial.

Page thirty-eight

PART F — LANGUAGE

Answers to questions on Language should refer to the text(s) and to such relevant features as register, accent, dialect, slang, jargon, vocabulary, tone, abbreviation . . .

16. Choose the language of newspaper reporting associated with sport **or** celebrity **or** crime **or** war **or** the environment.

    Identify the key language features and discuss the effectiveness of these features in communicating with the readership.

17. Choose the language of persuasion as used in the world of advertising **or** politics.

    Identify specific examples and discuss to what extent the language is effective.

18. Choose the language associated with a particular group in society which shares a common interest **or** work environment.

    Identify specific examples and discuss the advantages of these language features in aiding communication.

[END OF SECTION 2]

[END OF QUESTION PAPER]

Page thirty-nine

[BLANK PAGE]

DO NOT WRITE ON THIS PAGE

HIGHER
Answers

ANSWERS FOR

SQA HIGHER
ENGLISH 2017

HIGHER ENGLISH
2015

PAPER 1 — READING FOR UNDERSTANDING ANALYSIS AND EVALUATION

Marking Instructions for each question

Question	Expected Answer(s)	Max Mark	Additional Guidance
1.	Candidates should identify two positive aspects of Central Valley, California, given in lines 1—5. Candidates must use their own words. No marks for straight lifts from the passage. *Any two of the points in the "Additional Guidance" column for 1 mark each.*	2	Possible answers: • idyllic/pastoral ("almond trees", "sweet air", "orchards", "fields of …") • perfect/attractive ("sweet air", "vision") • diverse ("pomegranates, pistachios, grapes and apricots") • bountiful/fertile/productive ("million almond trees", "Beyond the almond orchards … fields of …", "two million dairy cows … six billion dollars' worth …") • vast/expansive/scale ("a million almond trees", "Beyond … were fields of …", "Somewhere in the distance")
2.	Candidates should analyse how the writer's use of language creates a negative impression of Central Valley in lines 6—10. For full marks there should be comments on at least 2 examples. 2 marks may be awarded for reference plus detailed/insightful comment; 1 mark for more basic comment; 0 marks for reference alone. *Possible answers shown in the "Additional Guidance" column.*	4	Possible answers: • "deeply disturbing" suggests unsettling/unnatural nature of agriculture in Central Valley • contrast e.g. "it may sound like … but it is …" — emphasises the unnatural qualities of Central Valley • repetition/list of "no birds, no butterflies, no beetles" — drives home the absence of nature/lack of wildlife • "single blade of grass" suggests that the most basic elements of nature have been eradicated here/wild nature is not tolerated • "only bees" highlights the strange lack of insect life • "arrive by lorry"/"the bees are hired by the day" — highlights the artificiality of Central Valley • "multibillion-dollar"/"industry" suggests anonymity/mass-produced for profit
3.	Candidates should analyse how the writer makes clear her disapproval of dairy farming methods used in Central Valley. For full marks there must be comment on both word choice and sentence structure, but these do not need to be evenly divided. 2 marks may be awarded for reference plus detailed/insightful comment; 1 mark for more basic comment; 0 marks for reference alone. Possible answers shown in the "Additional Guidance" column.	4	Possible answers: Word Choice • "last" suggests farmers see the cows as disposable objects, to be dismissed like rubbish when no longer productive • "crammed" suggests stifling, dangerous conditions • "barren" suggests emptiness, sterility, discomfort of the pens • "tiny patches" suggests restrictive, cramped areas in which cows are housed • "listlessly" suggests lack of life, lethargy, conditions weaken cows • "artificial (diets)" — emphasises the unnatural, unhealthy treatment of these cows • "pushed" suggests forceful manipulation • "grotesquely" suggests this type of dairy farming is monstrous, hideous • "worn out" suggests this type of farming is destructive • "short lives" — poignant description emphasises the tragic and unnatural consequences

146 ANSWERS FOR HIGHER ENGLISH

Question	Expected Answer(s)	Max Mark	Additional Guidance
3.	*(continued)*		**Sentence Structure** • positioning of "As for the cows," at the start of this paragraph creates a despairing tone and/or introduces the negative description of the cows' lives • inversion used in "Crammed … antibiotics." highlights the atrocious conditions in which the cows are kept • list "fed, milked or injected with antibiotics" emphasises the assembly line/uncaring manner of the farms, suggesting the cows are merely part of a repetitive industrial process • list of procedures ("selective breeding … hormones") highlights the seemingly scientific procedures involved, making this type of farming seem like a cold and uncaring experiment on animals • climactic final sentence ("In their short lives … grass.") emphatically/dramatically highlights the contrast between these cows and the environment with which we would normally associate them
4.	For full marks candidates should show understanding of the key point: the movement from farming methods in California to their application in the UK. 2 marks may be awarded for detailed/insightful comment supported by appropriate use of reference/quotation; 1 mark for more basic comment; 0 marks for reference alone. *Possible answers shown in the "Additional Guidance" column.*	2	Possible references include: • the writer's change of focus from the USA to UK is signalled by the question "Could the British … look like this?" • the writer's move to consider intensive farming in the UK is suggested by "Farming in Britain … intensification from America" • the writer goes on to suggest that some of the intensive farming methods used in the USA — "bees arrive by lorry"— may soon arrive in the UK — "Bees are disappearing" • the writer goes on to suggest that some intensive farming methods are already being adopted in the UK, "mega-dairies and mega-piggeries" • the writer highlights the impact of intensive farming already being witnessed in the UK "countryside too sterile … native birds"
5.	Candidates should summarise the differences between Government food policy and consumer wishes. For full marks, both sides must be dealt with but not necessarily equally divided. Candidates must attempt to use their own words. No marks for straight lifts from passage. *Any four points from the "Additional Guidance" column for 1 mark each.*	4	Possible answers include: Government food policy: • buy more British/regional produce ("urging families to buy British food") • buy less foreign food ("Choosing to buy fewer imports") • ease pressure on farmers ("churn out more for less") • be more environmentally aware ("more eco-friendly way of eating") • buy in-season/healthy food ("seasonal fruit and vegetables") Consumer wishes: • drawn to less expensive produce ("addicted to cheap meat … products") • not concerned about origins of food ("supply lines … globe") • previously exotic/expensive food now commonplace/inexpensive ("once delicacies … cheap as chips") • expectation of variety "supply lines … globe"

ANSWERS FOR HIGHER ENGLISH **147**

Question	Expected Answer(s)	Max Mark	Additional Guidance
6.	Candidates should analyse how imagery and sentence structure convey the writer's criticism of industrial farming. For full marks there should be comments on both imagery and sentence structure but these do not have to be evenly divided. 2 marks may be awarded for reference plus detailed/insightful comment; 1 mark for more basic comment; 0 marks for reference alone. *Possible answers shown in the "Additional Guidance" column.*	4	Possible answers: Imagery: • "dirty secret": suggests that the methods used in factory farming are so shocking that they cannot be revealed • "front line": suggests that industrial farming is a desperate struggle against competitors, with frequent business casualties • "treadmill": suggests that industrial farming is very hard work and consists of never-ending repetitive chores • "plummeting": suggests that proximity to an industrial farm causes a devastating drop in the value of local homes Sentence structure: • Parenthesis "to investigate … produced" makes clear the specific nature of the "truth" • List of countries "France … South America" indicates extent of intensive farming • Colon in line 38 introduces example of people directly affected • Dash in line 39 introduces example of people directly affected • Repetitive sentence openings "I talked … I also talked" emphasises the scale the problem, based on her evidence gathering/variety of people affected • List "their homes … pollution" emphasises range of stories by people affected
7.	Candidates should explain how the writer continues the idea that the Central Valley dairy farming is "nightmarish", by making 3 key points. Candidates must attempt to use their own words. No marks for straight lifts from passage. *Any three points from the "Additional Guidance" column for 1 mark each.*	3	Possible answers include: • visible contamination of air/pollution ("yellowish-grey smog") • waste products in the ground ("bovine population … people") • the animals are kept in terrible conditions ("mud, corrugated iron and concrete.") • the overpowering smell ("nauseating reek") • huge buildings are a blight on the landscape ("array of towering … muddy pens.") • (apocalyptic) sense of desolation ("human population is sparse")
8.	Candidates should evaluate the final paragraph's effectiveness as a conclusion to the writer's criticism of industrial farming. For full marks there must be appropriate attention to the idea of a conclusion but this does not have to be limited to points about structure. Candidates may make valid points about the emotive/rhetorical impact of the conclusion. 2 marks awarded for detailed/insightful comment plus reference. 1 mark awarded for a more basic comment. *Possible answers shown in the "Additional Guidance" column.*	2	Possible answers include: • by giving details of the proposed mega-dairy in Lincolnshire, the writer reminds us of her earlier point that the British countryside faces a similar fate to that of Central Valley • the writer reminds us of the ludicrous size of these factory farms by revealing the enormous number of cows planned for this mega-dairy • by including the ridiculous claim that "cows do not belong in fields" the writer forcefully reminds us that those who practise intensive farming have scant regard for nature or natural processes • the writer concludes the passage with a warning that factory farms are getting larger in a rather surreptitious way, suggesting that we are being duped by the unscrupulous owners of these farms • the writer's rather poignant final sentence reminds the readers of the unnatural nature of this transition from the outdoors to indoors

148 ANSWERS FOR HIGHER ENGLISH

Question	Expected Answer(s)	Max Mark	Additional Guidance
9.	Candidates should identify three key areas of agreement in the two passages. Candidates can use bullet points in this final question, or write a number of linked statements. *Approach to marking shown in the "Additional Guidance" column.* *Key areas of agreement shown in grid below. Other answers are possible.*	5	The following guidelines should be used: Five marks — identification of three key areas of agreement with detailed/insightful use of supporting evidence Four marks — identification of three key areas of agreement with appropriate use of supporting evidence Three marks — identification of three key areas of agreement Two marks — identification of two key areas of agreement One mark — identification of one key area of agreement Zero marks — failure to identify any key area of agreement and/or misunderstanding of task

	Area of Agreement	Passage 1	Passage 2
1.	Intensive farming is a highly productive process.	• size and fertility of the farms in Central Valley • high yields from dairy cows in Central Valley • farmers "churn out m ore or less"	• increased productivity of farms following introduction of intensive methods after Second Word War • higher numbers of chickens raised in less space • shorter time taken for animals to reach "edible size"
2.	Intensive farming yields affordable food for everyone.	• meat, fish and dairy products from factory farms are much cheaper • whole chickens sell for ridiculously low prices • farmers are under pressure to produce cheaper food	• factory farming fulfilled post-war policy of "cheap meat, eggs and cheese for everyone" • intensive farming allowed poorer people to have a much richer diet
3.	Intensive farming has brought about a change in people's dietary habits.	• previously expensive foods are now within the reach of everyone • exotic foods are now widely available • cheap meats contain more fat	• we have switched from a diet which was based on cereals/vegetable to one which is high in animal fats
4.	Intensive farming damages the environment and wildlife.	• nature is almost absent in Central Valley • bee populations are in decline • bird populations are in decline • natural habitats are disappearing • the UK countryside is increasingly barren • "desecration" of countryside • Central Valley is heavily polluted	• traditional, attractive farms are disappearing • hedgerows and wildlife are being lost • rivers and streams are being polluted
5.	Intensive farming causes undue stress and suffering to farm animals.	• factory farm animals are treated like machines rather than living creatures • these farm animals have shorter lifespans • conditions are very poor for these animals	• too many animals crammed into small spaces • unnatural for animals to be indoors all of the time • animal growth rates are unnatural • our misguided view that farm animals and pets have different needs causes suffering
6.	People who live beside or work in factory farms are adversely affected.	• property values are affected by industrial farms • people become ill because of pollution from these farms • air quality in Central Valley is worse than that of a big city • ruined aesthetics of Central Valley • farmers are under constant pressure to produce "more with less"	• introduction of intensive farming in the UK caused thousands of job losses in rural areas • the livelihoods of many traditional farmers have been badly affected

	Area of Agreement	Passage 1	Passage 2
7.	We need to restrict/oppose this development of intensive farming in the UK.	• the writer argues that factory farming is not the only way to produce affordable food • Central Valley is presented as a warning about what could happen in the UK • the writer notes that the movement of farm animals indoors is insidious and unnatural	• in the final paragraph, the writer provides us with a set of guidelines on what "we need to" do in order to return to the "environmentally friendly, humane and healthy" farming methods of the past
8.	Intensive farming may have a negative impact on human health	• cheap meats contain more fat • meat contaminated with drugs • quality of produce is low • health problems linked to pollution produced by intensive farms	• contaminated meat enters the human food chain • degenerative diseases connected to a high fat diet
9.	The unnatural nature of intensive farming	• limited lifespan of animals • animals prevented from living naturally outdoors • natural processes subject to human intervention	• animals denied natural living conditions • farm animals' lives considerably shortened in recent years • detrimental effects of unnatural animal diets

PAPER 2 – CRITICAL READING

SECTION 1 – Scottish Text

For all Scottish Texts, marking of the final question, for 10 marks, should be guided by the following generic instruction in conjunction with the specific advice given for the question on each Scottish Text:

Candidates can answer in bullet points in this final question, or write a number of linked statements.

0 marks for reference/quotation alone.

Up to 2 marks can be achieved for identifying elements of commonality as identified in the question.
A further 2 marks can be achieved for reference to the extract given.
6 additional marks can be awarded for discussion of similar references to at least one other part of the text (or other story or poem) by the writer.

In practice this means:

Identification of commonality (2) (e.g.: theme, characterisation, use of imagery, settng, or any other key element …)

from the extract:

1 × relevant reference to technique/idea/feature (1)
1 × appropriate comment (1)
(maximum of 2 marks only for discussion of extract)

from at least one other text/part of the text:

2 marks for detailed/insightful comment plus quotation/reference

1 mark for more basic comment plus quotation/reference

0 marks for quotation/reference alone

(Up to 6 marks).

150 ANSWERS FOR HIGHER ENGLISH

SCOTTISH TEXT (DRAMA)

Text 1 — Drama — *The Slab Boys* by John Byrne

Question	Expected Answer(s)	Max Mark	Additional Guidance
1.	Candidates should explain the contrast between the attitudes of Jack and Phil to Alan. For full marks both sides of contrast must be covered.	2	Possible answers include: • Jack: helpful, friendly, deferential, due to Alan's social position/family connections/youth • Phil: aggressive/hostile as he does not want to be patronised after being dismissed
2.	Candidates should analyse how the tension between Spanky and Phil is made clear in lines 16—31. 2 marks awarded for detailed/insightful comment plus quotation/reference. 1 mark for more basic comment plus quotation/reference. 0 marks for quotation/reference alone.	4	Possible answers include: • Spanky's use of questions/exclamations show his irritation with Phil eg 'How should I know? I've got all these dishes to wash! Can you not give us a hand?' • Spanky's wounding retaliation about Phil losing his job: 'At least I still am one (a Slab Boy)' • Phil's sarcastic response to Spanky's comment identifying himself with Alan: 'Aw, it's 'me and the boy' now, is it?' • Phil's disgust at Spanky's abandonment of him/conforming to the conventional work ethic 'I think I'm going to be sick'
3.	Candidates should analyse how language is used to convey the feelings of Phil and/or Curry. 2 marks awarded for detailed/insightful comment plus quotation/reference 1 mark for more basic comment plus quotation/reference. 0 marks for quotation/reference alone.	4	Possible answers include: **Curry:** • Dismissive towards Phil/gloating about his dismissal, shown in mock-helpful tone of 'Still here … any time' • Unsympathetic initially towards Phil/rules are rules attitude: formal language of 'Only urgent personal calls allowed' • Sympathetic (later) when discussing the plight of Phil's mother: 'She must've been badly injured' **Phil:** • Repeated questions demonstrating his incredulity and growing indignation that Curry is intruding into his personal life 'What … about it?' • Defiance/refusal to be an object of pity: use of blunt language/description emphasising the ludicrous visual effect rather than real pain of his mother's 'accident': 'What she done … simple'
4.	Candidates should discuss how humour is used to develop Phil's character. Candidates may choose to answer in bullet points in this final question or write a number of linked statements.	10	Up to 2 marks can be achieved for identifying elements of commonality as identified in the question, ie how humour is used to develop Phil's character. A further 2 marks can be achieved for reference to the extract given. 6 additional marks can be awarded for discussion of similar references from at least one other part of the text. <u>In practice this means:</u> Identification of commonality eg: Phil uses sarcasm/mockery/irony as a defence mechanism to help him cope with work or home problems From the extract: 2 marks for detailed/insightful comment plus quotation/reference; 1 mark for more basic comment plus quotation/reference; 0 marks for quotation/reference alone. eg "Nope … a Ford Prefect" use of bathos/name of car to 'correct' Curry's comment about the miracle shows his refusal to acknowledge the pain or seriousness of his mother's situation in front of Curry/humour used to protect/defend his own pride (2 marks)

ANSWERS FOR HIGHER ENGLISH **151**

Question	Expected Answer(s)	Max Mark	Additional Guidance
4.	*(continued)*		From at least one other text/part of the text: 2 marks for detailed/insightful comment plus quotation/reference; 1 mark for more basic comment plus quotation/reference; 0 marks for quotation/reference alone (Up to 6 marks). Possible answers include: • Phil and Spanky's witty banter and teasing of other characters/"Oh … what trade was that, Mr. Curry?" shows how he copes with his mundane life **(2)** • The farcical nature of Hector's "makeover"/reference to Phil forcing Hector into the clothes/the balaclava … shows Phil's cruelty towards others **(2)** • The use of black humour in the descriptions of Phil's mother/"The old dear's impromptu dip" — euphemism describes his mother's suicidal tendencies **(2)** • The attempts to get Lucille to accompany Hector to the Staffie shows that, underneath, Phil is a compassionate character **(2)** • Uses humour to show off/appear to be 'top dog'/put people down … — eg "You can't even get the tin trunks off a chocolate soldier, Jack" **(2)** Many other answers are possible.

Text 2 — Drama — *The Cheviot, the Stag and the Black, Black Oil* by John McGrath

Question	Expected Answer(s)	Max Mark	Additional Guidance
5.	Candidates should analyse how language is used to create different tones in the Duke's speeches, by referring to at least two examples. For full marks candidates must make reference to at least two distinct tones, but not necessarily in equal measure. 2 marks are awarded for detailed/insightful comment plus quotation/reference. 1 mark for more basic comment plus quotation/reference. 0 marks for quotation/reference alone	4	Possible answers include: Lines 1–4 • persuasive, evoking national pride and loyalty through "the Queen"/use of precedent and tradition through "as always" • business-like/authoritarian in evoking "My Commissioner informs me …" Lines 8–10 • patronising in the assumption that they can be bought off for personal gain: "6 golden sovereigns" • arrogant/presumptuous: "step up in an orderly manner" Lines 12–18 • angry in the demands for "an explanation" and swearing "damn it" because of Highland defiance • frustration that his argument has failed: "Have you no pride …?" • scaremongering tone in the use of hyperbole/threats: "the cruel Tsar of Russia installed in Dunrobin Castle" • accusatory/hectoring tone in the series of questions

152 ANSWERS FOR HIGHER ENGLISH

Question	Expected Answer(s)	Max Mark	Additional Guidance
6.	Candidates should analyse how both the stage directions and dialogue in lines 17–27 convey the local people's defiance of the Duke. For full marks candidates must cover both stage directions and dialogue, but not necessarily in equal measure 2 marks are awarded for detailed/insightful comment plus quotation/reference. 1 mark for more basic comment plus quotation/reference. 0 marks for quotation/reference alone.	4	Possible answers include: Stage Directions • *'Silence.'* Creates an unsettling atmosphere, showing the tension between the Highlanders and the Duke • *'Nobody moves.'* The inaction of the Highlanders shows a passive resistance • *'OLD MAN stands'* shows the shift from passive resistance to active resistance • *'in the audience'* makes the audience identify with the man as a representative of the people/puts the audience in the position of the tenants Dialogue • The old man's respectful, reasonable response adds weight to his argument: "I am sorry ..."/"your Grace" • The old man takes the Duke's threat as the basis of his counter-argument: "we could not expect worse treatment" • Use of personal pronouns "We ... you" emphasises the lack of identification that the Highlanders have with the Duke's cause • Climactically mocking the Duke by suggesting that the Duke conscripts the sheep • The humorous solidarity shown by the collective "Baa-aa"
7.	Candidates should explain how the MC's speech brings this section of the play to an ironic conclusion. 2 marks are awarded for detailed/insightful comment. 1 mark for more basic comment. 0 marks for quotation/reference alone.	2	Possible answers include: • Description of the fate of the one man who did enlist whose family was treated badly, in contrast to the promise of financial reward • Duke's expectations/efforts in contrast to the lack of response • The futility of the Highlanders' defiance: after they were cleared off the land they had to enlist anyway • Use of the phrase 'The old tradition of loyal soldiering' when it was based on desperation rather than duty
8.	Candidates should discuss how McGrath develops the theme of change/resistance to change in this and at least one other extract from the play. Candidates may choose to answer in bullet points in this final question, or write a number of linked statements.	10	Up to 2 marks can be achieved for identifying elements of commonality as identified in the question, ie the development of the theme of change/resistance to change in the play. A further 2 marks can be achieved for reference to the extract given. 6 additional marks can be awarded for discussion of similar references to at least one other part of the text. <u>In practice this means:</u> Identification of commonality (theme, characterisation, use of imagery, setting, or any other key element ...) eg Cultural/economical and social changes that have affected Scotland (1 mark) Variety of responses from the population to these changes (1 mark) From the extract: 2 marks for detailed/insightful comment plus quotation/reference;

ANSWERS FOR HIGHER ENGLISH **153**

Question	Expected Answer(s)	Max Mark	Additional Guidance
8.	*(continued)*		1 mark for more basic comment plus quotation/reference;
			0 marks for quotation/reference alone.
			eg Change in the attitude of the common people to authority from unquestioning obedience to resistance (2 marks)
			From elsewhere in the play:
			2 marks for detailed/insightful comment plus quotation/reference;
			1 mark for more basic comment plus quotation/reference;
			0 marks for quotation/reference alone
			(Up to 6 marks).
			Possible answers include:
			Role of women as defenders of the community in resisting the introduction of Cheviot sheep to the Highlands for example, female members' direct appeal to the audience when recounting Patrick Sellar's evictions in their community **(2)**
			The erosion of Gaelic culture through the banning of language, music etc for example, the role of the MC in disseminating historical information **(2)**
			Forced emigration to the colonies to maximise profit at the behest of figures of authority for example, the Duke of Selkirk's movement of his Lowland tenants to Canada **(2)**
			The continued eviction of tenants to free up land for hunting for example, Lady Phosphate's preference for gaming estates at the expense of the tenants in the area **(2)**
			The continued exploitation of the Highlands by entrepreneurial outsiders for example, Andy McChuckemup plans to exploit the landscape through commercialisation **(2)**
			Many other answers are possible.

Text 3 — Drama — *Men Should Weep* by Ena Lamont Stewart

Question	Expected Answer(s)	Max Mark	Additional Guidance
9.	Candidates should explain two of Jenny's reasons for visiting the family home.	2	Possible answers: • Jenny wants to correct her mother's misunderstanding of Bertie's situation: the hospital will not let him come back to Maggie's very unhealthy slum tenement • Jenny wants to make sure her parents actively pursue the Corporation about getting a Council house, using Bertie's ill-health as a lever • When Jenny was considering suicide by drowning, she thought of her father and all the love and kindness he had shown her when she was a child • Jenny regrets her ill-treatment, partly influenced by Isa, of her parents; she has come back to admit her guilt and regret

154 ANSWERS FOR HIGHER ENGLISH

Question	Expected Answer(s)	Max Mark	Additional Guidance
10.	Candidates should analyse how Lily and Jenny's differing attitudes are shown in lines 22—42. For full marks, both Lily and Jenny's attitudes must be covered, although equal coverage is not necessary. 2 marks awarded for detailed/insightful comment plus quotation/reference. 1 mark for more basic comment plus quotation/reference. 0 marks for quotation/reference alone.	4	Possible answers: Lily: • does not believe in couples living together unless they're married — "livin in sin" • is contemptuous, highly critical of the money or gifts Jenny has received; she implies that what Jenny is doing is little better than prostitution — "We've had an eye-fu o yer wages o sin"; "she'll hae earned it, Maggie. On her back." • suggests strongly that Jenny has damned herself in exchange for material possessions "The wages o sin's nae deith, it's fancy hairdos an a swanky coat an pur silk stockins" • assumes that a woman who lives with a man outwith marriage will inevitably be punished, disappointed, discarded — "till yer tired business man gets tired o you an ye're oot on yer ear" • is unswervingly conventional, is determined not to behave in a way society might find unacceptable — "I've kept ma self-respect" Jenny: • sees nothing wrong with couples living together outside marriage — "Aye, if ye want tae ca it sin! I don't." • is dismissive of conventional morality — "You seem tae ken yer Bible ... I never pretended tae." • favours happiness over convention — "kind", "generous", "I'm happy, an I'm makin him happy" • sees no point in sacrificing all hope of happiness, love or companionship just to follow the norms of society — "Aye. An that's aboot a ye've got."
11.	Candidates should analyse the dramatic impact of at least two of the stage directions in lines 43—62. 2 marks awarded for detailed/insightful comment plus quotation/reference. 1 mark for more basic comment plus quotation/reference. 0 marks for quotation/reference alone.	4	Possible answers: (Her hands to her head): • conveys the depth of Maggie's distress and unhappiness. The argument between Lily and Jenny, which she has just brought to an end, has pushed her to her wits' end • creates a dramatic pause before Maggie goes on to reflect that the happiness she had felt on seeing Jenny return has gone • emphasises Maggie prefers to avoid confrontation and often ignores the reality of her problems (She draws a couple of chairs together ... watching): • conveys Jenny's desire to discuss important matters with Maggie • Jenny only draws up two chairs, not three, clearly signaling she is excluding Lily from the discussion • Lily feels she is an important enough figure in the family and has the right to listen, so she withdraws but only a little (She doesn't even look at Lily): • conveys Jenny's determination to get somewhere with Maggie (Maggie nods): • shows the start of Maggie's acceptance that she must listen to Jenny and perhaps act on her advice. (She opens her handbag ... She gasps) • given the Morrisons' poverty, producing the "roll of notes" has a powerful physical impact on Maggie (John comes in ... lips tighten) • conveys his conflicting emotions about his daughter: initial pleasure at seeing her followed by his anger at her current situation

ANSWERS FOR HIGHER ENGLISH **155**

Question	Expected Answer(s)	Max Mark	Additional Guidance
12.	Candidates should discuss how Jenny's growing maturity is made clear and should refer to appropriate textual evidence to support their discussion. Candidates may choose to answer in bullet points in this final question, or write a number of linked statements.	10	Up to 2 marks can be achieved for identifying elements of commonality as identified in the question, ie how Jenny's growing maturity is made clear. A further 2 marks can be achieved for reference to the extract given. 6 additional marks can be awarded for discussion of similar references from at least one other part of the text. In practice this means: Identification of commonality eg: Jenny's concern for her family shows a sense of responsibility (1 mark) her earlier behaviour was self-centred and immature (1 mark) From the extract: 2 marks for detailed/insightful comment plus quotation/reference; 1 mark for more basic comment plus quotation/reference; 0 marks for quotation/reference alone. eg Jenny's admission of her previous lack of respect towards her mother shows her willingness to accept responsibility for her actions (2 marks) OR "Listen, Mammy. We canna wait for a hoose ... So while ye're waitin, ye're goin tae flit tae a rented hoose." shows that Jenny is now capable of taking control where her mother has been unable to do so (2 marks) From at least one other part of the play: 2 marks for detailed/insightful comment plus quotation/reference; 1 mark for more basic comment plus quotation/reference; 0 marks for quotation/reference alone (Up to 6 marks). Possible answers include: Jenny shows little sympathy for her parents' financial plight "I'm chuckin the shop"/she does not want to be disgraced by bringing home the "chipped apples and bashed tomaties" to help eke out the family budget **(2)** Jenny's late arrival home from the "pickshers" and her impudent response to John's concern shows that she is selfish and often irresponsible **(2)** Jenny's desperate attempts to carve her own identity often result in cruel, unloving behaviour towards her parents — "Ye needna worry! When I leave this rotten pig-stye I'm no comin back. There's ither things in life ... " **(2)** Jenny's guilt over abandoning her home and family becomes apparent through her attempts to reassure Maggie/"Ma, ye've got Dad and Alec and the weans. Ye'll no miss me oot of the hoose." **(2)** Mrs Bone and Mrs Harris' description of Jenny as "a right mess" reveals the difficult circumstances Jenny has managed to overcome before returning to the family home **(2)** Many other answers are possible.

156 ANSWERS FOR HIGHER ENGLISH

SCOTTISH TEXT (PROSE)

Text 1 — Prose — *Mother and Son* by Iain Crichton Smith

Question	Expected Answer(s)	Max Mark	Additional Guidance
13.	Candidates should analyse the writer's use of language in lines 1–22 to reveal the nature of the relationship between mother and son. 2 marks awarded for detailed/insightful comment plus quotation/reference. 1 mark for more basic comment plus quotation/reference. 0 marks for quotation/reference alone.	4	Possible answers include: <ul><li>pattern of relationship has been set/it had happened before/likely to happen again — "beginning again …"</li><li>Their conflict followed a regular pattern — "always …"/emphasis on repeated pattern of sentence structure — "You know well enough"</li><li>He is tired of the inevitable, repetitive conflicts — "spoke wearily"</li><li>She dominates him by hurtful comments — "same brutal pain stabbed him"</li><li>little chance of success in being understood/making his point — "retired defeated"</li><li>mother appears to give the son the chance to change/take responsibility but doesn't really mean it — "if you'll only say"</li></ul>
14.	Candidates should identify the tone of the mother's words in lines 27–28 and analyse how this tone is created. 1 mark awarded for identification of appropriate tone. Analysis: 2 marks awarded for detailed/insightful comment plus quotation/reference; 1 mark for more basic comment plus quotation/reference. 0 marks for quotation/reference alone.	3	Possible answers include: **Tone:** <ul><li>cruel/vicious/dismissive/critical …</li><li>dismissive put-down — "Lessons aren't everything."</li><li>repetition of accusatory "you" — "You aren't a mechanic."</li><li>Repeated use of negatives — "aren't"/"can't" …</li><li>short, quick-fire list of complaints/criticisms — "You … Why don't you hurry up with that tea?"</li><li>accusatory question — "Why don't you hurry up with that tea?"</li><li>escalating list of her perception of his inadequacies — "You aren't a mechanic … Fat good you'd be at a job."</li></ul>
15.	Candidates should analyse how the language of lines 29–38 conveys the son's reaction to his mother's words. 2 marks awarded for detailed/insightful comment plus quotation/reference. 1 mark for more basic comment plus quotation/reference. 0 marks for quotation/reference alone.		Possible answers include: <ul><li>defeated in the face of mother's constant criticism — "despairingly leaning"; "head on his hands"</li><li>acceptance of inadequacies — "wasn't a mechanic"; "never could understand"</li><li>deepening lack of self-esteem/self-doubt — "something had gone wrong"</li><li>unhappy/despairing — "sad look on his face"</li></ul>
16.	Candidates should discuss how Iain Crichton Smith uses contrasting characters to explore theme. Candidates may choose to answer in bullet points in this final question, or write a number of linked statements.	10	Up to 2 marks can be achieved for identifying elements of commonality as identified in the question, ie contrast used to explore character and/or theme. A further 2 marks can be achieved for reference to the extract given. 6 additional marks can be awarded for discussion of similar references from at least one other short story. <u>In practice this means:</u> Identification of commonality eg: Iain Crichton Smith will often create contrast between characters from different backgrounds (1 mark) with differing personalities (1 mark) **OR** the sense of an outsider in a closed community or alien environment (1 mark) such as restricted island setting or war-time situation (1 mark)

ANSWERS FOR HIGHER ENGLISH **157**

Question	Expected Answer(s)	Max Mark	Additional Guidance
16.	*(continued)*		From the extract:
			1 × relevant reference to technique/idea/feature
			1 × appropriate comment (2 marks)
			(maximum of 2 marks only for discussion of extract)
			eg The domineering mother contrasts with the submissive son — "her spiteful, bitter face"/"his head in his hands" (2 marks)
			The mother's directness contrasts with the son's tentative responses — "you'd be no good in a job"/"I'll take a job tomorrow ... if you'll only say" (2 marks)
			From at least one other text:
			2 marks for detailed/insightful comment plus quotation/reference;
			1 mark for more basic comment plus quotation/reference;
			0 marks for quotation/reference alone
			(Up to 6 marks).
			Possible answers include:
			• *The Telegram* — the fat woman and thin woman contrast as the thin woman is an incomer whereas the fat woman has always lived in this village — highlights small-mindedness of village "she was an incomer from another village and had only been in this one for thirty years or so" **(2)**
			• *The Telegram* — contrasting attitudes towards education/aspiration — "thin woman was ambitious: she had sent her son to university ..." whereas the fat woman has lived there all her life/is more conventional/her son was only an ordinary seaman but both are equally affected by the war **(2)**
			• *The Red Door:* Murdo contrasts with the rest of the islanders through his ultimate willingness to be different when he accepts the red door instead of re-painting it **(2)**
			• *The Painter:* painter sees the fight as an artistic opportunity whereas the other villagers are horrified by his apparent lack of concern for the violence — "... a gaze that had gone beyond the human and was as indifferent to the outcome as a hawk's might be." **(2)**
			• *The Crater:* contrast in attitude between Lt Robert Mackinnon and Sergeant Smith to the war. Mackinnon is sensitive/horrified by the brutality of war whereas Sergeant Smith is stolidly accepting — happy to be back **(2)**
			Many other answers are possible.

Text 2 — Prose — *The Wireless Set* by George Mackay Brown

Question	Expected Answer(s)	Max Mark	Additional Guidance
17.		For full marks, candidates should explain how Mackay Brown creates a sense of both community life and the role of the wireless set within it.	2	Possible answers include:
				• "passed the shop and the manse and the schoolhouse" — postman's journey encapsulates the centres of community life
		0 marks for reference/quotation alone.		• "the island postman" — suggests he is a central part of the community/small community requiring only one postman
				• "Joe Loss and his orchestra" — alien (from London) music intruding into island life via wireless set
				• Contrast traditional island life ("croft"/"track") with new, modern music (from outside/London)

158 ANSWERS FOR HIGHER ENGLISH

Question		Expected Answer(s)	Max Mark	Additional Guidance
18.	(a)	Candidates should analyse how Mackay Brown reveals the postman's attitude to Betsy in lines 6–15. 2 marks may be awarded for detailed/insightful comment plus quotation/reference. 1 mark for more basic comment plus quotation/reference. 0 marks for reference/quotation alone.	2	Possible answers include: • Repetition/parallel expressions in "Is there anybody with you?" and "There should be somebody with you" — reveals his insistence that she have support before he gives her the bad news — sympathetic/concerned • "miser parting with a twenty pound note" — image reveals his extreme reluctance to tell her/telling her the news is compared with parting with a thing that is precious : protective towards her/relishing power the knowledge gives him • "disappearing on his bike round the corner"- already left (by the time she has read the telegram) suggests he doesn't know how to deal with her/his concern is not deep/he has now moved on and left her to someone else to care for her (the missionary)
	(b)	Candidates should analyse how Mackay Brown uses language to convey the differing reactions of the missionary and Betsy to the news in lines 16–22. 0 marks for reference/quotation alone.	2	Possible answers include: Missionary: • "He died for his country"/"He made the great sacrifice" — platitudes/conventional clichés suggest insincerity/no real sympathy Betsy: • "It's time the peats were carted" suggests that Betsy is taken up with the work on the land rather than facing her personal tragedy/a coping strategy • "That isn't it at all" suggests Betsy's simple dismissal of the missionary's cliché/reveals her honesty in the face of his platitudes • "Howie's sunk with torpedoes. That's all I know" — blunt statement of the fact shows that she is forced to face up to the brutal reality of what has happened
19.		Candidates should refer to both sides of the contrast: the couple's real feelings and the missionary's perception of their feelings. 2 marks awarded for detailed/insightful comment plus quotation/reference. 1 mark for more basic comment plus quotation/reference. 0 marks for quotation/reference alone.	4	Possible answers include: The couple: • "How many lobsters … I got two lobsters … I got six crabs" determined focus on practicalities/modest numbers which define their frugal life/getting on with normalities of life as coping mechanism • "The wireless stood, a tangled wreck, on the dresser" — utter destruction of the object which 'brought the war' shows Hugh's agony The missionary's view: • "I'll break the news to him" — slightly officious/patronising attempt to take charge of the situation — he does not realise that Hugh already knows • "awed by such callousness" — complete failure to understand their stoical way of dealing with extreme grief • "slowly shaking his head" — demonstrates that the missionary doesn't understand their coping strategy/thinks they don't care • "My poor man" — tries to impose what he thinks their reaction should be

ANSWERS FOR HIGHER ENGLISH **159**

Question	Expected Answer(s)	Max Mark	Additional Guidance
20.	Candidates should discuss how the writer deals with the relationship between the island community and the outside world. Candidates may choose to answer in bullet points in this final question, or write a number of linked statements.	10	Up to 2 marks can be achieved for identifying elements of commonality as identified in the question, ie the relationship between the island community and the outside world. A further 2 marks can be achieved for reference to the extract given. 6 additional marks can be awarded for discussion of similar references from at least one other short story. <u>In practice this means:</u> Identification of commonality eg George Mackay Brown often reveals the intrusion of the modern or violent outside world (1 mark) into the traditional/safe/secure world of an island community (1 mark). From the extract: 2 marks for detailed/insightful comment plus quotation/reference; 1 mark for more basic comment plus quotation/reference; 0 marks for quotation/reference alone. eg The music belongs to another world outside the island — "The wireless was playing music inside, Joe Loss and his orchestra." (2 marks) **OR** The news of the Howie's death, arriving by telegram, shows the destructive intrusion of the war on the local community (2 marks) From at least one other text: 2 marks for detailed/insightful comment plus quotation/reference; 1 mark for more basic comment plus quotation/reference; 0 marks for quotation/reference alone (Up to 6 marks). Possible answers include: *Tartan* — the Vikings' journey through the village — apparently aggressive/predatory but villagers' silent, brooding presence follows them to shore — they leave hastily/gaining little from the raid **(2)** *Tartan* — the Vikings are searching for anything valuable to plunder but, ironically, give a silver coin to a child because of his wit (the only money to change hands in the raid) **(2)** *Tartan* — Vikings threaten violence/pillaging/attacking dark-haired woman but the only death is Kol, murdered by the villagers while he lies drunk **(2)** *The Eye of the Hurricane* — the narrator, Barclay's, slightly patronising attempt to relate to the island people shown in his description of them: "I had come to live … among simple, uncomplicated people" **(2)** *A Time to Keep* — the "missionary" (title suggests patronising attempt to bring enlightened religion to the community) offers comfort on death of Ingi but his words are hollow and meaningless and are rejected by Bill: "She's in the earth"/"The ground isn't a particularly happy place to be." **(2)** Many other answers are possible.

160 ANSWERS FOR HIGHER ENGLISH

Text 3 — Prose — *The Trick is to Keep Breathing* by Janice Galloway

Question	Expected Answer(s)	Max Mark	Additional Guidance
21.	Candidates should analyse how Galloway makes the reader aware of Joy's efforts to cope. 2 marks may be awarded for detailed/insightful comment plus quotation/reference. 1 mark for more basic comment + quotation/reference. 0 marks for quotation/reference alone.	2	Possible answers include: • Repetition of "I" eg "I wanted"; "I made"; "I kept going" emphasises all the things she was trying to do/creates a listing effect • Comparison to Bunyan's Pilgrim and Dorothy emphasises her determination • Reference to "endurance test" demonstrates the effort needed just to keep going • "all I had to do was last out" emphasises that she is trying to convince herself that she can cope
22.	Candidates should analyse how the writer uses language to convey Joy's desperation for Michael's presence. 2 marks awarded for detailed/insightful comment plus quotation/reference. 1 mark for more basic comment plus quotation/reference. 0 marks for quotation/reference alone.	4	Possible answers include: • Repetitive sentence structure in lines 9–14 emphasises her obsession with Michael • Use of list in sentence beginning "I saw him in cars" emphasises the number and variety of places she imagines seeing him • Use of question "How could he be …?" emphasises that she wants to believe/is trying to convince herself that he is still alive • Use of the senses eg smell ("I started smelling …") and sight ("I saw him …") emphasises that she can imagine his presence/wants his presence • "roaring past"; "drifting by"; "hovering in a cloud" emphasises that he is always just out of reach • "sunk my face into his clothes" emphasises how she totally immerses herself; wants to feel his presence • "howled" emphasises how much despair she feels at his absence • "invisible presence" emphasises her emptiness; imagines he is there but cannot see him
23.	Candidates should analyse how the writer conveys Joy's feelings of despair. For full marks at least two different examples must be commented on. 2 marks awarded for detailed/insightful comment plus quotation/reference. 1 mark for more basic comment plus quotation/reference. 0 marks for quotation/reference alone.	4	Possible answers include: • Sentence structure "Please god …" — plea/prayer emphasises her desire to die • "mashed remains"; "marrowbone jelly oozing" — word choice creates vivid visual image of the aftermath of boulders crashing through the roof; emphasises her desire to be wiped out completely • Use of humour in the Health Visitor's words emphasises her sarcasm/bitterness towards the medical professionals who are supposed to be helping her • "shrinking" emphasises that she feels as if she is disappearing • "shiver" emphasises her coldness/fear • Use of contrast in the final paragraph helps us to understand her despair at her situation
24.	Candidates should discuss how the writer conveys Joy's fear/anxiety about relating to other people and should refer to appropriate textual evidence to support their discussion. Candidates may choose to answer in bullet points in this final question, or write a number of linked statements.	10	Up to 2 marks can be achieved for identifying elements of commonality as identified in the question, ie evidence of Joy's fear/anxiety about relating to other people. A further 2 marks can be achieved for reference to the extract given. 6 additional marks can be awarded for discussion of similar references from at least one other part of the text. <u>In practice this means:</u> Identification of commonality eg Fear/anxiety is ever-present in Joy's view of the world around her and how she relates to other people (1 mark) shown through a range of narrative techniques/descriptions of her experiences (1 mark).

ANSWERS FOR HIGHER ENGLISH **161**

Question	Expected Answer(s)	Max Mark	Additional Guidance
24.	*(continued)*		From the extract:
			2 marks for detailed/insightful comment plus quotation/reference;
			1 mark for more basic comment plus quotation/reference;
			0 marks for quotation/reference alone.
			eg Health Visitor's clichéd comments reveal (Joy's perception of) her lack of understanding of the depth of Joy's problems and show that they cannot relate to one another (2 marks)
			OR
			Joy's direct statement ("Needing people ... wearing me out") reveals her inability to cope with forming relationships which she, nevertheless, recognises she needs (2 marks)
			From at least one other part of the text:
			2 marks for detailed/insightful comment plus quotation/reference;
			1 mark for more basic comment plus quotation/reference;
			0 marks for quotation/reference alone
			(Up to 6 marks).
			Possible references include:
			• Joy's attempts to distance herself from/avoid contact with her sister, Myra "Tell me where you live" **(2)**
			• Anxiety about visits from the Health Visitor — Joy refers to herself as a patient to distance herself from her illness and putting on a brave front by not being honest about how much she is struggling/how deep her depression is **(2)**
			• Anxiety about meeting doctors — eg referring to them by numbers, "Doctor 1, Doctor 2" which shows her refusal to engage with them on a personal level **(2)**
			• Fear of the phone — eg. after she self-harms she says "I can't face the phone tonight either" showing that, even when desperate, she cannot use the phone to seek help **(2)**
			• Fear/avoidance of communication — eg. despite having a landline, Joy prefers to use the phone box nearby because the landline represents people coming in/she can't control who is calling **(2)**
			Many other answers are possible.

Text 4 — Prose — *Sunset Song* by Lewis Grassic Gibbon

Question	Expected Answer(s)	Max Mark	Additional Guidance
25.	Candidates should explain how Chris is feeling in lines 1–8. 2 marks are awarded for detailed/insightful comment plus quotation/reference. 1 mark for more basic comment plus quotation/reference. 0 marks for quotation/reference alone.	2	Possible answers include: • Chris's desire to arrive at the Stones displays great mental strength like the strength of the metal iron; • the strength of Chris's will in her single-mindedness; • peace and restfulness of Chris lying down after her exertions; • sense of Chris's complete freedom from tension; Chris feels at peace with nature; • Physical symptoms indicative of exertion or distress
26.	Candidates should analyse how the writer conveys the impact her mother's death has had on Chris in lines 9–23. 2 marks are awarded for detailed/insightful comment plus quotation/reference. 1 mark for more basic comment plus quotation/reference. 0 marks for quotation/reference alone.	4	Possible answers include: • "as a dark cold pit" — the simile suggests Chris's misery and difficulty in escaping from so much sorrow; • "and the world went on ... the world went on and you went with it" — repetition reinforces the fact that Chris has no choice but to carry on with her life, despite her personal tragedy; • "something died in your heart and went down with her to lie" — suggests that emotionally Chris has suffered a loss which will accompany her mother to her grave;

162 ANSWERS FOR HIGHER ENGLISH

Question	Expected Answer(s)	Max Mark	Additional Guidance
26.	*(continued)*		• "the child in your heart died then" — shows Chris's acknowledgement of the abrupt end of childhood for her; • "hands ready to snatch you back … over-rough" — image conveys a past where Chris knew she would be rescued from harm; • "the Chris of the books and the dreams died with it" — all that might have been must be cast aside because reality has taken over from fantasy; • "the dark, quiet corpse that was your childhood" — stark image of death conveys the certainty of this childhood stage of Chris's life being over.
27.	Candidates should analyse how the writer conveys the horror of Chris's memory of her mother's death in lines 23–45. 2 marks are awarded for detailed/insightful comment plus quotation/reference. 1 mark for more basic comment plus quotation/reference. 0 marks for quotation/reference alone.	4	Possible answers include: • Description of Mistress Munro as a terrifying presence: "uncaring", "black-eyed futret", "snapping", "terrified" • Pathetic fallacy showing Chris's despair: "awful night", "rain-soaked parks" • Chris's initial feelings of shock/numbness: "dazed and dull-eyed" • Description of mother's body as beautiful heightening the horrific nature of Chris's loss: "sweet to look at" • Chris's movement from denial to the agony of grief: "hot tears wrung from your eyes like drops of blood" • Chris's thoughts conveyed directly to show her utter despair, including repetition: "Oh mother, mother, why did you do it?"
28.	Candidates should discuss how Grassic Gibbon presents Chris's growing to maturity in this and at least one other part of the novel. Candidates may choose to answer in bullet points in this final question, or write a number of linked statements.	10	Up to 2 marks can be achieved for identifying elements of commonality as identified in the question, ie Chris's growing to maturity. A further 2 marks can be achieved for reference to the extract given. 6 additional marks can be awarded for discussion of similar references to at least one other part of the text by the writer. In practice this means: Identification of commonality (theme, characterisation, use of imagery, setting, or any other key element …) Eg Her evolving identification with the land. (1 mark) This helps her to resolve her internal conflict and find her own identity at a time of personal and societal change. (1 mark) From the extract: 2 marks for detailed insightful comment plus quotation/reference; 1 mark for more basic comment plus quotation/reference; 0 marks for quotation/reference alone. eg During a time of change she finds comfort in the permanence of the Standing Stones (2 marks) **OR** Mistress Munro's role in reminding Chris of her familial responsibilities leads to her leaving behind her childhood and assuming the role of mother: "you'll find little time for dreaming and dirt when you're keeping house at Blawearie" (2 marks) From at least one other part of the text: 2 marks for detailed/insightful comment plus quotation/reference; 1 mark for more basic comment plus quotation/reference; 0 marks for quotation/reference alone (Up to 6 marks).

ANSWERS FOR HIGHER ENGLISH **163**

Question	Expected Answer(s)	Max Mark	Additional Guidance
28.	*(continued)*		Possible answers include: • Chris's loss of her father and decision to stay on the land which shows her increased sense of her identity being tied up with the land/taking responsibility for her own future **(2)** • Chris falling in love with and marrying Ewan further links her to the land as Ewan represents the agricultural way of life **(2)** • Her pregnancy and the birth of her son which shows her taking on responsibility and starting new life with her own family **(2)** • The return of Ewan as a soldier and the apparent destruction of their relationship when she displays resilience and determination to endure as an independent woman **(2)** • The death of Ewan which brings about redemption/ reconciliation in her eyes as he "went into the heart that was his forever" **(2)** Many other answers are possible.

Text 5 — Prose — *The Cone-Gatherers* by Robin Jenkins

Question	Expected Answer(s)	Max Mark	Additional Guidance
29.	Candidates should analyse how language is used to create a positive picture of Lady Runcie-Campbell in lines 1—19. 2 marks are awarded for detailed/ insightful comment plus quotation/ reference. 1 mark for more basic comment plus quotation/reference. 0 marks for quotation/reference alone.	4	Possible answers include: • Her attractiveness: "clear courteous musical voice"/"charming" speaker/"loveliness"/"outstanding beauty of face" • Her sense of fairness and justice: "earnestness of spirit"/"almost mystical sense of responsibility"/"passion for justice, profound and intelligent"/"determination to see right done, even at the expense of rank or pride" • Her ability to bring out the best in people: "ability to exalt people out of their humdrum selves" • Her Christian beliefs/altruism/spirituality: "almost mystical sense of responsibility"/"associated religion ... with her perfume"/"her emulation of Christ"
30.	Candidates should analyse two instances of the use of language to convey the contrast between the two characters in lines 23—43. 2 marks are awarded for detailed/ insightful comment plus quotation/ reference. 1 mark for more basic comment plus quotation/reference. 0 marks for quotation/reference alone.	4	Possible answers include: **Openness and duplicity:** Duror 's desire to corrupt Lady Runcie-Campbell' — "it would implicate her in his chosen evil"; in contrast she "looked at him frankly and sympathetically", suggesting her honesty and compassion **Beauty/Purity and ugliness:** Setting in the room suggests beauty — "sunny scented room" which contrasts with the evil thoughts in Duror's mind — "black filth" **Contrast in physical appearance** She is beautiful and "vital"; in contrast he is unkempt and ill-looking — "hadn't shaved". **Light and dark** Setting of the room suggests light/"glittering rings" contrasts with "black filth" **Good and evil:** Reference to the goodness of nature in the birdsong — "everywhere birds sang"-which contrasts with Duror's evil thought which "crept up until it entered his mouth, covered his ears, blinded his eyes, and so annihilated him"

164 ANSWERS FOR HIGHER ENGLISH

Question	Expected Answer(s)	Max Mark	Additional Guidance
31.	Candidates should explain why Lady Runcie-Campbell now feels more able to identify with Peggy's situation. 2 marks may be awarded for a detailed/insightful explanation. 1 mark for a more basic explanation.	2	Possible answers include: • The war (and the fact she is separated from her husband as a result) has demonstrated to Lady Runcie-Campbell what it is like to miss a loved one — she links this to Peggy Duror's illness as her 'war' and understands how she and Duror must feel • The war has stopped Lady Runcie-Campbell being able to appreciate aspects of everyday life: "flowers … friends", something Peggy has been deprived of for years • Word-choice such as "dreadful separations"/"cut off" may also be commented on, showing the hurt/pain caused by being apart • Candidates may also notice that her sympathies lie with Peggy rather than Duror — she empathises with a wife who is missing her husband (and perhaps fails to acknowledge his lack of emotion)
32.	Candidates should discuss how Duror is presented not just as an evil character, but one who might be worthy of sympathy or understanding, and should refer to appropriate textual evidence to support their discussion. Candidates can answer in bullet points in this final question, or write a number of linked statements. For the full 6 marks on elsewhere in the text, both evil and sympathy must be covered, although coverage will not necessarily be balanced.	10	Up to 2 marks can be achieved for identifying elements of commonality as identified in the question, ie how Duror is presented not just as an evil character, but one who might be worthy of some sympathy. A further 2 marks can be achieved for reference to the extract given. 6 additional marks can be awarded for discussion of similar references from at least one other part of the text. In practice this means: Identification of commonality eg: Duror's evil character is primarily shown through his persecution of those whom he perceives as imperfect (1 mark) yet some sympathy can be felt because of personal circumstances (1 mark) From the extract: 2 marks for detailed/insightful comment plus quotation/reference; 1 mark for more basic comment plus quotation/reference; 0 marks for quotation/reference alone. eg His duplicitous behaviour towards Lady Runcie-Campbell, yet some sympathy could be evoked by awareness of his own immorality (2 marks). **OR** his intention in this extract is to damage the cone gatherers, but we have some sympathy for the burden he carries with his wife (2 marks). From at least one other part of the text: 2 marks for detailed/insightful comment plus quotation/reference; 1 mark for more basic comment plus quotation/reference; 0 marks for quotation/reference alone (Up to 6 marks). Possible answers include: Duror as evil: • Duror lurking in the wood, spying on the cone-gatherers/aiming his gun at them suggests that he sees them as animals/inferior beings to be hunted/suggests his devious nature **(2)** • His determination to drive them out of the wood shows selfish protection of his own territory in the face of their geuine need **(2)** • The lies he spreads about Calum (eg. with reference to the doll) shows his desire to crush his innocence and/or destroy others' views of him **(2)**

ANSWERS FOR HIGHER ENGLISH **165**

Question	Expected Answer(s)	Max Mark	Additional Guidance
32.	(continued)		Sympathy for Duror: • His nightmare about Peggy before the deer drive/his collapse at the end of the deer drive shows that he is mentally ill — reflected in many of his thoughts **(2)** • His mother-in-law accuses him of spending more time with his dogs than with his wife suggests his loneliness and isolation **(2)** Many other answers are possible.

SCOTTISH TEXT (POETRY)

Text 1 — Poetry — *To a Mouse, On turning her up in her Nest, with the Plough, November 1785* by Robert Burns

Question	Expected Answer(s)	Max Mark	Additional Guidance
33.	Candidates should analyse how at least two aspects of the speaker's personality are established. 2 marks awarded for detailed/insightful comment plus quotation/reference. 1 mark for more basic comment plus quotation/reference. 0 marks for quotation/reference alone.	4	Possible answers include: Sympathetic • shows awareness of mouse's vulnerability — "poor, earth — born companion,/An' fellow-mortal" • apologetic tone of "I'm truly sorry" • reflected in the language emphasising the mouse's vulnerability — "wee", "cowrin", "tim'rous", "poor", "panic" Understanding • of the mouse's need to live/the modest nature of its needs — "A daimen icker in a thrave" Affectionate • tone of diminutives — "beastie"/"breastie"; • reassurance in direct address: "Thou need na start ..." Forgiving • the mouse's thieving put into the context of its need to "live" Reflective • his apologetic tone of "I'm truly sorry" suggests speaker's regret for man's destruction of the environment Generous • "'S a sma' request" suggests his willingness to share; "blessin" in allowing the mouse a living
34.	Candidates should analyse how the poet's language creates pity for the mouse and its predicament by dealing with at least two examples. These examples could be of the same, or of different technique(s). 2 marks awarded for detailed/insightful comment plus quotation/reference. 1 mark for more basic comment plus quotation/reference. 0 marks for quotation/reference alone.	4	**Possible answers include:** Word choice • "wee bit" or "wee bit heap" or "silly" underline the smallness and fragility of the mouse's nest • "housie" — as above; "house" (as opposed to nest) humanises the mouse • "strewin" — emphasises the power and harshness of the wind in the utter destruction of the nest; emphasises the fragility and flimsiness of the nest, so easily blown away • "bleak December's" — the harshness of the weather/season reinforces the desperation of the mouse's situation • "ensuing" — sense of inevitability, unavoidable harshness • "bare an' waste"; — emphasises/reinforces the devastation caused by winter and the hopelessness/harshness of the mouse's situation • "winds" or "snell" or "keen" or "blast" — (unrelenting) harshness of weather to emphasise vulnerability of mouse without its nest • "sleety dribble" — depicts the coldness and misery in store for the mouse without shelter

166 ANSWERS FOR HIGHER ENGLISH

Question	Expected Answer(s)	Max Mark	Additional Guidance
34.	(continued)		• "cruel coulter" — harshness/malice of the plough; sense of a force set against the mouse • "thole" — underlines suffering in store for mouse Personification • "housie"/"house or hald" — compares the mouse's nest to a human habitation encouraging empathy from the reader • "Now thou's turn'd out" — suggests forced eviction, homelessness Alliteration • "weary Winter" — underlines the difficulty/hopelessness posed by the coming cold • "Beneath the blast" — emphasises the harshness of the elements and the shelter the mouse might have had • "crash! the cruel coulter" — harsh sounds mirror the harsh action • "But house or hald" — underlines the complete loss the mouse has suffered • "Cranreuch cauld" — underlines the harshness of the cold the mouse will have to endure Onomatopoeia • "crash!" — adds drama to the sudden destruction; relives the experience from the mouse's perspective to make us feel the disaster Contrast • "cozie here" with "blast" (and any of the other weather words) — reinforce pity for mouse; hope for warmth and safety replaced with coldness and vulnerability • "thought to dwell" with " now thou's turned out" — reversal of fortune creates pity Repetition • "An'" — used at the start of lines to emphasise sense of all the problems/difficulties piling up to add to the mouse's predicament • words to do with harshness of weather — reinforce the mouse's vulnerability in face of the remorseless elements • "December — winter — winter" — emphasises the inescapable nature of the elements and the vulnerable mouse Tone • emotional, empathetic tone underlined by frequent use of exclamation marks, underlining the pitiful nature of the mouse's situation • empathetic — in the speaker putting himself in mouse's • situation — "Til crash! the cruel coulter" — and relating what has happened as a disaster • sympathetic — towards the effort now destroyed without hope of mending — "has cost thee mony a weary nibble"
35.	Candidates should explain how the final two verses highlight the contrast between the speaker and the mouse. 2 marks awarded for detailed/insightful comment plus quotation reference. 1 mark for more basic comment plus quotation/reference. 0 marks for quotation/reference alone.	2	Possible answers include: • the mouse is fortunate only living in the present whereas mankind must suffer the anxiety and trouble which come from being conscious of the past and the future • the penultimate verse deals with the mouse and the speaker's shared experience(s) whereas the final verse contrasts the emotions/feelings of the speaker and the mouse • the final verse starts with a direct comparison "Still thou are blest, compared wi'me!"

ANSWERS FOR HIGHER ENGLISH **167**

Question	Expected Answer(s)	Max Mark	Additional Guidance
36.	Candidates should discuss how Burns uses a distinctive narrative voice to convey the central concerns of *To a Mouse* and at least one *of* his other poems. Candidates can answer in bullet points in this final question, or write a number of linked statements.	10	Up to 2 marks can be achieved for identifying elements of commonality as identified in the question, ie how Burns uses a distinctive narrative voice to convey the central concerns in *To a Mouse* and at least one of his other poems. A further 2 marks can be achieved for the reference to the extract given. 6 additional marks can be awarded for discussion of similar references in at least one other poem by Burns. <u>In practice this means:</u> Identification of commonality eg the creation of a persona/speaker in a dramatic situation and/or communicating directly with reader (1 mark) allows Burns to explore a variety of themes — hypocrisy/social class/love religion/nature etc (1 mark) From the extract: 2 marks for detailed/insightful comment plus quotation/reference; 1 mark for more basic comment plus quotation/reference; 0 marks for quotation/reference alone. eg The regretful tone adopted by the persona allows Burns to reflect on man's destruction of nature and the impermanence of existence. (2 marks) **OR** The persona's compassion for the mouse allows Burns to comment on how even the "best laid plans" can be destroyed by fate. (2 marks) From at least one other text: 2 marks for detailed/insightful comment plus quotation/reference; 1 mark for more basic comment plus quotation/reference; 0 marks for quotation/reference alone (Up to 6 marks). Possible answers include: In comments on other poems by Burns, possible references include: • *A Poet's Welcome to his Love-Begotten Daughter* — the emotions of the defensive/combative speaker/persona are appropriate for the heartfelt challenge to contemporary religious and moral attitudes **(2)** • *Address to the Deil* — humorous, ironic speaker/persona is appropriate for poet's satirical critique of Calvinism **(2)** • *A Man's A Man For A' That* — a spokesman, champion of equality and fraternity speaking as the voice of a community/nation **(2)** • *Holy Willie* — creation of hypocritical character for dramatic monologue is an apt vehicle for poet's religious satire **(2)** • *Tam O'Shanter* — character of moralising, commentating narrator allows Burns to point out the vagaries of human nature/undermine the apparent moral 'message' of the poem **(2)** Many other answers are possible.

168 ANSWERS FOR HIGHER ENGLISH

Text 3 — Poetry — *War Photographer* by Carol Ann Duffy

Question	Expected Answer(s)	Max Mark	Additional Guidance
37.	Candidates should analyse how imagery is used to create a serious atmosphere. A detailed/insightful comment on one example may be awarded 2 marks. More basic comments can be awarded 1 mark each. Identification of image alone = 0 marks	2	Possible answers include: • The metaphor "spools of suffering" links the content of the photographic images in the spools to the subjects of the photographs to highlight the awareness of the (on-going, cyclical) misery endured by the subjects. • The image "spools … ordered rows" compares the meticulous arrangement of the spools to the graves in a (war) cemetery to highlight the scale of deaths witnessed/ the violent nature of the deaths. • The image of the "dark room" with its red light as a "church" compares the interior lighting within the darkroom to that of a church to highlight the gloomy, funereal atmosphere of the darkroom. • Word choice of "red" suggests danger (of war zone/ pictures) or blood (represents the horror of the war zone) • The image of the photographer as "a priest … intone a Mass" suggests a similarity between the role of the photographer and the priest in terms of the seriousness of the processes they are involved in/the importance of their roles in spreading the word. • The image "All flesh is grass" compares human life to short lived "grass" to highlight the transient nature of human life (especially in times of conflict).
38.	Candidates should analyse how Duffy conveys the contrast between the photographer's perception of life in Britain and life in the war zones he covers. For full marks both sides of the contrast should be dealt with but not necessarily in equal measure. 2 marks awarded for detailed/insightful comment plus quotation/reference. 1 mark for more basic comment plus quotation/reference. 0 marks for quotation/reference alone.	4	Possible answers include: • The word choice of "Rural England" suggests the idealised view of England as predominantly countryside which is leafy, peaceful, natural, wholesome. • The juxtaposition of "ordinary pain" suggests how trivial and unimportant the problems faced in Britain are compared to those in war zones. • The word choice of "simple weather" and/or "dispel" suggests how shallow/easily addressed the problems faced in Britain are. • The word choice of "explode" suggests the unpredictability and danger of life in the war zone. • The word choice of "nightmare heat" suggests extreme climactic conditions endured (with suggestion of oppressive or threatening atmosphere). • An extended contrast could be drawn between the stereotypical feature of "rural England" — "fields" and "running children" and how this is contrasted with reality of life in the war zone — "exploded" and "nightmare heat". • The word choice of "hand, which did not tremble then"- emphasises contrast between his ability to cope with the job at the time and the impact on him now as he reflects on it
39.	Candidates should analyse how poetic technique is used to convey the distressing nature of the photographer's memories. 2 marks awarded for detailed/insightful comment plus quotation/reference; 1 mark for more basic comment plus quotation/reference. 0 marks for reference/quotation alone.	2	Possible answers include: • Word choice — "twist" suggests the subject's body distorted by pain/injury; writhing in agony. • Word choice — "half-formed ghost" suggests memories of death/being haunted by the memories. • Word choice of "cries" suggests the anguish of the man's wife. • Enjambment "cries/of this man's wife" suggests emotional turmoil, uncontained by ordinary line structure. • Word choice of "blood stained" suggests the scale of the violence remembered/the indelible nature of the memory. • use of sense words such as "blood stained" and "cries" suggests the vivacity of the memory. • Word choice of "foreign dust" suggests abandoned and forgotten.

ANSWERS FOR HIGHER ENGLISH   **169**

Question	Expected Answer(s)	Max Mark	Additional Guidance
40.	Candidates should analyse how the poet's use of poetic technique conveys the indifference of the readership of the newspapers to the suffering shown in them. 2 marks awarded for detailed/insightful comment plus quotation/reference; 1 mark for more basic comment plus quotation/reference. 0 marks for reference/quotation alone.	2	Possible answers include: • Word choice — "A hundred agonies" suggests the emotional power/quantity of images that the public respond to in a limited way. • Word choice — "black and white" suggests the veracity of the images that the public respond to in a limited way. • The contrast in numbers, "hundred" with "five or six", illustrates the public's limited capacity for images of this horrific nature. • Word choice of "prick with tears" suggests the public's limited emotional response to the images • The juxtaposition/alliteration of "between the bath and the pre-lunch beers" suggests the brief impact of the suffering shown in the images. • The positioning/tone of "they do not care" reinforces sense of the British public's indifference to the suffering.
41.	Candidates should discuss the link between the past and present in this poem by Duffy and at least one other poem. Candidates may choose to answer in bullet points in this final question, or write a number of linked statements.	10	Up to 2 marks can be achieved for identifying elements of commonality as identified in the question, ie the way one's past influences one's present. A further 2 marks can be achieved for reference to the extract given. 6 additional marks can be awarded for discussion of similar references to at least one other poem by the poet. <u>In practice this means:</u> Identification of commonality eg Past exerts a powerful influence on the present (1 mark) this can be negative, haunting or add further complexity to life (1 mark). From the extract: 2 marks for detailed/insightful comment plus quotation/reference; 1 mark for more basic comment plus quotation/reference; 0 marks for quotation/reference alone. "half-formed ghost" suggests haunted by the memories of conflicts that he has witnessed (2 marks) From at least one other text: 2 marks for detailed/insightful comment plus quotation/reference; 1 mark for more basic comment plus quotation/reference; 0 marks for quotation/reference alone (Up to 6 marks). Possible answers include: • *Originally* — sense of childhood security lost in moving to unfamiliar environment still remembered vividly in adulthood shown in "big boys ... shouting words you don't understand" • *Anne Hathaway* — happy memories of the past with her late husband influencing her thoughts in the present "we would dive for pearls" **(2)** • *Mrs. Midas* — intimacy of past relationship intensifies pain of absolute separateness in present memory of "his hands, his warm hands on my skin" **(2)** • *Havisham* — pain of betrayal in youth has become the defining bitterness of age "ropes on the backs of my hands I could strangle with" **(2)** • *Havisham* "the dress yellowing" — wedding dress losing its bright whiteness symbolises the tarnishing/loss of her youthful dreams/ideals **(2)** Many other answers are possible.

170 ANSWERS FOR HIGHER ENGLISH

Text 3 — Poetry — *My Rival's House* by Liz Lochhead

Question	Expected Answer(s)	Max Mark	Additional Guidance
42.	Candidates should explain why the speaker feels uncomfortable in her rival's house. 2 marks may be awarded for detailed/insightful comment. 1 mark for more basic comment.	2	Possible answers may include: • the decorative materials look expensive but are cheap suggesting the rival's welcome is false/only superficial — "ormolu and gilt, slipper satin" • the furnishings seem luxurious at first glance but, in reality, are uncomfortable suggesting an unwelcoming atmosphere — "cushions so stiff … can't sink in" • disconcerting reflections in polished surfaces suggest deceptive nature of rival/too perfect to be true — "polished clear enough to see distortions in" • rival's almost aggressive pride in the perfection of the house — "ormolu and gilt, slipper satin"
43.	Candidates should analyse how the poet conveys a tense atmosphere by referring to at least two examples from these lines. 2 marks awarded for detailed/insightful comment plus quotation/reference. 1 mark for more basic comment plus quotation/reference. 0 marks for reference/quotation alone.	4	Possible answers may include: • "Silver sugar-tongs … salver" — suggests the rival is trying to intimidate the speaker with a display of wealth • "glosses over him and me" — gives the impression the rival thinks the speaker's relationship with the son is unimportant • "I am all edges … shell — suggests the speaker's sense of her own fragility/anxiety • "squirms beneath her surface" — suggests the speaker is aware that she will never be able to get to grips with her rival's hidden nature • "tooth … nail … fight" suggests the animalistic/visceral nature of the rivalry • "Will fight, fight foul …" — repetition of 'fight' emphasises the ongoing/intense nature of the rivalry • "Deferential, daughterly …" — irony as she is well aware of her rival's true feelings and is also putting up a façade
44.	Candidates should discuss how the speaker's resentment of her rival is made clear in at least two examples. 2 marks awarded for detailed/insightful comment plus quotation/reference. 1 mark for more basic comment plus quotation/reference. 0 marks for reference/quotation alone.	4	Possible answers may include: • "first blood to her" — grudging acknowledgement of mother's blood relationship/boxing imagery suggests speaker views this as a bitter match • "never, never can escape scot free" — repetition of "never" emphasises speaker's reluctant admission that she will never truly have her partner to herself • "sour potluck of family" suggests the speaker's bitter feelings about family ties • "And oh how close …" — mocking tone to suggest speaker's resentment • minor sentences "Lady of the house. Queen Bee." — suggest speaker's derogatory dismissal/summation of her rival's position • repetition of "far more" suggests the speaker's fearful view of the threat posed by her rival • "I was always my own worst enemy … taken even this from me" — speaker's sardonic comment reveals her awareness of her rival's power/destructive qualities • brevity of final two lines encapsulates the idea that the rivalry will never end
45.	Candidates should discuss how Lochhead uses descriptive and/or symbolic detail to explore personality in this and in at least one other poem. Candidates can answer in bullet points in this final question or write a number of detailed linked statements.	10	Up to 2 marks can be achieved for identifying elements of commonality as identified in the question, ie how Lochhead uses descriptive and/or detail to explore personality A further 2 marks can be achieved for the reference to the extract given. 6 additional marks can be awarded for discussion of similar references in at least one other poem by Lochhead. Ⓤ<u>In practice this means:</u> Identification of commonality eg details of description and/or symbolism of objects or activities (1 mark) can help to focus on key personality elements developed in the poem (1 mark).

ANSWERS FOR HIGHER ENGLISH **171**

Question	Expected Answer(s)	Max Mark	Additional Guidance
45.	*(continued)*		From the extract:
			2 marks for detailed/insightful comment plus quotation/reference;
			1 mark for more basic comment plus quotation/reference;
			0 marks for quotation/reference alone.
			eg Process of the rival's making tea for the speaker in such a superficially proper way is both patronising and, she senses, a precursor for more open hostility (2 marks)
			From at least one other text:
			2 marks for detailed/insightful comment plus quotation/reference;
			1 mark for more basic comment plus quotation/reference;
			0 marks for quotation/reference alone
			(Up to 6 marks). Possible answers include:
			• *Last Supper* — "So here she is, tearing foliage," reveals savagery of revenge underlying 'civilised' making of meal **(2)**
			• *Last Supper* — "cackling round the cauldron" in their desire to criticise the faithless boyfriend, the friends have become consumed by malice themselves **(2)**
			• *For my Grandmother Knitting* — "the needles still move/their rhythms" even though woman is old and frail, the need to provide for her family still defines her **(2)**
			• *For my Grandmother Knitting* — "deft and swift/you slit the still-ticking quick silver fish." evokes the dexterity and skill as a young woman **(2)**
			• *View of Scotland/Love Poem* "Down on her hands and knees … on Hogmanay" conveys mother's commitment to ritual, but not the spirit, of celebration **(2)**
			Many other answers are possible.

Text 4 — Poetry — *Visiting Hour* by Norman MacCaig

Question	Expected Answer(s)	Max Mark	Additional Guidance
46.	Candidates should analyse how the poet's use of language establishes his response to the surroundings. 2 marks awarded for detailed/insightful comment plus quotation/reference. 1 mark for more basic comment plus quotation/reference. 0 marks for quotation/reference alone.	2	Possible answers include: • Opening line of the poem "The hospital smell" is blunt and matter-of-fact defining the odour universal to all hospitals. • Unusual imagery of "combs my nostrils" combines the senses of touch and smell to convey the pungent nature of the odour. It is so strong it is almost palpable. • Quirky word choice of "bobbing" is designed to disguise his discomfort/shut out the unpleasant reality he is facing/The disembodied nature of "nostrils/bobbing" indicates how dislocated he feels at this point as he struggles to remain detached. • Reference to unpleasant colours "green/yellow" connote sickness and echo his inner turmoil as he prepares to face the reality of his situation. • Word choice of "corpse" hints at the seriousness of the patient's position/his preoccupation with death. The impersonal terminology creates a darker tone, thus foreshadowing the inevitable.

172 ANSWERS FOR HIGHER ENGLISH

Question	Expected Answer(s)	Max Mark	Additional Guidance
46.	*(continued)*		• "Vanishes" has connotations of magic/make-believe/disappearing forever suggesting that there is no afterlife and that, for him, death is final. • Religious imagery of "vanishes heavenward" introduces the hoped for final destination for those, unlike him, who believe in an afterlife. Ironic imitation of the "soul's" final journey is an observation conveying his view that this visiting hour will not be about recovery.
47.	Candidates should analyse how the poet's use of language conveys his sense of his own inadequacy. 2 marks awarded for detailed/insightful comment plus quotation/reference. 1 mark for more basic comment plus quotation/reference. 0 marks for quotation/reference alone.	4	Possible answers include: • Repetition in stanza 3 "I will not feel" emphasises the sharp contrast between the acuteness of his senses in his previous observations and his endeavours to keep his emotions entirely contained • "I" repeated three times illustrates the intensely personal difficulty he is experiencing in keeping his anguish in check. • Climax of "until I have to" shows his acknowledgement of his own avoidance. • Adverbs "lightly, swiftly" create a sense of immediacy and a change to a lighter tone. They suggest the tactful/sensitive/deliberate way in which the nurses work. This contrasts with his feelings of inadequacy. • Inversion of "here … there" echoes the busy and varied nature of the nurses' demanding jobs yet they remain focused. • Word choice of "slender waists" conveys their slight physical frames and sets up the contrast with the following expression — "miraculously … burden" — to highlight the poet's admiration for their dignified demeanour whilst working in this difficult environment whereas he is struggling to cope. • Word choice of "miraculously" has connotations of wonder and awe, suggesting he finds it inconceivable that the nurses could withstand so much emotional suffering. • Word choice of "burden/pain" echoes the emotional and physical responsibilities of their job highlighting its exacting nature. • Repetition of "so much/so many" illustrates his observations that a large proportion of a nurse's job is dealing with death and the dying ie it is a regular occurrence. • Word choice of "clear" shows their ability to remain professional and not form deep emotional attachments to their dying patients.

Question	Expected Answer(s)	Max Mark	Additional Guidance
48.	Candidates should analyse how the poet's use of language emphasises the painful nature of the situation for both patient and visitor. For full marks, both patient and visitor must be dealt with for full marks, although not necessarily in equal measure. 2 marks awarded for detailed/insightful comment plus quotation/reference. 1 mark for more basic comment plus quotation/reference. 0 marks for quotation/reference alone.	4	Possible answers include: Patient • Metaphor "white cave of forgetfulness" suggests that her reduced mental capacity offers her some protection/refuge from the horrors of her situation OR diminishes her insight into her own situations/lessens her ability to communicate • Imagery of a flower/plant "withered hand ... stalk" suggests her weakness and helplessness. The image is ironic as flowers are traditional tokens of recovery for hospital patients. • The unconventional inverted vampire image "glass fang/guzzling/giving" emphasises the reality that the patient is being kept alive medically as her body is decaying and death is imminent. Candidates may choose to deal with this as word choice/alliteration/onomatopoeia. All are acceptable approaches and should be rewarded appropriately. • Imagery of "black figure/white cave" suggests the patient is dimly aware of her surroundings but the "black figure" who has now entered her environment symbolises her approaching death. • Word choice of "smiles a little" indicates that the patient has, perhaps, accepted the reality of her situation/does have a sense of the caring nature of the visit Visitor • Personal pronouns "her/me/she/I" indicate that both are suffering albeit in different ways. The patient suffers the physical agony of dying but the visitor has to face the emotional anguish of her loss. • Repetition of "distance" highlights that on a literal level he has arrived at her bedside but there is still a gulf between them as he cannot help her. • Word choice "neither ... cross" conveys he is no longer an observer but a helpless participant who now feels acute emotional misery. • Word choice of "clumsily" highlights his feelings of inadequacy and ineptitude in the situation in which he finds himself. Either/both: • Symbolic reference to "books that ... read" creates a tone of futility/despair as the pleasure to be gained from reading will never be experienced again. • Oxymoron/pun "fruitless fruits" effectively conveys the hopelessness of the situation for both patient and visitor. Just as fruits are traditional gifts brought to hospital to aid recuperation, "fruitless" ironically reveals that this patient will never recover so there is no hope. The agony of her loss is, therefore, laid bare.

174 ANSWERS FOR HIGHER ENGLISH

Question	Expected Answer(s)	Max Mark	Additional Guidance
49.	Candidates should discuss the significance of loss in this poem and in at least one other by MacCaig and should refer to appropriate textual evidence to support their discussion. 0 marks for reference/quotation alone. Candidates can answer in bullet points in this final question, or write a number of linked statements.	10	Up to 2 marks can be achieved for identifying elements of commonality as identified in the question, ie MacCaig's presentation of the theme of loss. A further 2 marks can be achieved for reference to the extract given. 6 additional marks can be awarded for discussion of similar references to at least one other poem by the poet. <u>In practice this means:</u> Identification of commonality loss is a universal human experience(1 mark) Which can have a profound and long-lasting effect on the individual (1 mark) From the extract: 2 marks for detailed/insightful comment plus quotation/reference; 1 mark for more basic comment plus quotation/reference; 0 marks for quotation/reference alone. eg Fear of loss of the loved one influences the speaker's perception of everything in the hospital eg 'what seemed a corpse' (2 marks) OR Sense of despair at end of visit due loss of communication with the loved on- nothing has been achieved 'fruitless fruits; (2 marks) From at least one other text: 2 marks for detailed/insightful comment plus quotation/reference; 1 mark for more basic comment plus quotation/reference; 0 marks for quotation/reference alone (Up to 6 marks). Possible answers include: • *Sounds of the Day* — profound impact of loss when a relationship ends shown through contrast between sounds — meaning life — and the 'silence' after parting **(2)** • *Sounds of the Day* use of 'numb' as final word emphasizes finality and intensity of negative feelings associated with the relationship ending **(2)** • *Memorial* — all consuming, all pervading nature of loss in the death of a loved one shown in 'Everywhere she dies' **(2)** • *Memorial* — despite passage of time, his life is now a 'memorial' devoted to her memory 'I am her sad music' **(2)** • *Aunt Julia* loss of opportunity to communicate with his aunt shown in 'absolute silence' of her death/grave, by the time he could have spoken Gaelic to her **(2)** Many other answers are possible.

ANSWERS FOR HIGHER ENGLISH   **175**

Text 5 — Poetry — *An Autumn Day* by Sorely MacLean

Question	Expected Answer(s)	Max Mark	Additional Guidance
50.	Candidates should analyse how the poet's use of language emphasises the impact of this experience. 2 marks awarded for detailed/insightful comment plus quotation/reference. 1 mark for more basic comment plus quotation/reference. 0 marks for quotation/reference alone.	4	Possible answers include: • Reference to "that slope" suggests that the specific place is imprinted on the mind of the persona • "soughing" is surprising, suggesting the deadly shells make a gentle noise • "six dead men at my shoulder" — a matter-of-fact tone, suggesting that the persona has become accustomed to the extraordinary and the traumatic. • "waiting ... message" suggests a communication with a higher power, as if the dead soldiers are in a state of limbo • "screech" conveys the disturbing nature of the noise from shells • "throbbing" suggests pain and discomfort • "leaped ... climbed ... surged" makes clear the rapid spread of deadly fire • "blinding ... splitting" shows how the shell robs the persona of his senses.
51.	Candidates should analyse how the poet uses at least two examples of language to emphasise the meaninglessness of the men's deaths. 2 marks awarded for detailed/insightful comment plus quotation/reference. 1 mark for more basic comment plus quotation/reference. 0 marks for quotation/reference alone.	4	Possible answers include: • "the whole day" suggests that their deaths have been ignored • "morning ... midday ... evening" emphasising the time continues as normal/is never-ending • "sun ... so indifferent" — the sun, rather than being a primary life-force, is portrayed as being cold and lacking in nurturing qualities • juxtaposition of "painful" and "comfortable/kindly" highlights the ironic nature of the landscape ignoring the men's deaths • "In the sun ... under the stars" highlight the starkness of death in the midst of the continuous nature of time/life's cycle • contrast of "six men dead" and "stars of Africa/jewelled and beautiful" emphasises the triviality of the men's deaths beside the greatness/majesty of nature
52.	Candidates should explain what the speaker finds puzzling when he reflects on the men's deaths. 2 marks may be awarded for detailed/insightful comment. 1 mark for more basic comment	2	Possible answers include: • he is puzzled by the random/indiscriminate nature of death —"took them and did not take me" • he is puzzled as these deaths seem to contradict the beliefs/religious teaching of his background — the notion of the Elect

176 ANSWERS FOR HIGHER ENGLISH

Question	Expected Answer(s)	Max Mark	Additional Guidance
53.	Candidates should discuss how MacLean uses nature to convey the central concern(s) of this and at least one other poem. Candidates may choose to answer in bullet points in this final question, or write a number of linked statements.	10	Up to 2 marks can be achieved for identifying elements of commonality as identified in the question, ie how MacLean uses nature to convey the central concerns of his poetry A further 2 marks can be achieved for the reference to the extract given. 6 additional marks can be awarded for discussion of similar references from at least one other poem by MacLean. In practice this means: Identification of commonality eg vivid images from nature (1 mark) allow MacLean to explore a variety of themes — war/heritage and tradition/love/ relationships etc (1 mark) From the extract: 2 marks for detailed/insightful comment plus quotation/reference; 1 mark for more basic comment plus quotation/ reference; 0 marks for quotation/reference alone. eg The grandeur contained in the imagery of the "stars of Africa, jewelled and beautiful" highlights humanity's insignificance. (2 marks) **OR** Autumn is used to suggest the transience of life/ inevitability of death in the continuous cycle of nature. (2 marks) From at least one other text: 2 marks for detailed/insightful comment plus quotation/reference; 1 mark for more basic comment plus quotation/ reference; 0 marks for quotation/reference alone (Up to 6 marks). Possible answers include: • *Hallaig*: the native trees of Raasay are used to symbolise the traditional ways of life/inhabitants who have been removed as a consequence of The Clearances **(2)** • *Screapadal*: the beauty of the natural setting allows the persona to reflect on his connection with the Hebrides **(2)** • *Screapadal*: the peaceful nature of the seal and basking shark is contrasted with the submarine/ threat of destruction from humans **(2)** • *Shores*: the sea coming into "Talisker bay forever" depicts the fulfilling qualities of love **(2)** • *I gave you Immortality*: **the permanence of nature symbolises his undying love for Eimhir (2)** Many other answers are possible.

ANSWERS FOR HIGHER ENGLISH   **177**

Text 6 — Poetry — *Two Trees* by Don Paterson

Question	Expected Answer(s)	Max Mark	Additional Guidance
54.	Candidates should analyse how the poet's use of poetic technique in lines 1—12 emphasises the importance of the story of the trees. 2 marks are awarded for detailed/insightful comment plus quotation/reference. 1 mark for more basic comment plus quotation/reference. 0 marks for quotation/reference alone.	4	Possible answers include: • Temporal sequence of 'One morning … Over the years …' suggests the ever-present/universal nature of the story • Interest in character of Don Miguel as obsessive: 'one idea rooted' • Allegorical representation/characterisation/symbolism of trees: 'the magic tree' suggest powerful nature of the story • Impact of the tree on the villagers: 'not one kid in the village didn't know'
55.	Candidates should analyse how language is used to create an impression of 'the man'. 2 marks will be awarded for 1 detailed/insightful comment plus reference. 1 mark for more basic comment plus reference. 0 marks for reference/quotation alone.	4	Possible answers include: • "The man" is unnamed, remains faceless/anonymous • "had no dream" suggests lack of imagination or empathy • "dark" suggests sense of foreboding • "malicious" suggests evil intent • "whim" suggests casual, thoughtless act • "who can say" suggests his actions were inexplicable/unaccountable • "axe"/"split the bole" suggests a violence/brutality in his actions
56.	Candidates should explain the irony of the final two lines. 2 marks awarded for one detailed/insightful comment. 1 mark for more basic comment.	2	Possible answers: • Idea of trees having no human qualities despite earlier allusions • Trees are essentially prosaic with no magical qualities • The definitive statement that the poem is only about trees when it is clearly not
57.	Candidates should discuss how Paterson develops the theme of relationships. Candidates may choose to answer in bullet points in this final question, or write a number of linked statements.	10	Up to 2 marks can be achieved for identifying elements of commonality as identified in the question, ie the theme of relationships. A further 2 marks can be achieved for reference to the extract given. 6 additional marks can be awarded for discussion of similar references to at least one other short story by the writer. <u>In practice this means:</u> Identification of commonality eg the profound and complex nature of intimate relationships on the individual (1 mark) and the potential fragility of human relationships (1 mark). From the extract: 2 marks for detailed/insightful comment plus quotation/reference; 1 mark for more basic comment plus quotation/reference; 0 marks for quotation/reference alone. eg "so tangled up" suggests complex mutual dependency which can be either damaging or productive (2 marks)

178 ANSWERS FOR HIGHER ENGLISH

Question	Expected Answer(s)	Max Mark	Additional Guidance
57.	*(continued)*		**OR**
			"nor did their unhealed flanks weep every spring" suggests the resilience of the human spirit/the pain of separation/longing for intimacy (2 marks)
			From at least one other text:
			2 marks for detailed/insightful comment plus quotation/reference;
			1 mark for more basic comment plus quotation/reference;
			0 marks for quotation/reference alone
			(Up to 6 marks).
			Possible answers include:
			• *Waking with Russell* — father/son bond explored through transformative power of love showing it is unconditional — "pledged myself forever" **(2)**
			• *Waking with Russell* — "lit it as you ran" suggests love providing mutual benefit, enriching lives **(2)**
			• *The Ferryman's Arms* — relationship with self when he plays pool alone, suggesting the conflict between different aspects of the self **(2)**
			• *The Thread* — development of the thread image shows fragility of family relationship/resilience gained through trauma **(2)**
			• *The Thread* — "the great twin-engined wingspan of us" suggests the uplifting exhilaration of sharing experiences with loved ones **(2)**
			Many other answers are possible.

Section 2 — CRITICAL ESSAY
Supplementary marking grid

	Marks 20-19	Marks 18-16	Marks 15-13	Marks 12-10	Marks 9-6	Marks 5-0
Knowledge and understanding **The critical essay demonstrates:**	thorough knowledge and understanding of the text	secure knowledge and understanding of the text	clear knowledge and understanding of the text	adequate knowledge and understanding of the text	limited evidence of knowledge and understanding of the text	very little knowledge and understanding of the text
	perceptive selection of textual evidence to support line of argument which is fluently structured and expressed	detailed textual evidence to support line of thought which is coherently structured and expressed	clear textual evidence to support line of thought which is clearly structured and expressed	adequate textual evidence to support line of thought, which is adequately structured and expressed	limited textual evidence to support line of thought which is structured and expressed in a limited way	very little textual evidence to support line of thought which shows very little structure or clarity of expression
	perceptive focus on the demands of the question	secure focus on the demands of the question	clear focus on the demands of the question	adequate focus on the demands of the question	limited focus on the demands of the question	very little focus on the demands of the question
Analysis **The critical essay demonstrates:**	perceptive analysis of the effect of features of language/filmic techniques	detailed analysis of the effect of features of language/filmic techniques	clear analysis of the effect of features of language/filmic techniques	adequate analysis of the effect of features of language/filmic techniques	limited analysis of the effect of features of language/filmic techniques	very little analysis of features of language/ filmic techniques
Evaluation **The critical essay demonstrates**	committed evaluative stance with respect to the text and the task	engaged evaluative stance with respect to the text and the task	clear evaluative stance with respect to the text and the task	adequate evidence of an evaluative stance with respect to the text and the task	limited evidence of an evaluative stance with respect to the text and the task	very little evidence of an evaluative stance with respect to the text and the task
Technical Accuracy **The critical essay demonstrates:**	few errors in spelling, grammar, sentence construction, punctuation and paragraphing the ability to be understood at first reading				significant number of errors in spelling, grammar, sentence construction, punctuation and paragraphing which impedes understanding	

180 ANSWERS FOR HIGHER ENGLISH

HIGHER ENGLISH
2016

PAPER 1 — READING FOR UNDERSTANDING, ANALYSIS AND EVALUATION

Marking Instructions for each question

Question		Expected Answer(s)	Max Mark	Additional Guidance
1.		For full marks there should be comments on at least two examples. Possible answers are shown in the "Additional Guidance" column.	2	Possible answers: • emphatic/categorical nature of opening sentence conveys the topic in an unequivocal manner • "hugely important" conveys the gravity of the topic • use of question/repeated use of questions invites the reader to think about the topic • humorous tone created, e.g. mockery of their lack of basic political awareness • use of stereotypical teenage concerns leads the reader to agree or disagree with the writer • climactic nature of final sentence
2.	(a)	Candidates must attempt to use their own words. No marks for straight lifts from the passage. 2 marks may be awarded for detailed/insightful comment. 1 mark for more basic comment. Possible answers are shown in the "Additional Guidance" column.	2	Possible answers: Writer's viewpoint: • assumption that today's teenagers will be just like her generation ("my younger self") • no idea how to make important decisions/lack of awareness or knowledge ("clueless") • preoccupied with relationships with contemporaries ("increased obsession with their peer group") • distracted/influenced by technology ("unpatrolled access to social media", "constant barrage of entertainment") Scientific research: • the teenage brain is not fully formed ("undeveloped teenage brain") • (inadequate frontal lobes means) higher order thinking/judgements are challenging for teenagers ("think in the abstract...impulses") • teenagers' inability to make personal choices precludes them from influencing issues affecting other people ("life-changing decisions for themselves")
	(b)	For full marks there should be comments on at least two examples. 2 marks may be awarded for detailed/insightful comment plus quotation/reference. 1 mark for more basic comment plus quotation/reference. 0 marks for quotation/reference alone. Possible answers are shown in the "Additional Guidance" column.	4	Possible answers: • the delaying of the final clause of the first sentence ("when I would have agreed .... status quo") suggests the plausibility of the case against lowering the voting age • "clueless" suggests an inability to make responsible decisions • "(increased) obsession" suggests an irrational fixation with social standing • "unpatrolled" suggests the potential damage of unlimited access/malign influence of social media on young people • "constant" suggests the unremitting distraction of media products • "barrage", an intense military bombardment, suggests the destructive influence of the media • the list "social media... entertainment" suggests range of lifestyle features on which they place greater importance

ANSWERS FOR HIGHER ENGLISH **181**

Question		Expected Answer(s)	Max Mark	Additional Guidance
2.	(b)	*(continued)*		• "disengagement" suggests an apathetic attitude towards politics • "smartphone-fixated" suggests the supposedly trivial/self-absorbed nature of the teenagers' concerns • "undeveloped" suggests that the brain is not fully functioning/is not capable of fully undertaking a task • the list "enables us to think in the abstract … control our impulses" suggests the seeming amount/variety of mental processes teenagers can't properly engage in
3.		2 marks may be awarded for detailed/insightful comment. 1 mark for more basic comment. Possible answers are shown in the "Additional Guidance" column.	2	Possible answers: The example of Malala's achievements at such a young age is used to show that young people should be allowed to vote/challenge the view that young people are too irrational or immature. Someone with Malala's qualities could not vote in the UK elections merely because of age shows how ridiculous the age restriction is/adults with ridiculous views can vote, yet someone like Malala would not be allowed to. Candidates could approach this question in a number of ways (e.g. Malala reference acts as a link between negative views of young people and more positive views).
4.		For full marks, candidates must deal with both word choice and sentence structure, but not necessarily in equal measure. 2 marks may be awarded for detailed/insightful comment plus quotation/reference. 1 mark for more basic comment plus quotation/reference. 0 marks for quotation/reference alone. Possible answers are shown in the "Additional Guidance" column.	4	Possible answers: Word choice: • "scarcely (exempt)" suggests a scathing condemnation of adult failings • "limited brain power/inadequately brained" suggests adults' lack of intelligence • "incivility" suggests the rude behaviour exhibited by adults • "tantrums" suggests immature outbursts of temper • "profanity" suggests the offensive nature of the language used by adults • "prejudice" suggests the intolerance displayed by adults • "time-wasting" suggests a lack of commitment/desire to shirk work • "unedifying" suggests setting a poor example • "illiterate" suggests lack of sophistication in opinion • "non-taxpaying" suggests devious, unwilling to accept civic responsibilities • "ignorant" suggests ill-mannered/lack of awareness Sentence structure: • parenthesis "as politicians must hope" emphasises/isolates the writer's point about political hypocrisy • list "incivility, tantrums, …. tabloid websites" emphasises the variety/scale of the unacceptable behaviour exhibited by adults (a comment on the anti-climactic nature of the list, introducing a mocking tone is also possible) • parallel sentence structure of the lists "sport, music, creating computer software" and "incivility, tantrums, … tabloid websites" to emphasise the negative behaviour of adults in comparison to teenagers

ANSWERS FOR HIGHER ENGLISH

Question	Expected Answer(s)	Max Mark	Additional Guidance
4.	*(continued)*		• parallel sentence structure of the lists "incivility, tantrums, ... tabloid websites" and "inadequately brained, illiterate, non-taxpaying or ignorant" to reinforce the negative behaviour exhibited by adults • climactic nature of final sentence culminating in condemnatory use of "chilling"
5.	2 marks may be awarded for detailed/ insightful comment. 1 mark for more basic comment. Possible answers are shown in the "Additional Guidance" column.	3	Possible answers: • from their earliest years they have been exposed to technological advances • they have the capacity to absorb a variety of sources to establish their own outlook on important issues • they have enough knowledge of how the media works not to be taken in by those who try to deceive them
6.	For full marks there should be comments on at least two examples. 2 marks may be awarded for detailed/ insightful comment plus quotation/reference. 1 mark for more basic comment plus quotation/reference. 0 marks for quotation/reference alone. Possible answers are shown in the "Additional Guidance" column.		Possible answers: • sequence "No ... Yes ... But" builds to climactic turnaround emphasising the positive qualities of teenagers • positioning of "But" in the paragraph/sentence to indicate change to positive view of teenagers • parenthesis of "idealism ... open-mindedness" to identify/clarify the "more loveable teenage qualities" • list of "loveable teenage qualities" to emphasise the scale/variety of qualities • "idealism" suggests lack of cynicism/belief in making the world a better place • "energy" suggests passion and commitment to making a difference • "sense of injustice" suggests their desire to right wrongs in the world • "open-mindedness" suggests their tolerance and lack of prejudice • "starved" suggests that at the moment politics is in dire need of/sorely lacks/is deprived of the positive qualities young people exhibit • "inject some life" suggests the rejuvenating effect of young people on political debate OR the sudden force/strength/impact of their introduction into political debate
7.	For full marks candidates must deal with both tone and contrast, but not necessarily in equal measure. 2 marks may be awarded for detailed/ insightful comment plus quotation/reference. 1 mark for more basic comment plus quotation/reference. 0 marks for quotation/reference alone. Possible answers are shown in the "Additional Guidance" column.	4	Possible answers: Tone: • conversational tone of "Naturally" suggests shared understanding between writer and reader about validity of teenage concerns • tongue-in-cheek tone. "If voting has to be rationed ..." Writer uses humour to approach the topic in a subversive manner • ironic tone of "only have a year to wait" builds on previous examples of irony e.g. the reference to "epistocracy"/the irony of the powers of old and teenage voters, to mock the opposing viewpoint • blunt, matter-of-fact tone of "We could compromise" suggests the initial plausibility of this solution • incredulous tone created by listing the responsibilities currently conferred ("after they have already married ... fight for their country") highlights the absurdity/inconsistencies of current policy • scathing tone of "believe they know so much better" underlines the arrogance of adults

ANSWERS FOR HIGHER ENGLISH **183**

Question	Expected Answer(s)	Max Mark	Additional Guidance
7.	*(continued)*		• sarcasm/mockery of the final sentence ("doing our young people a great big favour") to suggest the absurdity of not recognising a teenager's right to vote
			Contrast:
			• development of old vs young argument — old allowed to vote but not around to live with the consequences, young not allowed to vote but have to live with the consequences • list of fairly trivial things ("fireworks") contrasted with life-changing decisions ("donated an organ") — stresses random/illogical nature of what people are and are not allowed to do • final sentence emphasises the contrast between adults who consider themselves superior set against the young people whose rights are being denied
8.	Candidates can use bullet points in this final question, or write a number of linked statements. Key areas of disagreement are shown in the grid. Possible answers are shown in the "Additional Guidance" column.	5	The following guidelines should be used: 5 marks — identification of three key areas of disagreement with detailed/insightful use of supporting evidence 4 marks — identification of three key areas of disagreement with appropriate use of supporting evidence 3 marks — identification of three key areas of disagreement 2 marks — identification of two key areas of disagreement 1 mark — identification of one key area of disagreement 0 marks — failure to identify any key areas of disagreement and/or misunderstanding of the task **NB** A candidate who identifies only two key areas of disagreement may be awarded up to a maximum of 4 marks, as follows: • 2 marks for identification of two key areas of disagreement **plus**: **either** • a further mark for appropriate use of supporting evidence to a total of 3 marks **or** • a further 2 marks for detailed/insightful use of supporting evidence to a total of 4 marks A candidate who identifies only one key area of disagreement may be awarded up to a maximum of 2 marks, as follows: • 1 mark for identification of one key area of disagreement • a further mark for use of supporting evidence to a total of 2 marks

184 ANSWERS FOR HIGHER ENGLISH

	Areas of Disagreement	Passage 1	Passage 2
1.	Intellectual ability	Teenagers are capable of intellectual maturity, for example reference to Malala	Young people may have political knowledge but not the intellectual development of an adult, for example the writer refers to her daughter
2.	Areas of political debate	Teenagers would focus on issues of relevance to them like student debt, minimum wage	Debate will continue to focus on traditional areas of concern like the economy and the NHS
3.	Independence of thought	As part of iGeneration, they have developed an independent political stance	Influenced by parents to turn out to vote
4.	Response to manipulation	Too media aware to be taken in by politicians/spin doctors	Susceptible to media manipulation by cynical politicians
5.	Commitment	Potential to sustain long term commitment to political issues, for example the environment	Give up on voting very quickly
6.	Responsibilities/rights	Teenagers already have a large number of rights/responsibilities and therefore should be allowed to vote	Teenagers have a limited number of rights/responsibilities and therefore should not be allowed to vote
7.	Impact of teenage voters	Teenager voters would invigorate/ energise political life	Teenage voters would be detrimental/would make no difference to the political process

PAPER 2 — CRITICAL READING

SECTION 1 — Scottish Text

For all Scottish Texts, marking of the final question, for 10 marks, should be guided by the following generic instruction in conjunction with the specific advice given for the question on each Scottish Text:

Candidates can answer in bullet points in this final question, or write a number of linked statements.

0 marks for reference/quotation alone.

Up to 2 marks can be achieved for identifying elements of commonality as identified in the question.
A further 2 marks can be achieved for reference to the extract given.
6 additional marks can be awarded for discussion of similar references to at least one other part of the text (or other story or poem) by the writer.

<u>In practice this means:</u>

Identification of commonality (2) (e.g.: theme, characterisation, use of imagery, settng, or any other key element ...)

from the extract:

1 × relevant reference to technique/idea/feature (1)
1 × appropriate comment (1)
(maximum of 2 marks only for discussion of extract)

from at least one other text/part of the text:

2 marks for detailed/insightful comment plus quotation/reference

1 mark for more basic comment plus quotation/reference

0 marks for quotation/reference alone

(Up to 6 marks).

ANSWERS FOR HIGHER ENGLISH **185**

Detailed Marking Instructions for each question

SECTION 1 — Scottish Text

SCOTTISH TEXT (DRAMA)

Text 1 — *Drama — The Slab Boys* by John Byrne

Question	Expected Answer(s)	Max Mark	Additional Guidance
1.	2 marks may be awarded for detailed/ insightful comment plus quotation/reference. 1 mark for more basic comment plus quotation/reference. 0 marks for quotation/reference alone.	2	Possible answers include: • Challenging/obstructive: "What're you wanting him for?" • Assertive: repetition of "I'll take it." • Taking control away from Jack: "That's all right. I'll take it." • Defiant: "I'll take it, I said."/"I'm authorised!" • No respect for Jack/ignoring him shown by *(Exits.)* to take the call when Jack has said not to
2.	2 marks may be awarded for detailed/ insightful comment plus quotation/reference. 1 mark for more basic comment plus quotation/reference. 0 marks for quotation/reference alone.	4	Possible answers include: • Sadie's incongruous casting of herself as a martyr: "Too bloody soft, that's my trouble…" • Incongruity of reference to casters instead of feet. • Lucille's shocked overreaction to finding Sadie in the slab room: "Waaaahh! God!" • Play on word "shy": Sadie means "fifteen bob shy" whereas Lucille thinks she means lacking in confidence (opposite of what Spanky is) • Ludicrousness of description of Sadie's husband's antics at last year's dance — "leapfrogging over … beehive hairdo" • Juxtaposition of Lucille's question about leg injury sustained during this behaviour
3.	For full marks both Sadie and Lucille should be covered but not necessarily in equal measure. 2 marks may be awarded for detailed/ insightful comment plus quotation/reference. 1 mark for more basic comment plus quotation/reference. 0 marks for quotation/reference alone.	4	Possible answers include: Sadie: • Critical of men/contemptuous/thinks they are useless: reference to negative connotations of "real rubbish" and "dross" • Impossibility of finding a decent man: anti-climactic effect of "sift through the dross … real rubbish" • Blames her choice of husband for her disappointment with life: dismissive tone of "all you've got to show's bad feet and a display cabinet" Lucille: • She is confident in her own chance of finding a better man than Sadie's: powerful rebuttal of Sadie's viewpoint of men "They're not all like that, for God's sake" • Determined not to define herself by choice of man: confident assertion of "Not this cookie, Lucille Bentley … Woman of the World"
4.	Candidates can answer in bullet points in this final question, or write a number of linked statements.	10	Up to 2 marks can be achieved for identifying elements of commonality as identified in the question, i.e. the role of women. A further 2 marks can be achieved for reference to the extract given. 6 additional marks can be awarded for discussion of similar references to at least one other part of the text by the writer. In practice this means: Identification of commonality **(2)** E.g. play is mainly about men/the male experience of work/thwarted ambition **(1)** but women important in terms of what they represent/the relationships they offer to the men **(1)**

186 ANSWERS FOR HIGHER ENGLISH

Question	Expected Answer(s)	Max Mark	Additional Guidance
4.	(continued)		From the extract: 2 marks for detailed/insightful comment plus quotation/reference 1 mark for more basic comment plus quotation/reference 0 marks for quotation/reference alone Maximum of 2 marks only for discussion of extract. E.g. Lucille represents the confident young woman who sees herself as independent/equal to any man and does not need to validate herself through a relationship **(2)** From at least one other part of the text: as above for up to 6 marks Possible references include: • Lucille "every slab boy's dream" — she is seen as a traditional representation of femininity/objectified in terms of her desirability **(2)** • Phil's mother — source of worry for Phil/reverse of the nurturing role of mother, e.g. his story about her breakdown and its impact on him **(2)** • Lucille provides the motivation/cause of the extreme mockery of Hector: he is dressed up ridiculously to impress her **(2)** • Sadie's role as "surrogate mother" providing food (tea trolley cakes) and nagging the slab boys to behave properly **(2)** • Sadie is represented as a clichéd/stock female character in a male-dominated world, providing humour in the play on the receiving end of Phil and Spanky's banter/scene where she hits Phil on the head **(2)**

Text 2 — *Drama* — *The Cheviot, the Stag and the Black, Black Oil* by John McGrath

Question	Expected Answer(s)	Max Mark	Additional Guidance
5.		2	Possible answers include: Tone: • Astonishment • Incredulity • Outrage Analysis: • Dismissive nature of "Re" contrasts with the serious nature of the accusation • Repeated use of questions suggests inability to believe they could think this of him • "Can you believe" emphasises the unlikely nature of the accusation • Repetition of "no" emphasises the obvious lack of motivation
6.	2 marks are awarded for detailed/insightful comment plus quotation/reference. 1 mark for more basic comment plus quotation/reference. 0 marks for quotation/ref alone.	4	Possible answers include: Language: • use of "Therefore" implies unquestioning acceptance of Sellar's defence • understatement of the crimes with language such as "ignored a custom" • directing the jury with phrases such as "I would ask them ..." • using language which suggests the crime — damaged property ("barns" and "the burning of the house of Chisholm") — whilst ignoring the deaths of the tenants

ANSWERS FOR HIGHER ENGLISH **187**

Question	Expected Answer(s)	Max Mark	Additional Guidance
6.	*(continued)*		• "contradictory nature" contrasts with "real evidence" suggesting that the judge gives greater credence to evidence which defends Sellar • use of "And ... And ..." suggests an accumulation of evidence for Sellar's defence • he directs the jury to ignore contradictory evidence and focus on character assessment with references to the accused "humanity" and being "in all cases ... most humane" • the inappropriately friendly greeting, "hello, Archie" suggests he is complicit in Sellar's defence
7.	2 marks are awarded for detailed/insightful comment plus quotation/reference. 1 mark for more basic comment plus quotation/reference. 0 marks for quotation/ref alone.	4	Possible answers include: • "Every reformer of mankind" suggests he/those he works for are bringing about grand-scale improvement as many others have before • "errors, frauds and quackery" suggests that he dismisses the opposition as duplicitous and mistaken: • "at bottom" suggests the fundamental truth/rightness of what the reformers are doing • "patience" suggests resilience and commitment in the face of adversity • his references to "zeal and enthusiasm" present the reformers as being motivated, committed and dynamic • "generous" suggests reformers are selflessly working for the good of mankind • "exertions" suggests the tireless efforts to make improvements • "public yet unostentatious" suggests generosity combined with modesty • "distresses of the widow, the sick and the traveller" list of clichéd examples of needy people to emphasise Sutherland's wide-ranging philanthropic role
8.	Candidates may choose to answer in bullet points in this final question, or write a number of linked statements.	10	Up to 2 marks can be achieved for identifying elements of commonality as identified in the question, i.e. McGrath's presentation of authority A further 2 marks can be achieved for reference to the extract given. 6 additional marks can be awarded for discussion of similar references to at least one other part of the text by the writer. <u>In practice this means:</u> Identification of commonality **(2)** E.g. the self-seeking nature of authority in a variety of guises **(1)** Their cruel treatment of the people over whom they should exercise stewardship **(1)** From the extract: 2 marks for detailed/insightful comment plus quotation/reference; 1 mark for more basic comment plus quotation/reference; 0 marks for quotation/reference alone. Maximum of 2 marks only for discussion of extract. E.g. The judge's involvement with the defence illustrates collusion within the establishment **(2)** Sellar's speech shows hypocrisy by presenting the inhumane actions of Lord and Lady Stafford in a positive light **(2)**

188 ANSWERS FOR HIGHER ENGLISH

Question	Expected Answer(s)	Max Mark	Additional Guidance
8.	*(continued)*		From elsewhere in the text: as above for up to 6 marks Possible answers include: • List of Sutherland's estates, properties and sources of wealth, e.g. "huge estate in Yorkshire", "a large slice of the Liverpool-Manchester Railway" suggests his self- serving, selfish and materialistic view of his privileges as a lord **(2)** • Hypocrisy of Sellar and Loch in lamenting the problems of the lifestyle of the crofters as an excuse to remove them and exploit the land they live on **(2)** • Cruelty and violence towards vulnerable crofters shown in example of old woman and her grandchildren forced to live in an exposed sheep-cot when their home was seized **(2)** • Sinister behaviour of Lord Crask and Lady Phosphate turning guns on audience to show threat their kind pose "We'll show you we're the ruling class" **(2)** • Sutherland's attempts to manipulate the people into enlisting suggests that they are seen as a resource to be exploited, not people to be respected **(2)**

Text 3 — *Drama* — *Men Should Weep* by Ena Lamont Stewart

Question	Expected Answer(s)	Max Mark	Additional Guidance
9.	For full marks, both relationships should be covered but not necessarily in equal measure. 2 marks awarded for detailed/insightful comment plus quotation/reference. 1 mark for a more basic comment plus quotation/reference. 0 marks for quotation/reference alone.	4	Possible answers include: Relationship with Maggie: • "…gives Maggie a pat" — gesture suggests an easy intimacy between them • "they exchange warm smiles" — suggests their affection is mutual, natural, spontaneous • "Ye dry, John? I'll pit the kettle on." — suggests Maggie anticipates his needs and wants to care for him • "He didna mean onythin." — Maggie's assertion is an attempt to justify his behaviour, to keep the peace with Lily Relationship with Lily: • "turning to Lily" — lack of respect shown by the fact John only acknowledges Lily after being in the room some time • "with as much of a smile as he can muster" — suggests being polite to Lily requires considerable effort on his part, is not natural or easy • "An how's Lil?" — suggests deliberate provocation by using a form of her name he knows she dislikes • "Don't you two stert up!" — Maggie's remark shows an awareness of repeated confrontations between John and Lily/highlights childish nature of John's behaviour towards Lily • "Goad help us!" — John finds Lily's constant criticism and undermining of him tiresome/ irritating/exasperating

ANSWERS FOR HIGHER ENGLISH | **189**

Question	Expected Answer(s)	Max Mark	Additional Guidance
10.	For full marks both Lily and Maggie should be covered, though not necessarily in equal measure. 2 marks awarded for detailed/insightful comment plus quotation/reference. 1 mark for a more basic comment plus quotation/reference. 0 marks for quotation/reference alone.	4	Possible answers: Lily: • ridicules him by presenting an idealised vision of the domestic world he believes men would create. "if you was a wumman"/"everythin just perfect"/"the weans a washed and pit tae bed at six"/"everythin' spick an span"/"naethin tae dae till bedtime but twiddle yer thumbs" • points out the impracticalities of his ideas in the face of the reality of the demands placed on Maggie every day "hoose-fu o weans"/"and a done aul granny tae look after." • Emphatic nature of "And ony wumman'll tell ye" undermines his status as a man Maggie: • mocks his ability to do anything useful around the house despite his claims that he could organise things more efficiently. "Ye should see him tryin tae mak the breakfast on a Sunday; ye'd get yer kill." • highlights his inability to multi-task when he actually tries to do household chores. "If he's fryin bacon, he's fryin bacon, see? ... intae the pan a at the same time." Lily and Maggie • mock John, showing how silly they think his ideas are by throwing his words back at him in unison. "He'd hae a system!"
11.		2	Possible answers include: • Lily is annoyed by John's insinuation that she is expecting the Morrisons to feed her • She feels a lack of appreciation for the fact that she often provides the family with food/has brought the tin of beans • She is annoyed by John's suggestion that she would chase after a man if she had the opportunity • She is annoyed at their ingratitude in the light of the fact that (their son) Alec still owes her money
12.	Candidates may choose to answer in bullet points in this final question, or write a number of linked statements.	10	Up to 2 marks can be achieved for identifying elements of commonality as identified in the question, i.e. John's role within the family. A further 2 marks can be achieved for reference to the extract given. 6 additional marks can be awarded for discussion of similar references to at least one other part of the text by the writer. <u>In practice this means:</u> Identification of commonality **(2)** E.g. John conforms to assumptions about the male role within the family **(1)** however he often does not fulfil this traditional role and feels frustrated/despondent as a result **(1)** From the extract: 2 marks for detailed/insightful comment plus quotation/reference; 1 mark for more basic comment plus quotation/reference; 0 marks for quotation alone. Maximum of 2 marks only for discussion of extract

190 ANSWERS FOR HIGHER ENGLISH

Question	Expected Answer(s)	Max Mark	Additional Guidance
12.	*(continued)*		E.g. John's obvious consideration for Maggie does not stop him from accepting her assumption that she should make him tea when he comes in, although she is exhausted **(2)** From elsewhere in the text: as above for up to 6 marks Possible answers include: • John's willingness to share in Maggie's household duties is very limited/he sees domestic work as very much the preserve of women Maggie: "Ye couldna even wash up a dish for me!" • John sees his role as father of Jenny is to protect her and be respected shown by his anger when she is out in the close with a man • He feels ashamed of his inability to provide for the family "Ye end up a bent back and a heid hanging wi shame for whit ye canna help." • He responds to Isa's flirtation/criticism of Maggie even though this is a betrayal of his wife for feelings which are much more superficial • He is proud and happy when he is able to provide for the family, in the traditional male role for example the Christmas present of the red hat for Maggie in Act 3 - a reminder of their "courting" days

SCOTTISH TEXT (PROSE)

Text 4 – *Prose* – *The Crater* by Iain Crichton Smith

Question	Expected Answer(s)	Max Mark	Additional Guidance
13.	2 marks awarded for detailed/insightful comment plus quotation/reference. 1 mark for more basic comment plus quotation/reference. 0 marks for quotation/reference alone.	2	Possible answers include: • Repetition of questions suggests his nervousness/confusion/frustration at a situation he cannot control • "We're like a bunch of actors" – comparison suggests a sense of unreality • Emphatic statement/repetition of "I'm" "I'm leading these men, I'm an officer" suggests self-doubt as he is trying to convince/reassure himself • "a huge mind breeding thought after thought" – suggests that he believes that something/someone beyond earthly beings must be controlling their actions
14.	2 marks awarded for detailed/insightful comment plus quotation/reference. 1 mark for more basic comment plus quotation/reference. 0 marks for quotation/reference alone.	4	Possible answers include: • "I am frightened." – simple statement/child-like language suggests the sudden realisation of the danger that he is in • Repetition of "fear" reinforces the pervasive nature of the feeling • "It was an older fear"/"the fear of being buried"/"the fear of wandering" use of repetition/word choice to emphasise the deep-rooted atavistic nature of the fear • "grey figures like weasels" symbolises the unknown/unnatural/indeterminate nature of the threat • reference to "web"/"spiders" – primitive fears/idea of being trapped

ANSWERS FOR HIGHER ENGLISH **191**

Question	Expected Answer(s)	Max Mark	Additional Guidance
15.	2 marks awarded for detailed/insightful comment plus quotation/reference. 1 mark for more basic comment plus quotation/reference. 0 marks for quotation/reference alone.	4	Possible answers include: • sequence of "thrustings", "hackings", "scurryings", "flowing" suggests unrelenting nature of the action • "thrustings and flashes" – dramatic language emphasises sudden combat/forceful violence • "scurryings and breathings as of rats" – evokes primitive fears • "Back. They must get back." – urgency of short sentences/repetition emphasises panic • "Mills bombs, hackings ..." – listing of horrors emphasises the range of danger they are in • "Over the parapet. They were over the parapet. Crouched they had run and scrambled" – staccato nature of sentence structure creates a sense of relief that they were safe for the moment • "Wright ... one arm seemed to have been shot off" use of ellipsis emphasises his sudden realisation of the horror of combat • "all those dead moons" description of desolate landscape evocative of death/emptiness is ever present
16.	Candidates can answer in bullet points in this final question, or write a number of linked statements.	10	Up to 2 marks can be achieved for identifying elements of commonality as identified in the question – i.e. the impact of extreme situations on characters A further 2 marks can be achieved for reference to the extract given. 6 additional marks can be awarded for discussion of similar references to at least one other part of the text. <u>In practice this means:</u> Identification of commonality **(2)** E.g. extremity of situation can bring out positive qualities in a character **(1)** and/or bring about their destruction **(1)** From the extract: 2 marks for detailed/insightful comment plus quotation/reference; 1 mark for more basic comment plus quotation/reference; 0 marks for quotation/reference alone. E.g. Sergeant Smith's practical, phlegmatic response to war is underlined by his matter of fact comment to the soldier who has lost his arm, focusing on the positive benefits **(2)** From at least one other text/part of the text: as above for up to 6 marks Possible answers include: • *In Church* when Colin MacLeod is faced with the threat of death from the 'priest' during his sermon we see his growing sense of unease and stoicism • *The Telegram* the thin woman's quiet heroism, coping with (apparent) reality of the bad news of her son's death as the elder seems to be approaching her house – she is able to comfort the fat woman at that moment • *The Painter* William Murray's detached attitude of the artist is developed as he coolly observes the fight and the emotional reactions of the villagers – isolates him further

192 ANSWERS FOR HIGHER ENGLISH

Question	Expected Answer(s)	Max Mark	Additional Guidance
16.	*(continued)*		• *Mother and Son* the mother's unrelenting criticism of her adult son creates tension in the household resulting in his feelings of hopelessness and despair • *The Red Door* the mysterious painting of Murdo's door prompts him to consider the difficulty — and attractiveness - of breaking away from the conformity of his community.

Text 5 — *Prose — The Whaler's Return* by George Mackay Brown

Question	Expected Answer(s)	Max Mark	Additional Guidance
17.	Up to 2 marks awarded for detailed/insightful comment plus quotation/reference. 1 mark for more basic comment plus quotation/reference. 0 marks for quotation/reference alone.	4	Possible answers include: • "standing at a mirror … drove a pin through it" her actions reveal her vanity, determined focus on her appearance • "yellow hair … fine burnished knot" — build-up of 'golden' images suggests attractive, almost magical/captivating quality • "At last she got a fine …" suggests the length of time she spends on her hair and the length of time he watches her • Use of the list with repeated use of "and" emphasises her snobbish attitude towards the working men • "Out of her pretty mouth she spat on the stone floor" — contrast between daintiness of "pretty mouth" and coarseness of "spat" emphasises her unpleasant action which contrasts with her lovely appearance
18.	Up to 2 marks awarded for detailed/insightful comment plus quotation/reference. 1 mark for more basic comment plus quotation/reference. 0 marks for quotation/reference alone.	4	Possible answers include: • "wearing his decent suit" suggests he is pleased he is looking his best in order to impress her • "smiled at him sweetly" suggests the special nature of the moment because of the perceived approval/acceptance by 'unattainable' barmaid • "touched rims" suggests intimacy/gentle coming together • "whisky trembled" suggests nervous, tremulous excitement • "transported" — shows intensity of experience for Flaws taken beyond normality • "glittered at him with eyes, teeth, hair, rings" word choice/listing suggests the all-encompassing nature of her allure
19.		2	Possible answers include: • "shame" because he was being dishonest about what he is in order to be accepted • "resentment" because he has been unfairly rejected/humiliated/missed his opportunity

ANSWERS FOR HIGHER ENGLISH **193**

Question	Expected Answer(s)	Max Mark	Additional Guidance
20.	Candidates can answer in bullet points in this final question, or write a number of linked statements.	10	Up to 2 marks can be achieved for identifying elements of commonality as identified in the question, i.e. the importance of journeys, both literal and metaphorical.
			A further 2 marks can be achieved for reference to the extract given.
			6 additional marks can be awarded for discussion of similar references from at least one other short story.
			<u>In practice this means:</u> Identification of commonality **(2)** E.g.: journeys can be physical challenges for survival **(1)** and these are mirrored by metaphorical journeys as a rite of passage **(1)**
			From the extract: 2 marks for detailed/insightful comment plus quotation/reference; 1 mark for more basic comment plus quotation/reference; 0 marks for quotation alone. E.g. The episode in the bar, when Flaw's deception is rewarded with humiliation, is a learning moment on his journey to fulfilment **(2)**
			From at least one other text: as above for up to 6 marks
			Possible answers include:
			• *The Eye of the Hurricane* — Cpt. Stevens' speech on the 'voyage' of life is a quiet moment in the final storm of his life • *A Time to Keep* — journey through the year in time and life involving marriage, birth, death and rebirth • *Tartan* — the Vikings' journey across the island seeking treasure: allegorical journey meeting the human condition in the form of death, fear, betrayal... • *The Bright Spade* — the men set off on a physical/metaphorical journey into the snow to save the community which leads to their heroic, but pointless, deaths • *The Bright Spade* — the community's journey through winter reflects the harsh nature of life and the ever-present threat of death faced by the community

Text 6 – *Prose – The Trick Is To Keep Breathing* by Janice Galloway

Question	Expected Answer(s)	Max Mark	Additional Guidance
21.	2 marks may be awarded for detailed/insightful comment plus quotation/reference. 1 mark for more basic comment plus quotation/reference. 0 marks for quotation/reference alone.	3	Possible answers include: • Word-choice shows attempt to think positively, e.g. "cheap"/"opened up"/"fresh" • "it also meant travel"/"it made me feel free" suggests the idea of freedom as the bus stop is outside the door • Repetition — "my own place, my home" emphasises she is pleased/proud to possess the cottage/be independent • Sentence structure — lists the number and variety of domestic chores she undertook to try to be positive about her new home "I papered ... the place fresh" • Use of short sentences makes it sound matter-of-fact/keeping her emotions in check — "The parting wasn't bitter. We wanted to be civilised and polite" • "I figured they were good signs. Everybody needs to cry now and then" — she turns a negative into a positive

194 ANSWERS FOR HIGHER ENGLISH

Question	Expected Answer(s)	Max Mark	Additional Guidance
22.	Up to 2 marks awarded for detailed, insightful comment plus quotation/reference. 1 mark for more basic comment plus quotation/reference. 0 marks for quotation/reference alone.	3	Possible answers include: • Word-choice "uneasy" suggests her feelings of concern as she is worried/uncomfortable • Word-choice "tried" suggests she did not succeed in forgetting/continues to be concerned • Personification of the mushroom — "where it had settled"/"left a little pink trail like anaemic blood"/"baby mushrooms"/"just to let them alone in case"/"dangerous"/emphasises that she sees them as almost human/actions are deliberately menacing • "LOOK" in bold and/or capitals emphasises her panic • Minor sentence "In case" suggests they are a real threat
23.	Candidates should deal with both sides of the contrast but not necessarily in equal measure. Up to 2 marks awarded for detailed, insightful comment plus quotation/reference. 1 mark for more basic comment plus quotation/reference. 0 marks for quotation/reference alone.	4	Possible answers include: Cottage: • "Dry rot." abrupt statement/repetition/positioning at the start of both paragraphs emphasises the scale and the extent of the problem • "Sinister" emphasises that Joy sees the dry rot as something evil/deliberately menacing • Metaphor "eaten from the inside by this thing" emphasises that she sees her cottage as a victim of something alien/evil/monstrous • "multiply … as we slept" emphasises the sense of menace as the rot creeps up on them while they are vulnerable • Word choice "silent spores" also increases the feeling of an invisible evil presence • Word choice "creeping red clouds" emphasises the silent predatory nature of the rot/like it is alive House: • Word choice "cheerful"/"bright" emphasises the attractiveness of and happiness within the house • "full of windows" gives the impression of openness and light • Emphasis on colour — "yellow walls and white woodwork" is bright/cheerful symbolising a new start
24.	Candidates may choose to answer in bullet points in this final question, or write a number of linked statements.	10	Up to 2 marks can be achieved for identifying elements of commonality as identified in the question, i.e. the impact of Joy's relationship with Michael A further 2 marks can be achieved for reference to the extract given. 6 additional marks can be awarded for discussion of similar references from at least one other part of the text. In practice this means: Identification of commonality (2) E.g. Michael brings a short period of happiness to Joy (1) and, therefore, his sudden, tragic death is all the more shocking for her (1). From the extract: 2 marks for detailed/insightful comment plus quotation/reference; 1 mark for more basic comment plus quotation/reference; 0 marks for quotation alone.

ANSWERS FOR HIGHER ENGLISH **195**

Question	Expected Answer(s)	Max Mark	Additional Guidance
24.	*(continued)*		E.g. throughout the extract Joy repeats "We" to suggest a sense of unity/belonging as she feels protected and complete when she is with Michael **(2)**
			From at least one other part of the text: as above for up to 6 marks
			Possible answers include:
			• The effect of Michael's death and its contribution to Joy's depression — reference to the flashbacks of Michael's drowning convey the still-present horror of that experience
			• The effect on her ability to cope with day to day life, e.g. work — the Head Teacher doesn't want her to make a fuss when Michael's wife is invited to the Memorial Service
			• Her casual relationships with men following Michael's death reveal her difficulties in coping with his loss
			• Her unwillingness to accept Michael's death shows the power of the relationship, still, in her life, e.g. deliberately spilling his aftershave to create a sense of his presence
			• Her anorexia develops after Michael's death and this allows her some control — she realises she has gone past her time for eating/she bakes but doesn't eat any of it

Text 7 – *Prose – Sunset Song* by Lewis Grassic Gibbon

Question	Expected Answer(s)	Max Mark	Additional Guidance
25.	2 marks awarded for detailed/insightful comment plus quotation/reference.	4	Possible answers include:
	1 mark for more basic comment plus quotation/reference.		• "a cold and louring day" — sense of gloom is heightened by the combination of the two adjectives
	0 marks for quotation/reference alone.		• "under the greyness" — dullness which seems all-encompassing
			• "squelched" — onomatopoeic word which catches the gurgling and sucking sound when walking in wet mud emphasising the sodden conditions she's walking through
			• "oozing" — again suggests the unpleasantness of the gradual flow of a smell of decay from the wet earth
			• "sodden" — suggests a thorough soaking which adds to the disagreeable impression of the conditions
			• "sheltered" is contrasted with "drenched" to highlight the extent of the rain damage to the crops
			• The very long sentence from "The wet fields" to "*endures*" gives a sense of the much wider world beyond, which is emphasised by the constant movement south to several places beyond Chris's immediate world
			• "ancient tower that the Pictish folk had reared" suggests Chris's awareness of the achievements of settlers long ago
			• "below the hands of the crofter folk" shows Chris's awareness of previous generations of farmers working this land
			• "Standing Stones" their presence provides a link with ancient times emphasising her sense of connection to the many generations before (and their worship)
			• General awareness that people are transient — "they lasted but as a breath" — but the landscape remains constant

196 ANSWERS FOR HIGHER ENGLISH

Question	Expected Answer(s)	Max Mark	Additional Guidance
26.	2 marks awarded for detailed/insightful comment plus quotation/reference. 1 mark for more basic comment plus quotation/reference. 0 marks for quotation/reference alone.	4	Possible answers include: • "weeping"/"stricken and frightened" suggests Chris has now realised that her plans to leave the land were foolish and she recognises that the land is part of who she is • "she could never leave it" sums up what Chris has realised/accepted about her relationship with the land • "this life … acrid" — repeated use of "and" shows a build up of all the challenging aspects of the constant physical effort which Chris (ironically) does not want to leave behind • "bound and held as though they had prisoned her here" suggests no possibility of escape • "fine bit plannings" suggests Chris's plans had been childish and vague, without a basis in reality • "the dreamings of a child" suggests that Chris's plans were unrealistic, fantasy, immature • "over toys it lacked" suggests a peevish desire for a passing childish phase • "toys that would never content it when it heard the smore of a storm …" suggests that Chris's previous plans were part of a childish world of playthings which cannot compare to the more lasting pleasures of nature and farming the land • "She could no more teach a school than fly" suggests how unrealistic her dreams were by comparing them to the fantasy idea of flying • "for all the fine clothes and gear she might get and hold" suggests that her desire to pursue her education was at least in part a desire for superficial possessions • "hated and loved" explains the dilemma that Chris has with the land
27.	2 marks awarded for detailed/insightful comment plus quotation/reference. 1 mark for more basic comment plus quotation/reference. 0 marks for quotation/reference alone.	2	Possible answers include: • *"Mighty be here, Chris, where are you going?"* — Auntie's words suggest she feels she should have power over Chris/treats her as though she were a child who needs to ask permission • *"I'm away to Stonehaven to see Mr Semple, can I bring you anything?"* — Chris' determination to make her own decisions and establish her independence • *"Away to Stonehive? What are you jaunting there for? I'll transact any business you have"* — Uncle Tam reacts as though Chris is wasting time on an outing, when he, as the man, should deal with business/legal matters
28.	Candidates can answer in bullet points in this final question, or write a number of linked statements.	10	Up to 2 marks can be achieved for identifying elements of communality as identified in the question, i.e. the idea that "nothing endures". A further 2 marks can be achieved for reference to the extract given. 6 additional marks can be awarded for discussion of similar references to at least one other part of the text by the writer. In practice this means: Identification of commonality **(2)** E.g. Chris's life undergoes constant change as a result of family deaths and changes in her circumstances. **(1)** just as the farming community changes as a result of the devastating effects of the war **(1)**

ANSWERS FOR HIGHER ENGLISH **197**

Question	Expected Answer(s)	Max Mark	Additional Guidance
28.	*(continued)*		From the extract: 2 marks for detailed/insightful comment plus quotation/reference; 1 mark for more basic comment plus quotation/reference; 0 marks for quotation alone. E.g. Chris's growing independence reflects her transition from child to woman when she makes a mature decision to stay on the land and stands up to her Aunt and Uncle who try to dictate what she should do **(2)**.
			From at least one other part of the text: as above for up to 6 marks
			Possible answers include:
			• The death of Jean Guthrie forces Chris to relinquish her childhood dreams and educational aspirations and adopt the role of the woman of the house • The impact of the war on the landscape with the felling of the trees leads to soil erosion making the land harder to farm • Post-war economic exploitation of the land leads to the loss of small farms and the crofters' way of life • The mechanisation of farming, e.g. at the harvest demonstrates agricultural change and progress and the emergence of a new technological world • The end of an era as indicated in the "Morning Star" eulogy suggesting the end of a way of life, culture and a community

Text 8 – *Prose – The Cone-Gatherers* by Robin Jenkins

Question	Expected Answer(s)	Max Mark	Additional Guidance
29.	2 marks awarded for detailed/insightful comment plus quotation/reference. 1 mark for more basic comment plus quotation/reference. 0 marks for quotation/reference alone.	4	Possible answers include: • "yew trees" suggests evil/death as they are often found in graveyards • "dark caverns" suggests underground places (possibly idea of Hades?) where Roderick cannot see/place which is creepy/frightening/dangerous … • "evil presences" extremity of word choice suggests someone/something undefined there to do wrong/cause hurt/create danger • "lurker" suggests someone watching and waiting with harmful intent • "No sunshine" negative term suggests darkness/cold and, therefore, connotations of evil/danger • Reference to Roderick's feelings suggests sinister atmosphere as he is uneasy, e.g. "cold"/"frightened"/"sick at heart". These suggest he is clearly upset/rattled/scared by the presence in the wood
30.	2 marks awarded for detailed/insightful comment plus quotation/reference. 1 mark for more basic comment plus quotation/reference. 0 marks for quotation/reference alone.	4	Possible answers include: • Roderick begins to work out what is going on in Duror's mind, e.g. he realises Duror is spying on the cone-gatherers to collect evidence of their "wrong-doing" (although he does not realise how sinister Duror's thoughts actually are, yet he is closer to the truth than any of the other characters) • He recognises some of the hypocrisy/irony in Duror's thinking – "Duror himself shot deer on Sundays", yet he might use working on a Sunday as an example of the cone-gatherers' "wrong-doing"

198 ANSWERS FOR HIGHER ENGLISH

Question	Expected Answer(s)	Max Mark	Additional Guidance
30.	(continued)		• He is insightful enough to recognise that Duror dislikes the cone-gatherers and wants them removed from the wood: "Why then did he hate the cone-gatherers and wish to drive them away?" • Roderick has an understanding of the "struggle between good and evil" — and recognises the cone-gatherers as good and Duror as evil • He understands that "Good did not always win" based on his reading (references to Christian from *The Pilgrim's Progress* and Sir Galahad's struggles) • He recognises there is something wrong with Duror — "Had Duror gone mad" — and links this to the "change" his mother and Mrs. Morton had been discussing • He makes the link between Duror and the "perils in the wood" which Mrs. Morton had warned him about: without understanding fully, intuitively, he is the closest to understanding what is going on with Duror
31.	2 marks may be awarded for a detailed/ insightful comment plus reference. 1 mark should be awarded for a more basic comment plus reference. 0 marks for reference/quotation alone.	2	Possible answers include: • Duror's presence is responsible for Roderick hiding rather than going to the cone-gatherers' hut as intended • Duror is responsible for Roderick's feelings of fear • Roderick's thoughts and fears involve Duror — his imaginings and his attempt to work out why Duror thinks and acts as he does • Duror motivates Roderick to think about the battle between good and evil
32.	Candidates may answer in bullet points in this final question, or write a number of linked statements.	10	Up to 2 marks can be achieved for identifying elements of commonality as identified in the question, i.e. the conflict between good and evil. A further 2 marks can be achieved for reference to the extract given. 6 additional marks can be awarded for discussion of similar references to at least one other part of the text by the writer. In practice this means: Identification of commonality **(2)** E.g. Conflict between good and evil is symbolised through Duror's irrational hatred of the innocent Calum **(1)** Calum has an affinity with nature whereas Duror destroys it **(1)** From the extract: 2 marks for detailed/insightful comment plus quotation/reference; 1 mark for more basic comment plus quotation/ reference; 0 marks for quotation alone. E.g. Roderick works out that the cone-gatherers represent goodness and Duror evil shown by his perceptive reaction to Duror's presence outside the hut and is beginning to understand that the struggle between good and evil never ends **(2)** From at least one other text/part of the text: as above for up to 6 marks

ANSWERS FOR HIGHER ENGLISH **199**

Question	Expected Answer(s)	Max Mark	Additional Guidance
32.	*(continued)*		Possible answers include: • References to the war as an influence of evil, destroying the landscape/many men/families contrasts with the gentleness of Calum/nature as a life force • Calum is presented as a Christ-like figure of goodness, sacrificed in a Biblical way at the end of the novel whereas Duror is presented as evil in his thoughts and deeds, e.g. lurking at the start of the novel • Roderick is presented as the future of hope/goodness, having inherited a sense of fairness and justice from his grandfather and mother — his desire to be like the cone gatherers identifies him with Calum's innocence • Lady Runcie-Campbell's faith is presented as goodness as this encourages her to visit Peggy Duror/be lenient towards the cone-gatherers following the deer drive/weeps at the end of the novel, yet she sends the cone-gatherers into the storm rather than allowing them to stay in the beach-hut — corrupted by Duror • Mr. Tulloch's continued support of the cone-gatherers is seen as good; he demonstrates fairness and justice following the deer drive and their expulsion from the beach-hut and at the end when Lady Runcie-Campbell insists they rescue Roderick from the tree — this contrasts with influence of Duror

SCOTTISH TEXT (POETRY)

Text 9 — *Poetry — A Poet's Welcome to His Love-Begotten Daughter; The First Instance that entitled him to the Venerable Appellation of Father* by Robert Burns

Question	Expected Answer(s)	Max Mark	Additional Guidance
33.	2 marks awarded for detailed/insightful comment plus quotation/reference. 1 mark for more basic comment plus quotation/reference.	2	Possible answers include: • "Thou's welcome, wean" suggests warm/congratulatory/proud tone in defiance of convention • "My sweet wee" acknowledges ownerships/suggests intimacy and protectiveness • "My (sweet wee) lady!" — deliberately gives the child status despite the circumstances of her birth • "Daddy" — familiar/informal title underlines the closeness of the bond he acknowledges between them • "mishanter fa' me" — determination not to feel shame/embarrassment
34.	2 marks awarded for detailed/insightful comment plus quotation/reference. 1 mark for more basic comment plus quotation/reference.	4	Possible answers include: • "fornicator" — blunt statement of their accusation showing his refusal to be intimidated/troubled by it • "kintry clatter" — reduces the accusations to trivial gossip/alliteration emphasises the noisy meaninglessness of it • "the mair they talk, I'm kent the better" — balance in the comparatives suggests relishing his notoriety • "clash!" makes all the gossip seems like discordant noise/climactic nature of positioning at end of the short line

200 ANSWERS FOR HIGHER ENGLISH

Question	Expected Answer(s)	Max Mark	Additional Guidance
34.	*(continued)*		• "auld wife's tongue's" belittling connotations — people who think like this are old-fashioned/out of touch/not worth listening to • "I hae fought for"/"Baith kirk and queir" defiant tone emphasises his determination to take them on/individual taking on authority and institution
35.	2 marks awarded for detailed/insightful comment plus quotation/reference. 1 mark for more basic comment plus quotation/reference. 0 marks for quotation/reference only.	4	Possible answers include: • "Tho' I should be the waur bestead...bienly clad" juxtaposition/contrast of "I" and "thou" to emphasise his commitment to support her, whatever the cost to himself • word choice of "brat" and "wedlock's bed" emphasises his defiant attitude in the face of social convention • "fatherly I kiss and daut thee" use of terms of physical tenderness as an expression of his love for her/the attention he lavishes on her • "Thy mither's person, grace an' merit" list of conventional female virtues emphasises his loyalty and commitment to the baby's mother despite the circumstances • "An' thy poor, worthless daddy's spirit" word choice creates self-deprecating humour showing that he doesn't take himself too seriously
36.	Candidates can answer in bullet points in this final question, or write a number of linked statements.	10	Up to 2 marks can be achieved for identifying elements of commonality as identified in the question, i.e. Burns' treatment of the religious and/or moral concerns of his time A further 2 marks can be achieved for the reference to the extract given. 6 additional marks can be awarded for discussion of similar references in at least one other poem by Burns. <u>In practice this means:</u> Identification of commonality **(2)** E.g. Burns challenges/criticises the rigid/intrusive/hypocritical aspects of moral/religious beliefs of his time **(1)** while presenting a warmer, more human alternative **(1)** From the extract: 2 marks for detailed/insightful comment plus quotation/reference; 1 mark for more basic comment plus quotation/reference; 0 marks for quotation/reference alone. E.g. "But be a loving father to thee, And brag the name o' 't." demonstrates his love for and commitment to her, as well as his pride, despite the criticism he will face from those representing conventional religion and morality **(2)** From at least one other text: as above for up to 6 marks Possible references include: • *Address to the Deil* — humorous, ironic speaker/persona is appropriate for poet's satirical critique of Calvinism • *A Man's A Man For A' That* — a spokesman, champion of equality and fraternity speaking as the voice of a community/nation as he criticises the hierarchical nature of society • *Holy Willie* — creation of self-righteous character who justifies his own sins as an apt vehicle for his critique of the perceived religious hypocrisy of the time

ANSWERS FOR HIGHER ENGLISH **201**

Question	Expected Answer(s)	Max Mark	Additional Guidance
36.	*(continued)*		• *Tam O'Shanter* — character of moralising, commentating narrator allows Burns to point out the vagaries of human nature/undermine the apparent moral 'message' of the poem • *To a Mouse* uses the symbol of the homeless mouse to make a comment about the suffering of the tenant farmers of his day.

Text 10 — *Poetry* — *Mrs Midas* by Carol Ann Duffy

Question	Expected Answer(s)	Max Mark	Additional Guidance
37.	Both sides of the contrast must be dealt with for full marks but not necessarily in equal measure. 2 marks awarded for detailed/insightful comment plus quotation/reference. 1 mark for more basic comment plus quotation/reference. 0 marks for quotation/reference alone.	4	Possible answers include: Stanza 1 — the atmosphere of ordinariness/security suggested by: • "poured a glass of wine/started to unwind/relaxed" all suggest the routine process of starting to enjoy the free time at the end of the day • "kitchen filled ... itself" conveys the domesticated/homely environment • "blanching the windows/opened one/wiped the other" suggest the mundane activities involved in the preparation of the meal Stanza 2 — the atmosphere of extraordinariness/threat/disbelief suggested by: • "visibility poor/dark" signals a change in mood from previous stanza to one of mystery • "twig in his hand ... gold" suggests a supernatural occurrence • "pear ... like a lightbulb" suggests the unnatural appearance of her husband • "fairy lights" the incongruity of putting these up in September/connotations of something magical
38.	2 marks awarded for detailed/insightful comment plus quotation/reference. 1 mark for more basic comment plus quotation/reference. 0 marks for quotation/reference alone.	2	Possible answers include: • "He drew the blinds" the furtive action suggests a concealment/attempt to isolate them from the outside world • "strange, wild, vain" conveys her confusion/concern at the change in his demeanour • "spitting out the teeth ... rich" suggests the negative effects of his greed/inappropriateness of his behaviour at the table • "shaking hand" demonstrates the anxiety she feels over his actions • "glass, goblet, golden chalice" suggests the stages of the unnatural transformation of the glass before her eyes
39.	2 marks awarded for detailed/insightful comment plus quotation/reference. 1 mark for more basic comment plus quotation/reference. 0 marks for quotation/reference alone.	4	Possible answers include: • "I finished the wine/I made him sit" highlights her practical nature/ability to regain her composure • Sequencing of "I made/I locked/I moved" suggests she quickly takes control of the situation demonstrating her strength of character/domineering nature • "The toilet I didn't mind" shows her pride in material possessions/keeping up appearances • Use of statement/(rhetorical) questions "I couldn't believe my ears"/"But who has .../about gold?" suggests her no-nonsense approach to life's problems • "keep his hands to himself ... lock the cat in the cellar ... At least ... smoking for good" all suggest a humorous side to her character in being able to make light of such a serious situation

202 ANSWERS FOR HIGHER ENGLISH

Question	Expected Answer(s)	Max Mark	Additional Guidance
40.	Candidates can answer in bullet points in this final question, or write a number of linked statements.	10	Up to 2 marks can be achieved by identifying elements of commonality as identified in the question, i.e. attempts of characters to cope with life-changing situations.
			A further 2 marks can be achieved for reference to the text given.
			6 additional marks can be awarded for discussion of similar references to at least one other poem by the poet.
			<u>In practice this means:</u>
			Identification of commonality **(2)** E.g. Duffy presents characters who develop various coping "strategies" either consciously or unconsciously **(1)** some more successful in allowing them to accept or move on, whilst others are still struggling **(1)**
			From this extract: 2 marks for detailed/insightful comment plus quotation/reference; 1 mark for more basic comment plus quotation/reference; 0 marks for quotation/reference alone.
			E.g. she attempts to cope by using humour to make light of the horrifying implications of the situation **(2)**
			From at least one other text: as above for up to 6 marks
			Possible comments include:
			• *Anne Hathaway* she focuses on happy memories of when her husband was alive and the depth of their passionate love for one another to cope with the pain of her loss • *Havisham* the speaker imagines violent acts against her one time lover in order to cope with the rejection she feels but is still stuck in the past • *War Photographer* the inability of the photographer to rid himself of his experiences in warzones despite his attempts to adopt a professional distance • *Originally* the speaker attempts to adapt her language in order to fit in to her new environment but feels a sense of loss as a result of this • *Valentine* the speaker attempts to cope with the loss of her illusions about love by rejecting the clichés of love in favour of a more cynical view

Text 11 — *Poetry — The Bargain* by Liz Lochhead

Question	Expected Answer(s)	Max Mark	Additional Guidance
41.	At least two examples should be included for full marks. 2 marks awarded for detailed/insightful comment plus quotation/reference. 1 mark for more basic comment plus quotation/reference. 0 marks for quotation/reference alone.	4	Possible answers include: • "river fast and high" suggests the relationship isn't going smoothly/could run into trouble • "You and I" Individual personal pronouns separated by "and" suggests that even though they seem physically together, they are drifting apart • "twitch and fret" — connotations of unsettled, jumpy. Refers not only to the police horses but the speaker's awareness of her failing relationship • "rubbing the wrong way" — beginnings of disagreement/discomfort of being in the crowd echoes their feelings towards each other

ANSWERS FOR HIGHER ENGLISH **203**

Question	Expected Answer(s)	Max Mark	Additional Guidance
41.	*(continued)*		• "ready to let fly" — the impending violence of the fans suggests conflict/her fear that her lover is preparing to leave her • "looking back, looking forward" — repetition to highlight the uncertainty in the relationship/don't know whether to look to the past or the future
42.	2 marks awarded for detailed/insightful comment. 1 mark for more basic comment. 0 marks for quotation/reference alone.	2	Possible answers include: • Alliteration of "b" in "but the boy...beautiful Bakelite/Bush" suggests energy/upbeat attitude of boy to activity • Positive connotations of "beautiful/Bakelite" suggests bright, upbeat mood • Fast pace/internal rhyme of "buttonpopping stationhopping" suggests enthusiastic enjoyment of music • List of three positive aspects of boy's experience in "doesn't miss a beat", "sings along", "it's easy" suggests the boy's happiness
43.	At least two examples should be included for full marks. 2 marks awarded for detailed/insightful comment plus quotation/reference. 1 mark for more basic comment plus quotation/reference. 0 marks for quotation/reference alone.	4	Possible answers include: • "splintering city" — suggests city is broken or divided, just as the relationship is fractured • "wintry bridges" — cold and uninviting, which suggests the distance/lack of connection in the relationship • "black" — suggests neglect and poverty in this area, which reflects the deteriorating nature of the relationship • "every other tenement … on its gable end" — pun suggests the open and frank nature of the people which contrasts with lack of openness in the relationship now • "I know it's cold" — pathetic fallacy suggests lack of harmony/closeness in their relationship • "wet dog reek … damp clothes" — emphasises the unpleasant smell which permeates the area, symbolic of the state of their relationship
44.	Candidates can answer in bullet points in this final question, or write a number of linked statements.	10	Up to 2 marks can be achieved for identifying elements of commonality as identified in the question, i.e. Lochhead's exploration of the theme of difficult relationships. A further 2 marks can be achieved for reference to the extract given. 6 additional marks can be awarded for discussion of similar references to at least one other poem. In practice this means: Identification of commonality **(2)** E.g. Lochhead explores the various problems in relationships **(1)** and in doing this gives us new insights/increases our understanding of universal human problems **(1)** From the poem: 2 marks for detailed/insightful comment plus quotation/reference; 1 mark for more basic comment plus quotation/reference; 0 marks for quotation/reference alone. E.g. the projection of the disintegrating relationship onto the surroundings "splintering city … wintry bridges" **(2)**

204 ANSWERS FOR HIGHER ENGLISH

Question	Expected Answer(s)	Max Mark	Additional Guidance
44.	*(continued)*		OR
			The portrayal of the tension/uncertainty within the relationship "looking back … which way" **(2)**
			From at least one other text: as above for up to 6 marks
			Possible answers include:
			• *My Rival's House* the difficult relationship of the speaker and her prospective mother-in-law due to her overprotectiveness of her son "this son she bore … never can escape"
			• *My Rival's House* the awkwardness and insecurity of the speaker in the face of the unwelcoming attitude of the rival "I am all edges, a surface, a shell"
			• *Last Supper* the bitterness and resentment as a result of the disintegration of a relationship "betrayal with a kiss"
			• *Last Supper* the predatory nature of the spurned as they seek new relationships "get hungry and go hunting again"
			• *For my Grandmother Knitting* repetition of "there is no need" emphasises the grandmother's diminishing importance within the family

Text 12 — *Poetry* — *Memorial* by Norman MacCaig

Question	Expected Answer(s)	Max Mark	Additional Guidance
45.	2 marks awarded for detailed/insightful comment plus quotation/reference. 1 mark for more basic comment plus quotation/reference.	3	Possible answers include: • Blunt/matter-of-fact opening statements convey the simple truth that her death surrounds him • Repetition of "everywhere" and/or "dies" reinforces the fact that he cannot escape from this • Present tense shows it is still vivid in his mind • Patterned list of phrases "no sunrise … mountain" emphasises the inescapable nature of her death as these are places not usually associated with death. Placement of "but" after the list highlights the pleasure he previously took has become tainted by her death • Paradox "silence of her dying sounds" conveys the devastating impact of her death as its intensity blocks out everything else. It, in itself, is his only focus • Imagery of "carousel of language" is intricate and candidates may consider it in different ways. Sensible interpretations should be rewarded which link/contrast it to the ideas suggested by "the silence of her dying". E.g. the frivolous, noisy, joyous nature of a fairground; the endless, circular movement which has no purpose other than to entertain; the connotations of childhood freedom and innocence • Imagery of "web" connotes: a deadly trap possibly suggesting his grief is so powerful it eliminates all other emotions/interconnectedness or interwoven human emotions — no escape from absolute quiet • Word choice/imagery of "stitches" further illustrates that his despair is so firmly secured in his psyche that all future happiness will be overpowered/vanquished

ANSWERS FOR HIGHER ENGLISH **205**

Question	Expected Answer(s)	Max Mark	Additional Guidance
45.	*(continued)*		• Candidates may also make a case for "web/ stitches" having more positive connotations, e.g. of his memories of happier times being secured/ fastened/locked away. As before, sensible interpretations, which are justified with evidence, should be considered • Rhetorical question "How can ..." creates a pessimistic tone highlighting that his grief is so prevalent he can see no escape • Word choice of "clasp" suggests a tight grip showing the close bond and the strength of his feelings towards his loved one. Thus, this conveys the impact her death has had on him • Imagery of "thick death" portrays death as something impenetrable which he can never break through or recover from emotionally • Word choice of "intolerable distance" conveys his feelings on the inevitable, unbearable barrier between the living and the dead. Highlights his wider beliefs about the finality of death being a gap which can never be bridged
46.	2 marks awarded for detailed/insightful comment plus quotation/reference. 1 mark for more basic comment plus quotation/reference.	4	Possible answers include: • Repetition/echoing in opening line "she grieves ... grief" informs of her sympathy/comfort for him in his sorrow, thus reinforcing their love • Present tense of "dying" and "she tells me" conveys his vivid recollection that at the end of her life she was still concerned about the impact, on him, of her death • References to nature "bird ... fish" are contradictions of the normal order of things. He sees death as a reversal of existence and so their relationship has been permanently altered./Equally death is being presented as part of the natural cycle of things symbolised by the bird and the fish • Imagery of "crocus is carved ….shapes my mind" offers a brief respite in mood as he appreciates her invocation of nature to highlight that death is part of the circle of life. As such, her death inspires him to be more creative in his work/be precise in the words he uses • The dash/"But" introduces a contrast/change of mood to one of melancholy about his loved one being forever lost to him • Word choice of "black words" continues this mood and hints at his despair about the finality of death forever separating them • Oxymoron "sound of soundlessness" echoes his anguish in stanza 1 about the intense nature of his all-consuming grief • Word choice of "that name" is vague and unspecific highlighting his view of the implausibility of reunion after death • Imagery of "nowhere …. continuously going into" is ambiguous in nature conveying his bleak outlook that her death is a never-ending journey with no certainty or hopeful conclusion

206 ANSWERS FOR HIGHER ENGLISH

Question	Expected Answer(s)	Max Mark	Additional Guidance
47.	2 marks awarded for detailed/insightful comment plus quotation/reference. 1 mark for more basic comment plus quotation/reference.	3	Possible answers include: • "she can't stop dying" shows how her death is constantly on his mind. The present (continuous) tense illustrates its vividness and clarity which threatens to overwhelm him • "she makes me" conveys their bond and the strength of his love for her, which will prevail through time • "elegy" shows he has become a living testament to the profound nature of grief as an elegy would usually be written as a tribute to her. Instead he subverts the notion to show how profound his melancholy is • "masterpiece" normally relates to an outstanding piece of work/impressive creation. This satirically conveys his belief that his grief is so penetrating it has transformed him into a work of art/treasure/monument • "true fiction" — oxymoron suggests that unlike a story, his anguish is real and links to the "ugliness of death" to convey his horror and anger regarding his fundamental belief in the reality of the situation • "sad music" sums up the central idea about the pervasive nature of grief and despair. The pessimistic ending highlights the all-consuming nature of grief and how it remains forever with him
48.	Candidates may choose to answer in bullet points in this final question, or write a number of linked statements.	10	Up to 2 marks can be achieved for identifying elements of commonality as identified in the question, i.e. reaction to suffering A further 2 marks can be achieved for reference to the extract given. 6 additional marks can be awarded for discussion of similar references to at least one other poem. In practice this means: Identification of commonality **(2)** E.g. reaction to suffering is part of the human condition **(1)** can be experienced as life-affirming or life-denying **(1)** From the poem: 2 marks for detailed/insightful comment plus quotation/reference; 1 marks for more basic comment plus quotation/reference; 0 marks for quotation alone. E.g. the all-consuming and enduring impact of his grief "Everywhere I go she dies" **(2)** From at least one other text: as above for 6 marks Possible answers include: • *Visiting Hour* the speaker's denial/numbness in reaction to severity of the patient's condition and his refusal to accept the inevitable • *Aunt Julia* the speaker's mental pain and regret over the loss of his Aunt and all that she represents in terms of Scotland's heritage • *Assisi* the beggar's reaction to physical suffering: acceptance and gratitude for the little he has in the face of neglect and hypocrisy

ANSWERS FOR HIGHER ENGLISH **207**

Question	Expected Answer(s)	Max Mark	Additional Guidance
48.	*(continued)*		• *Sounds of the Day* the speaker underestimates the depth and enduring nature of his suffering when the relationship ends • *Visiting Hour* the all-consuming despair felt by the speaker at the futility of his efforts to communicate with or to alleviate the suffering of his loved one

Text 13 — *Poetry — Shores* by Sorley MacLean

Question	Expected Answer(s)	Max Mark	Additional Guidance
49.	2 marks awarded for detailed/insightful comment plus quotation/reference. 1 mark for more basic comment plus quotation/reference. 0 marks for quotation/reference alone.	4	Possible answers include: • Sense of immense scale of the landscape conveyed by place names, word choice of "ocean", reference to "between Scotland and Tiree" • Use of Gaelic place names in English translation emphasises speaker's appreciation of the depth of history/his sense of heritage • The enormity of the physical landscape suggested by personification/comparison with a giant of "great white mouth"/"two hard jaws" • "while the ocean was filling ... forever" suggests speaker is appreciative of the never ending power of nature • "Prishal bowed his stallion head" comparison to intimidating, wild, elemental force • Use of hyperbole: of "between the world and eternity" emphasises his sense of wonder at the vast timeless quality of nature
50.	2 marks awarded for detailed/insightful comment plus quotation/reference. 1 mark for more basic comment plus quotation/reference. 0 marks for quotation/reference alone.	4	Possible answers include: • "till doom"/"measuring sand, grain: by grain"/ "for the sea draining drop by drop" geological timescale to highlight depth of speaker's commitment, devotion and patience • "And if ... Mull"/"And if ... Moidart" — parallel structure and references to places that he wishes they could be together in, suggests that his strong love for these places is mirrored in his love for the person/wishes to share them with his lover • "that wide solitude ... wait there forever" extreme nature of the vocabulary emphasises that even in this vast, empty setting he is willing to wait for his lover • "a synthesis of love" suggests the link between his love for sea and land and love for his woman • Reference to "ocean and sand" emphasises the never ending nature of his love by comparison with never- ending natural phenomena/gives a sense of his love as elemental, like the force of nature itself
51.	Candidates may choose to comment on either language or ideas or both. 2 marks awarded for detailed/insightful comment plus quotation/reference. 1 mark for more basic comment plus quotation/reference. 0 marks for quotation/reference alone.	2	Possible answers include: Language: • Personification of "unhappy" contrasting the sea with his own contented state as conveyed in the rest of the poem • Nature is shown as powerful/threatening "surging sea"/"dragged the boulders"/"threw them over us" as it was earlier • Promise of "I would build the rampart wall" reaffirms his desire to preserve his love from threats and make sure that it will endure • Threat is described as "an alien eternity" linking back to the idea of infinite time and its sublime power

208 ANSWERS FOR HIGHER ENGLISH

Question	Expected Answer(s)	Max Mark	Additional Guidance
51.	*(continued)*		Ideas: • Desire to protect his love emphasises the strong feelings that he has conveyed in the rest of the poem for his lover • Nature as a powerful, frightening force is emphasised here, and in the rest of the poem • Eternity of his love is compared to the eternity of natural, elemental forces
52.	Candidates can answer in bullet points in this final question, or write a number of linked statements.	10	Up to 2 marks can be achieved for identifying elements of commonality as identified in the question, i.e. discuss how MacLean explores the impact of time on human experience. A further 2 marks can be achieved for reference to the extract given. 6 additional marks can be awarded for discussion of similar references to at least one other poem by the poet. <u>In practice this means:</u> Identification of commonality **(2)** E.g.: human experience is essentially transitory **(1)** but aspects of life, e.g. love, appreciation of nature have greater permanence **(1)** From the extract: 2 marks for detailed/insightful comment plus quotation/reference; 1 mark for more basic comment plus quotation/reference; 0 marks for quotation/reference alone. E.g. declaration of love which will never end — the constant quality of his love emphasised by comparisons with measuring the sea "drop by drop" and the sand, "grain by grain" **(2)** From at least one other text: as above for up to 6 marks Possible answers include: • *Screapadal* the elemental beauty of the place has outlived its human occupation, which is essentially ephemeral • *An Autumn Day* death in war can be sudden and without warning or time and opportunity to prepare • *I Gave You Immortality* the immortality bestowed by the celebration of love in the poem contrasts with actual human response of the woman • *Heroes* youth, inexperience of the soldier who is killed emphasises the lack of heroism/common vulnerability of humanity and transience of human life • *An Autumn Day* the indifference of nature to the suffering of humanity shown in the passing of a whole day as the men's bodies lie in the sunshine

ANSWERS FOR HIGHER ENGLISH

Text 14 — *Poetry — The Thread* by Don Paterson

Question	Expected Answer(s)	Max Mark	Additional Guidance
53.	2 marks awarded for detailed/insightful comment plus quotation/reference. 1 mark for more basic comment plus quotation/reference.	4	Possible answers include: • "Made his landing … so hard … ploughed" echoes a crash landing suggesting his arrival on earth was potentially life-threatening • positioning of "so hard" emphasises the intensity of the danger • "ploughed straight back into the earth" alludes to the burial of the dead suggesting the fragility of life • "They caught him" conveys the medical team's active role/intervention in saving his life • "by the thread" suggests how precarious his survival was • "pulled him up" suggests last minute intervention to save his life
54.	2 marks awarded for detailed/insightful comment plus quotation/reference. 1 mark for more basic comment plus quotation/reference.	2	Possible answers include: • "I thank what higher will" suggests his continuing gratitude for the intervention of a benign force guiding their destiny/looking after them • structure of "to you and me and Russ" suggests a unified, cohesive group • "great twin-engined … us" suggests the stability and resilience of the family grouping • "roaring" suggests life and vitality of the family • "somehow" suggests the miraculous nature of his survival • "out-revving … universe" suggests immense energy and power of the family unit and their activities
55.	2 marks awarded for detailed/insightful comment plus quotation/reference. 1 mark for more basic comment plus quotation/reference.	4	Possible answers include: • "All that trouble … dead" reprises the trauma of the boy's birth • "all I thought … week" contrasts with the present happiness • "thread holding all of us" returns to fragility of life/ suggests bond which holds family together • "look at our tiny house" concludes flight metaphor suggesting take-off/elation/joy • "tiny house" symbolic of vulnerability/closeness of small family unit • "white dot … mother waving" suggests the traditional, supportive role of the mother within the family unit

210 ANSWERS FOR HIGHER ENGLISH

Question	Expected Answer(s)	Max Mark	Additional Guidance
56.	Candidates may choose to answer in bullet points in this final question, or write a number of linked statements.	10	Up to 2 marks can be achieved for identifying elements of commonality as identified in the question, i.e. the fragility of human life.
			A further 2 marks can be achieved for reference to the extract given.
			6 additional marks can be awarded for discussion of similar references to at least one other poem by the poet.
			<u>In practice this means:</u> Identification of commonality (2) E.g. the threat of death is ever-present in our sense of ourselves as human beings (1) anticipation/survival of this threat can be a powerful force at all stages of life (1)
			From the extract: 2 marks for detailed/insightful comment plus quotation/reference; 1 mark for more basic comment plus quotation/reference; 0 marks for quotation/reference alone. E.g. image of the 'thread' fastening Jamie to life reinforces the sense of the fragile and precarious nature of life as death is always a possibility (2)
			From at least one other text: as above for up to 6 marks
			Possible answers include:
			• *Nil Nil* reference to gall stone — all that's left of pilot — kicked into gutter emphasises how casually life can be disposed of and a human being can be reduced to an object • *The Ferryman's* Arms speaker waiting for the ferryman — reference to Greek mythology — ferry journey to afterlife suggests sense that we as living human beings are waiting for death/passing the time until the inevitability of death happens • *Nil Nil* decline of football team from (modest) glory days to no one coming to see their match creates a nihilistic picture of the inevitable decline of humanity towards death • *11.00: Baldovan* the boys' return to world where they no longer feel part of things/world seems to have changed suggests sense that life moves on without us and individuals are forgotten and dispensable • *Waking with Russell* the speaker, faced with the vulnerability of his new born child, commits himself to nurture and protect him from danger.

SECTION 2 — Critical Essay

Please see the assessment criteria for the Critical Essay on page 79.

ANSWERS FOR HIGHER ENGLISH   **211**

HIGHER ENGLISH
2017

PAPER 1 — READING FOR UNDERSTANDING, ANALYSIS AND EVALUATION

Marking Instructions for each question

Question		Expected Response	Max Mark	Additional Guidance
1.	(a)	Read lines 1–12. Analyse how the writer's word choice in lines 1–3 emphasises the "conventional wisdom" that reading books is better than playing video games. 2 marks may be awarded for reference plus detailed/insightful comment; 1 mark for reference plus more basic comment; 0 marks for reference alone. Possible answers are shown in the "Additional Guidance" column. (Marks may be awarded 2 or 1 + 1)	2	Possible answers include: • "enriches" suggests that reading adds to one's knowledge, awareness; is rewarding, beneficial; improves one • "the mind" suggests reading is influencing something greater than just the brain; it influences our consciousness: thought, perception, emotions and imagination • "deadens" suggests video games make kids less aware, less sensitive, less vigorous; they make kids think less; lifeless • "zoning out" suggests video games make kids detached from people and things around them, unresponsive, unstimulated
	(b)	Explain in your own words "the question" the writer asks in line 6 about "other forms of culture". Candidates must attempt to use their own words. No marks for straight lifts from the passage. 2 marks may be awarded for detailed/insightful comment plus quotation/reference 1 mark for basic comment plus quotation/reference 0 marks for quotation/reference alone	2	Possible answers include: • the writer is asking if these other forms of culture involve discrete thinking skills/have qualities which benefit, stimulate, challenge, stretch our minds in ways which are different from — but just as important as — reading
	(c)	By referring to at least two features of language in lines 8–12 ("Where … books"), analyse how the writer emphasises the contrast between his positive view of "other forms of culture" and the negative view held by "most critics". 2 marks may be awarded for reference plus detailed/insightful comment; 1 mark for reference plus more basic comment; 0 marks for reference alone. Possible answers are shown in the "Additional Guidance" column. (Marks may be awarded 2 + 2, 2 + 1 + 1, 1 + 1 + 1 + 1)	4	Possible answers include: *Imagery* • "(progressive) story": just as a "story" is a developing, organised narrative, so the writer sees the positive influence of popular culture as gradual, logical, coherent, interesting … • "our brains sharper": just as sharpening involves giving cutting tools a better edge, this suggests making our brains keener, more accurate … • "we soak in": soaking in is a process of absorption, of taking in as much liquid as possible; this suggests we become immersed in popular culture, that its influence is natural, irresistible, all-consuming, profound, deep … • "(lowbrow) fluff": fluff is light, downy material (for example, small pieces of wool); its use suggests critics believe popular culture is light, trivial, worthless, superficial, irrelevant, trifling … • "honing": just as honing is a (refined) process of giving cutting tools a perfect edge, this suggests gradually making our brains as sharp as possible, more and more precise, accurate, productive … *Word choice* • "allege" suggest doubt, calls the critics' views into question • "dumbing down" suggests popular culture offers people a reduced intellectual challenge **or** is responsible for making people less educated, less intelligent, more lowbrow

212 ANSWERS FOR HIGHER ENGLISH

Question		Expected Response	Max Mark	Additional Guidance
	(c)	*(continued)*		• "progressive" suggests developing, advancing, moving forward steadily, leading to improvement • "steadily" suggests reliable, consistent progress • "imperceptibly" suggests change is gradual, subtle • "sharper" suggests keener, more precise, more accurate • "soak in" suggests it's not a superficial process; influence is deep; we are fully engaged, absorbed • "dismissed" suggests brushed aside, considered beneath contempt, irrelevant, unimportant, trivial • "lowbrow" suggests vulgar, anti-intellectual, uncultured, plebeian • "fluff" suggests worthless, trivial, inconsequential, superficial • "honing" suggests sharpening, perfecting, refining *Sentence structure* • balanced structure/contrast of "Where ... story" allows the writer to trump the critics' argument; this is heightened by the greater certainty of his "see" set against the dubious nature of what they "allege" • use of colon to introduce a full development of his "progressive story" argument • use of parenthesis "but ... imperceptibly" to explain that this positive development is so gradual that it's easy for the less astute (like the critics) to miss it • positioning of "I hope to persuade you" at the start of the final sentence alerts the reader to the fact that the writer is about to make what he believes is his most important point • positioning of "increasingly" just before his key statement stresses that the point he is about to make is more and more relevant, true • balanced nature of final statement, hinging on the "just as important as" comparison stresses skills developed by popular culture are of a comparable standard to the skills developed by reading
2.		By referring to lines 13–19, analyse how the writer uses both sentence structure and imagery to convey the difficulty of playing video games. For full marks there must be reference to both features. 2 marks may be awarded for reference plus detailed/insightful comment; 1 mark for reference plus more basic comment; 0 marks for mere identification of a feature of sentence structure. Possible answers are shown in the "Additional Guidance" column. (Marks may be awarded 2 + 2, 2 + 1 + 1, 1 + 1 + 1 + 1)	4	Possible answers include: *Sentence structure* • the positioning of **and/or** rhythmic/repetitive nature of "And the first and last thing" conveys the definitive 'Alpha and omega' nature of this phrase, especially when placed at the start of the sentence, suggests the difficulty of video games is a fundamental point to the writer • use of parenthesis "the thing ... hear" adds to the mystery, adds to the dramatic build-up to the final announcement of video games' difficulty • additional phrase "sometimes maddeningly" has two functions: again adds to the build-up **and/or** ramps up the notion of extreme difficulty that "fiendishly" has introduced

ANSWERS FOR HIGHER ENGLISH **213**

Question		Expected Response	Max Mark	Additional Guidance
2.		*(continued)*		• use of climax in the sentence "The dirty … fun." — the somewhat awkward/unusual construction of this sentence is designed to stress the "not having fun" element of its conclusion • repetition of the "you may be" structure stresses — and this is heightened by the use of the inclusive direct address — the variety of problems playing video games may cause • repetition of adjectives ("frustrated", "confused", "disorientated", "stuck") — rat-a-tat run of adjectives suggests 'the sea of troubles' playing video games may involve • anticlimax of "you may be stuck" in its definitive downbeat simplicity, it is a stark summation of the seemingly insoluble challenge these games present • use of the continuous tense in final sentence — an argument might be made that this reflects the ongoing, nagging nature of the problems involved *Imagery* • "wrestling": just as wrestling involves close, physical combat with a single opponent, so it suggests a demanding, exhausting battle with an unforgiving enemy • "worrying a loose tooth": just as this involves the constant working away at a persistent physical annoyance, so it suggests that the difficulties presented by video games are nagging frustrations that constantly prey on one's mind • "stuck": just as to be stuck is to be fixed immovably, so it suggests being trapped in a situation which offers no escape • "dirty little secret": usually used in the realms of ethics or morality, a deliberate attempt to hide the truth, a cover-up of some sort, a hidden scandal; used in relation to the difficulty of video games, it heightens the potentially damaging nature of this feature, suggests it is a very negative feature that is deliberately glossed over
3.		Read lines 20–33. Identify three reasons why "reward" is so important to the learning process involved in playing video games. Use your own words as far as possible. Candidates must attempt to use their own words. No marks for straight lifts from the passage. (Marks awarded 1 + 1 + 1)	3	Possible answers include: • people are hard-wired to respond strongly to rewards • people find rewards a great stimulus to action, learning etc. • video games are designed to be full of rewards • rewards in video games are precise, with clear outcomes (explanation of "clearly defined") • the rewards are attractive • the rewards are presented in a variety of forms • players are constantly reminded about the rewards • the rewards are vitally important to achieving success in the games • the rewards are more intense, striking, colourful than in real life • players aren't always aware that they are learning (explanation of "without realising …")

214 ANSWERS FOR HIGHER ENGLISH

Question		Expected Response	Max Mark	Additional Guidance
4.		Read lines 34–47. Identify two criticisms and two defences the writer makes of video games. Candidates must attempt to use their own words. No marks for straight lifts from the passage. (Marks awarded 1 + 1 + 1 + 1) NB Maximum 2 marks awarded for criticism and 2 marks awarded for defence.	4	Possible answers include: *Criticisms* • the games may seem attractive but the attractions flatter to deceive, are rather superficial, blind one to the truth (explanation of "dazzled") • the games are addictive (explanation of "hooked") • the subject matter is infantile, petty, puerile, trivial … (explanation of "actual content … childish") • unnecessarily threatening, unjustifiably scary (explanation of "gratuitously menacing" — but explanation of "menacing" alone: 0) • the subject matter is very limited **and/or** moves between the two extremes of violence and childish fantasy (explanation of "alternates … princess-rescuing") • the games are violent (explanation of "drive-by shooting") • the games are pure fantasy (explanation of "princess-rescuing") *Defences* • the activities involved are beneficial for mental training/development ("good for the brain") • the skills developed will be of use in other spheres ("come in handy elsewhere") • it resembles learning algebra, which might seem pointless and abstract but exercises the brain • like chess, games might seem very basic (and aggressive in concept), but they are every bit as cerebral and mind-developing as chess; they develop strategic, tactical thinking
5.	(a)	Read lines 48–54. Explain in your own words the key distinction the writer makes between reading a novel and playing a video game. Candidates must attempt to use their own words. No marks for straight lifts from the passage. (Marks awarded 1 + 1)	2	Possible answers include: *reading a novel* • can get us thinking in a creative way, transport us to in different situation (explanation of "activate our imagination") • can affect our feelings, arouse passions (explanation of "conjure up powerful emotions") *playing a game* • makes you explore, study carefully (explanation of "analyse") • makes you weigh up options (explanation of "choose") • makes you evaluate options (explanation of "priotitise") • makes you reach a conclusion (explanation of "decide")

ANSWERS FOR HIGHER ENGLISH **215**

Question		Expected Response	Max Mark	Additional Guidance
	(b)	Analyse how the writer's use of language in lines 50—54 ("From … strategies") conveys the contrast between what a gamer looks like from "the outside" and what is happening "inside the gamer's mind". For full marks there must be reference to both "outside" and "inside"; 2 marks may be awarded for reference plus detailed/insightful comment; 1 mark for reference plus more basic comment; 0 marks for reference alone. Possible answers are shown in the "Additional Guidance" column. (Marks may be awarded 2 + 2, 2 + 1 + 1, 1 + 1 + 1 + 1)	4	Possible answers include: *the gamer from "the outside"* • "looks like" suggests this may be an unreliable perspective, a superficial, unquestioning way to approach an analysis of gamers • "fury" suggests the gamer is behaving in an impulsive, uncontrolled way; everything is being done at top speed, in a blur of unthinking activity • "clicking" suggests mindless, repetitive activity • "shooting" suggests destructive, homicidal activity • "clicking and shooting" automatic, unthinking, mechanical, robotic, repetitive … • the general simplicity of the penultimate sentence (especially when compared to the much more complex final sentence) heightens the impression that this is a naïve, simplistic way to view gamers *the gamer on the inside* • "peer" suggests an active approach involving close examination • "turns out" suggests a sense of some kind of revelation, surprise, discovery • "another creature" suggests something mysterious, surprising, unexpected, interesting but hard to define, a new form of life we didn't know existed • use of colon introduces a detailed description of the full range of intellectual activities involved in gaming • balance/repetition of "some of them" stresses range of activities involved • contrast in "snap judgements … long-term strategies" shows range of important decision-making skills involved from quick, smart thinking to overall planning • "judgements" suggests wise, fair thinking • "strategies" suggests considered, creative thinking

Passage 2

Question		Expected Response	Max Mark	Additional Guidance

6.		Look at both passages.
		
		 The writers disagree about video games.
		
		 Identify three key areas on which they disagree.
		
		 You should support the points by referring to important ideas in both passages.
		
		 You may answer this question in continuous prose or in a series of developed bullet points.
		
		 Candidates can use bullet points in this final question, or write a number of linked statements.
		
		 Approach to marking is shown in the "Additional Guidance column.
		
		 Key areas of disagreement are shown in the grid below. Other answers are possible.
			5	The following guidelines should be used:
				 Five marks — identification of three key areas of agreement with detailed/insightful use of supporting evidence
				 Four marks — identification of three key areas of agreement with appropriate use of supporting evidence
				 Three marks — identification of three areas of agreement
				 Two marks — identification of two key areas of agreement
				 One mark — identification of one key area of agreement
				 Zero marks — failure to identify any key areas of agreement and/or misunderstanding of the task
				 NB: a candidate who identifies only two key areas of agreement may be awarded up to a maximum of four marks, as follows
				 • two marks for identification of two key areas of agreement
				   plus:
				   either
				 • a further mark for appropriate use of supporting evidence to a total of three marks
				   or
				 • a further two marks for detailed /insightful use of supporting evidence to a total of four marks
				 A candidate who identifies only one key area of agreement may be awarded up to a maximum of two marks, as follows
				 • one mark for identification of one key area of agreement
				 • a further mark for use of supporting evidence to a total of two marks

ANSWERS FOR HIGHER ENGLISH

	Area of Disagreement	Steven Johnson	Boris Johnson
1	general status	they are viewed as pointless, but they are not	they are harmful, narcotically addictive
2	intellectual benefits	they develop the brain in a number of ways	they require no thought or effort
3	educational benefits	high level thinking skills are developed	they may pretend to be educational but are totally lacking in educational value; a threat to literacy
4	the challenge involved	they can appear simple but are often very complex the process is more important than the (often simplistic) content	they encourage slovenly behaviour and thinking
5	the reward(s) involved	they are at times extremely hard unlike other entertainment, pleasure is not immediate	they offer immediate and simple pleasures

PAPER 2 — CRITICAL READING

SECTION 1 — Scottish Text

- Candidates should gain credit for their understanding, analysis and evaluation of the extract and either the whole play or novel, or other poems and short stories by the writer.
- In the final 10-mark question the candidate should answer the question in either a series of linked statements, or in bullet points.

Detailed marking instructions for each question

SCOTTISH TEXT (DRAMA)

Text 1 — *Drama* — *The Slab Boys* by John Byrne

Question	Expected Answer(s)	Max Mark	Additional Guidance
1.	2 marks awarded for detailed/insightful comment plus quotation/referenche; 1 mark for more basic comment plus quotation/reference; 0 marks for quotation/reference alone. Possible answers are shown in the "Additional Guidance" column. (Marks may be awarded 2 + 1, 1 + 1 + 1)	3	Possible answers include: - Spanky's hesitation in e.g. "We'd like to present this little...er...this token of ...er..." suggests sympathy for loss of his job and awkwardness about being sincere now, due to their previously mocking behaviour towards him - "Are you going to shut your face...Shorty?" offhand and insulting vocabulary suggest the familiar exasperation expressed towards Hector, despite current sympathy for him - Spanky's skirting around the subject/use of euphemism to describe losing his job, "We know it's come as a bit of a surprise...you having to leave" suggests attempt to be tactful and not embarrass or hurt Hector - Phil's unsuccessful attempt to be more articulate than Spanky — "What Spanky ... och, here" suggests he, too, feels uncomfortable in the unusual role of kindness towards Hector
2.	2 marks awarded for detailed/insightful comment plus quotation/reference; 1 mark for more basic comment plus quotation/reference; 0 marks for quotation/reference alone. Possible answers are shown in the "Additional Guidance" column. (Marks may be awarded 2 + 2, 2 + 1 + 1, 1 + 1 + 1 + 1)	4	Possible answers include: - Hector's comical repetition of "Eh?" emphasises his lack of understanding as Phil and Spanky try to commiserate with him for the (supposed) loss of his job - Repetition of "Till you get another job" by Phil and Spanky, culminating in climax of their saying it together builds up sense of their frustration that he does not seem to understand what they are commiserating with him about - Hector's statement of "I've already got another job" is a bathetic moment, echoing their repeated statements about his needing another job - Phil's question "Is there a mobile Broo outside?" emphasises the absurdity of the idea that he might have another job already - Spanky and Phil's exclamation in unison, "What????" is a comical climax which conveys their incredulity that he has been promoted - Hector's comment that he feels unwell is echoed by Spanky, "Me too", with the contrasting meaning: Spanky is sickened that Hector should be promoted; Hector feels sick with excitement

ANSWERS FOR HIGHER ENGLISH **217**

Question	Expected Answer(s)	Max Mark	Additional Guidance
3.	2 marks awarded for detailed/insightful comment plus quotation/reference; 1 mark for more basic comment plus quotation/reference; 0 marks for quotation/reference alone. Possible answers are shown in the "Additional Guidance" column. (Marks may be awarded 2 + 1, 1 + 1 + 1)	3	Possible answers include: • Repetition of questions: "...guess what?...how about that?" suggests his excitement about starting work and/or insensitivity to the fact that he is given this chance because of Phil losing his job • "Where are the gum crystals kept again?" matter of fact question suggests that he is getting started right away, with no regard for the trauma being suffered by Phil • "Oh...message on..." broken sentences said while looking for gum crystals suggests his offhand attitude to the message which is so important to Phil/his selfish interest in small concerns of his own rather than vital issues of others • Blunt statement of "You didn't get in" suggests his indifference to the blow this message will cause for Phil/an element of enjoyment of Phil's devastation • "...something like that..." lack of specific detail conveys how unimportant this information is to him/dismissive approach to something so important to another person
4.	Candidates may choose to answer in bullet points in this final question, or write a number of linked statements. Possible answers are shown in the "Additional Guidance" column.	10	Up to 2 marks can be achieved for identifying elements of commonality as identified in the question, i.e. theme of opportunity. A further 2 marks can be achieved for reference to the extract given. 6 additional marks can be awarded for discussion of similar references to at least one other part of the text. <u>In practice this means:</u> Identification of commonality (2) e.g. Opportunity is not equally or fairly available: it depends on factors such as social class, education, family connections (1) Lack of real opportunity leads to feelings of cynicism and disillusion, exemplified by the attitudes of Phil and Spanky (1) From the extract: 2 marks for detailed/insightful comment plus quotation/reference; 1 mark for more basic comment plus quotation/reference; 0 marks for quotation alone. e.g. Phil, though talented, is rejected by the art college, therefore not given the opportunity to develop his talent: there is a sense that this background, from 'Feegie', and lack of formal education is held against him (2) From at least one other part of the text: as above for 6 marks Possible answers include: • Phil and Spanky resent the lack of opportunities open to them since joining the slab room, claiming that they would be rewarded more if they were masons • Frustration of the slab boys at being stuck in the slab room, with no desk in sight, is clear e.g. Spanky who has been in the slab room for three years and, at the end, is told he might get a desk in eighteen months • Alan, with his education, social class and family commitments has expectations of greater opportunity e.g. he is not over-impressed with his salary of £3 (which is a lot of money to the slab boys) • Opportunities in love also come to those with more money etc., shown by Lucille agreeing to go to the Staffie with Alan, as long as he picks her up in his father's car • Jack accuses Phil and Spanky of destroying Hector's opportunities by mocking him for his eagerness to learn : he wants to give Hector a chance as a designer

218 ANSWERS FOR HIGHER ENGLISH

Text 2 — *Drama — The Cheviot, the Stag and the Black, Black Oil* by John McGrath

Question	Expected Answer(s)	Max Mark	Additional Guidance
5.	For full marks candidates should deal with both characters but not necessarily in equal measure. 2 marks awarded for detailed/insightful comment plus quotation/reference; 1 mark for more basis comment plus quotation/reference; 0 marks for quotation/reference alone. Possible answers are shown in the "Additional Guidance" column. (Marks may be awarded 2 + 2, 2 + 1 + 1, 1 + 1 + 1 + 1)	4	Possible answers include: Lady Phosphate • Reference to Queen implies personal friendship, suggesting over-inflated sense of her own importance • Repetition of "what?" affectation suggests social posturing/shallowness of character • Over-blown and clichéd language — "divine", "rugged beauty", "abound" — suggests lack of sincerity/pretentiousness • Use of literary quotation "Oh listen … sound" to convey supposed intellectual superiority/lack of authenticity Lord Crask • "Has your ladyship sampled the salmon?" shows eagerness to ingratiate/impress • Unnecessary use of full title to stress status/joint membership of upper classes suggests his pride and arrogance • "120,000 acres … most of it" — comical juxtaposition of large figure with comment on true extent of land suggests boastfulness
6.	2 marks awarded for detailed/insightful comment plus quotation/reference; 1 mark for more basic comment plus quotation/reference; 0 marks for quotation/reference alone. Possible answers are shown in the "Additional Guidance" column. (Marks may be awarded 2 + 2, 2 + 1 + 1, 1 + 1 + 1 + 1)	4	Possible answers include: • Lord Crask's misunderstanding of "capital" suggests the upper class's obsession with wealth and power • Comic exchange of "Wapping … Topping … No Wapping" mocks the upper class's/highlights their ridiculous nature • Lord Crask offers Lochinver when Lady Phosphate asks for "a small port", demonstrating his limited understanding/lack of thought for the local population • Lord Crask offers a bush as toilet facilities suggesting that the sophistication of the upper classes is just a veneer/they are no different from anyone else • Reference to Lady Phosphate's "sten gun" — inappropriately over the top for grouse shooting — suggests her lack of regard for the natural environment • Ironic understatement "Thon was a nice wee boy" suggests complete disregard for human life
7.	1 mark for comment plus quotation/reference (x2); 0 marks for quotation/reference alone. Possible answers are shown in the "Additional Guidance" column. (Marks may be awarded 1 + 1)	2	Possible answers include: Local people • Repetition of "We'll clear" suggests their determination to let nothing stand in their way/not to be stopped or criticised • Derogatory use of plural — "the locals" — suggests dismissive/superior attitude to the community Environment • Juxtaposition of "ni-i-ice" with killing of various creatures suggest selfish lack of concern for environment • Pronunciation of "grice" and "trite" suggests unwillingness to learn about the environment

ANSWERS FOR HIGHER ENGLISH **219**

Question	Expected Answer(s)	Max Mark	Additional Guidance
8.	Candidates may choose to answer in bullet points in this final question, or write a number of linked statements. Possible answers are shown in the "Additional Guidance" column.	10	Up to 2 marks can be achieved for identifying elements of commonality as identified in the question, i.e. how the writer explores the issue of social class and its effects. A further 2 marks can be achieved for reference to the extract given. 6 additional marks can be awarded for discussion of similar references to at least one other part of the text. <u>In practice this means:</u> Identification of commonality (2) e.g. land-owning classes in the Scottish Highlands exhibit selfish and exploitative behaviour (1) leading to suffering and destitution of the poor (1) From the extract: 2 marks for detailed/insightful comment plus quotation/reference; 1 mark for more basic comment plus quotation/ reference; 0 marks for quotation/reference alone. e.g. the callous killing of the little boy reveals the contemptuous attitude of the upper classes to the local population (2) From at least one other part of the text: as above for up to 6 marks. Possible answers include: <ul><li>Sellar evicts lower classes from their homes and destroys their livelihood, callously referring to them as "a set of savages"</li><li>International developers are encouraged as long as they adhere to the laws of capitalism, where the end justifies the means, despite the suffering of the poor in the name of 'progress'</li><li>Lord Selkirk, a member of the aristocracy, has a plan to exploit, develop and maximise profits with no regard for the consequences to the local people</li><li>Collective solidarity by the dispossessed against the upper classes has met with varying success, particularly at "The Battle of the Braes", emphasising that ultimately they are powerless</li><li>Many of the indigent characters are known only by their employment or gender — Ghillie, Aberdonian Rigger, First woman — contrasting with the use of titles and individual names of the upper class characters, showing the anonymity of and disregard for the poor</li></ul>

220 ANSWERS FOR HIGHER ENGLISH

Text 3 — *Drama* — *Men Should Weep* by Ena Lamont Stewart

Question	Expected Answer(s)	Max Mark	Additional Guidance
9.	For full marks, both stage directions and dialogue should be covered but not necessarily in equal measure. 2 marks awarded for detailed/insightful comment plus quotation/reference; 1 mark for a more basic comment plus quotation/reference; 0 marks for quotation/reference alone. Possible answers are shown in the "Additional Guidance" column. (Marks may be awarded 2 + 2, 2 + 1 + 1, 1 + 1 + 1 + 1)	4	Possible answers include: Stage directions • "a hard-faced harridan" suggests Lizzie is a mean, cold, aggressive woman • "ignoring the others" suggests Lizzie has no time for social niceties or being pleasant to people • "Mrs Bone goes to help her" suggests Lizzie is quite happy for Granny to struggle on her own whereas Mrs Bone sees the need to lend a hand • "taking the pension book from Mrs Bone" suggests Lizzie's aggressive, greedy personality • "They both stare hard at Lizzie, then shake their heads at each other" suggests their general disbelief/incredulity at Lizzie's attitude towards life Dialogue • "An yer pension book?"/"See's a look at it."/"Ye got the money?" suggests Lizzie's mercenary outlook on life • "Well, it's no Maggie's, it's mines" suggests Lizzie's utterly selfish attitude • "If ye're comin tae bide wi me, ye're no comin tae bide *aff* me" suggests Lizzie's greed and/or her determination not to be taken advantage of • "And whit does she think you're gonna live on for the next week? Air?" aggressive questioning reveals her hard-hearted outlook • "Ach, leave...tae feed." Mrs Harris' speech underlines how lacking in compassion or humanity Lizzie is • "I'm no takin...no room in ma hoose" — suggests Lizzie's cold hearted, uncompromising nature • "That's jist whit I said: *anything human*" emphasises that Mrs Bone feels Lizzie is so lacking in compassion and pity that she is scarcely human
10.	2 marks awarded for detailed/insightful comment plus quotation/reference; 1 mark for a more basic comment plus quotation/reference; 0 marks for quotation/reference alone. Possible answers are shown in the "Additional Guidance" column. (Marks may be awarded 2 + 2, 2 + 1 + 1, 1 + 1 + 1 + 1)	4	Possible answers include: • "ye aul miser"/"at fifty percent" suggests outrage at Lizzie's obsession with making money • "A bargain? Frae you?" suggests incredulity that Lizzie could act in a generous manner • "Veloory hat...bird on tap" mockery suggests their contempt for Lizzie's pretensions • "A bit whit? Pinchin?" suggests recognition of Lizzie's true nature • "No roon aboot here ye couldnae. They a ken ye." conveys a contemptuous awareness of Lizzie's reputation
11.	2 marks awarded for a detailed/insightful explanation; 1 mark for a more basic explanation; 0 marks for quotation/reference alone. Possible answers are shown in the "Additional Guidance" column. (Marks may be awarded 2, 1 + 1)	2	Possible answers include: • Granny represents the older generation who are dependent on others • Granny's situation highlights the poverty which often accompanied old age at that time • As a woman, she has no status or independence in the society of the time • She represents the vulnerable in a harsh world as she moves from household to household • Her lack of autonomy highlights the devastating effects of poverty • She represents the difficulty of family responsibility e.g. there is no room for her when Isa and Alec are made homeless

ANSWERS FOR HIGHER ENGLISH **221**

Question	Expected Answer(s)	Max Mark	Additional Guidance
12.	Candidates may choose to answer in bullet points in this final question, or write a number of linked statements. Possible answers are shown in the "Additional Guidance" column.	10	Up to 2 marks can be achieved by identifying elements of commonality as identified in the question, i.e. how the writer develops the theme of community. A further 2 marks can be achieved for reference to the extract given. 6 additional marks can be awarded for discussion of similar references to at least one other part of the text. <u>In practice this means:</u> Identification of commonality (2) e.g. community is important in this society because of the support and compassion people offer each other (1) although they can also be judgmental, opinionated, intrusive (1) From the extract: 2 marks for detailed/insightful comment plus quotation/reference; 1 mark for more basic comment plus quotation/reference; 0 marks for quotation/reference alone. e.g. Mrs Bone and Mrs Harris support Maggie by sitting with Granny while she is waiting to be collected/by defending Maggie from attack by Lizzie and are not afraid to openly pass judgement on Lizzie's behaviour and morals (2) From elsewhere in the text: as above for up to 6 marks Possible answers include: • Maggie's neighbours often help her with Granny, with baby-sitting and the support neighbours offer each other is an integral part of how this impoverished society operates. Maggie says, "Folks like us hev tae depend on their neighbours when they're needin help." • Maggie's neighbours are mostly compassionate and kind: they really worry about Bertie's serious illness; they keep up Granny's spirits; they take pleasure in Maggie's improved fortunes in the final act. As Maggie says, "Oh, they're no bad — they're coorse but kind." • Women play a central role in this community and there is a sense that they share lives which men do not understand or in which men contribute to women's problems • Members of the community are quite open in passing judgements and voicing criticisms of their husbands, of the younger generation, even of Maggie's new hat: "Whit the hell made ye tak *red*?" • Maggie and John worry about community opinions, whereas the younger generation, such as Jenny and Isa, are happy to flout the traditional values that their neighbours largely represent. Jenny says to her father, "Whit do I care whit the neighbours thinks?"

222 ANSWERS FOR HIGHER ENGLISH

SCOTTISH TEXT (PROSE)

Text 1 — *Prose* — *The Red Door* by Iain Crichton Smith

Question	Expected Answer(s)	Max Mark	Additional Guidance
13.	For full marks, candidates must deal with both the door and the surroundings, but not necessarily in equal measure. 2 marks awarded for detailed/insightful comment plus quotation/reference; 1 mark for more basic comment plus quotation/reference; 0 marks for quotation/reference alone. Possible answers are shown in the "Additional Guidance" column. (Marks may be awarded 2 + 2, 2 + 1 + 1, 1 + 1 + 1 + 1)	4	Possible answers include: Door • "painted very lovingly" suggests care had been taken to ensure the door looked beautiful and was not just functional • "shone with a deep inward shine" suggests that the door stood out against its backdrop/had an alluring quality which radiated from within • "looked like a picture/work of art" suggests the door was attractive and now had an importance of its own • "stood out" suggests the door was striking/out of the ordinary Surroundings • "wasn't at all modern/old" suggests the house was dated/behind the times • "intertwined…rusty pipes like snakes" conveys the idea that the house was in need of maintenance/had been neglected • Imagery "intertwined/snake" suggests the house was constricting/restraining its occupant • "drab landscape" implies that it was uninspiring/dull/gloomy set against the brightness of the door • Dismissal of more harmonious colours "blue/green" highlights the surroundings were now tedious/uninspiring to Murdo
14.	2 marks awarded for detailed/insightful comment plus quotation/reference; 1 mark for more basic comment plus quotation/reference; 0 marks for quotation/reference alone. Possible answers are shown in the "Additional Guidance" column. (Marks may be awarded 2 + 2, 2 + 1 + 1, 1 + 1 + 1 + 1)	4	Possible answers include: • "morning was breaking/blue smoke was ascending" symbolises that the new day for the villagers was a new beginning for Murdo • "a cock was crowing" biblical allusion to signal Murdo's 'betrayal' of his current way of life • "belligerent and heraldic…metallic breast" military connotations suggest that a new assertive/combative spirit had been awakened in Murdo • "oriental and strange" suggests that this feeling was foreign and unfamiliar to him • Murdo's inner dialogue "I have always/I go/I do…" conveys his admission of his disillusionment with his life up to this point • "never had the courage…coloured waistcoat/jacket" reveals Murdo's realisation of his long held desire to be an individual/be different from others/stand out from the crowd • "whiteness of the frost…glimmerings of snow" contrast emphasises the striking physical impact of the door and the symbolic significance of a new beginning for Murdo • "seemed to have its own courage" personification represents Murdo's inner thoughts and wishes

ANSWERS FOR HIGHER ENGLISH **223**

Question	Expected Answer(s)	Max Mark	Additional Guidance
15.	2 marks awarded for detailed/insightful comment plus quotation/reference; 1 mark for more basic comment plus quotation/reference; 0 marks for quotation/reference alone. Possible answers are shown in the "Additional Guidance" column. (Marks may be awarded 2, 1 + 1)	2	Possible answers include: • Use of the question "was he happy?" highlights his uncertainty/doubts about his current way of life • Repetition of "he didn't like" emphasises the level of his discontent/frustration with his situation • "had to keep...smiling face" conveys his inner conflict over the image he projected to others • Climactic nature of "hated them" reveals the strength and depth of his true feelings
16.	Candidates may choose to answer in bullet points in this final question, or write a number of linked statements.	10	Up to 2 marks can be achieved by identifying elements of commonality as identified in the question, i.e. Crichton Smith's exploration of the conflict between individuality and conformity. A further 2 marks can be achieved for reference to the extract given. 6 additional marks can be awarded for discussion of similar references to at least one other short story by Crichton Smith. In practice this means: Identification of commonality (2) e.g. Crichton Smith shows that the impact of trying to fit in with one's surroundings (1) can cause some to suffer and deny their true feelings whilst others find the courage to break free (1) From the extract: 2 marks for detailed/insightful comment plus quotation/reference; 1 mark for more basic comment plus quotation/reference; 0 marks for quotation/reference alone. e.g. the discovery of the red door acts as a catalyst for Murdo to begin a new life where he can be true to himself (2) From at least one other text: as above for up to 6 marks Possible comments include: • *The Telegram* the thin woman has lived in the village for many years yet she is isolated by others as she does not make the same choices as them • *The Painter* William challenges the conventions of the village by painting a realistic picture of the fight and is ostracised as a result • *Mother and Son* John feels trapped by his overbearing, critical mother but is compelled by a sense of duty to stay with her thus denying his true self • *In Church* the 'priest' is a deserter who becomes a murderer as he could not conform to the expectations of war • *The Crater* the need to conform to the expected nature of an officer leads Robert to conceal his fears on the battlefield

224 ANSWERS FOR HIGHER ENGLISH

Text 2 — *Prose* — *Tartan* by George Mackay Brown

Question	Expected Answer(s)	Max Mark	Additional Guidance
17.	2 marks awarded for detailed/ insightful comment plus quotation/ reference; 1 mark for more basic comment plus quotation/reference; 0 marks for quotation/reference alone. Possible answers are shown in the "Additional Guidance" column. (Marks may be awarded 2 + 2, 2 + 1 + 1, 1 + 1 + 1 + 1)	4	Possible answers include: • "muttering and sighing" suggests ongoing nature of deep grief/despair at loss of the future • Contrast between Kol's energy "leapt...loud beserk yell" and the stillness and quiet in the room • "might have been a fly buzzing...paid to him" comparison with "fly buzzing" conveys how completely unimportant/ irrelevant the Viking raid — normally an event of fear and danger — is in comparison to loss of child • Parallel structure of the old woman's sentences "I thought to see you a shepherd...Or maybe you would be a man...Or you might have been a holy priest" suggests repetitive chant to convey the primal sense of grief • "...shepherd...fisherman...man with lucky acres...holy priest" conveys the range of possible futures/hope which have been destroyed by the child's death • "cross...tangled in his cold fingers" conveys bleak finality of the human loss by creating a picture of the child's fingers, already cold • "crossed themselves in the door": simple description of the Vikings' action conveys the sense that even they are awed and moved by his death • "slunk out like a dog" suggests Kol's shame at the inappropriateness of his leap into the room
18.	2 marks awarded for detailed/ insightful comment plus quotation/ reference; 1 mark for more basic comment plus quotation/reference; 0 marks for quotation/reference alone. Possible answers are shown in the "Additional Guidance" column. (Marks may be awarded 2 + 2, 2 + 1 + 1, 1 + 1 + 1 + 1)	4	Possible answers include: • "Strangers from the sea...you are welcome...I ask you to accept ale" exaggerated nature of welcome, under the circumstances i.e. they are Viking raiders, suggests insincerity/attempt to manipulate them • "They are good people here, except for the man who lives..." use of "they" distances himself from the other people of Durness/sees himself as superior and in a position to judge the others • "he will not pay me for the cloth I wove for him last winter" accusatory tone by which he attempts to gain the support of the Vikings against one of his own community • "he and his wife and his snovelly-nosed children" dismissive and distasteful description of Duncan's family suggests his feelings of superiority towards them • "Take it, take it by all means" repetition of "take it" suggests his eagerness to please the Vikings, to ingratiate himself with them • "John has been on the hill all week...I think she is lonely" apparently simple statement of facts suggests her isolation and vulnerability and even hints at the idea that she is sexual prey, indicating how low and disloyal his attitude is
19.	1 mark for comment plus quotation/ reference (x2); 0 marks for quotation/reference alone. Possible answers are shown in the "Additional Guidance" column. (Marks awarded 1 + 1)	2	Possible answers include: • Havard's 'retrospective' threat to Malcolm: "If it (the ale) had been sour, we would have stretched you..." suggests his aggression/bullying quality (though perhaps said in a jocular way) • Arnor's decision to "settle matters" with Duncan on behalf of Malcolm, along with "Now we need our cups filled again" suggests his desire to be seen as in command • Kol's staggering, combined with his bravado claim "Doubtless somebody will pay for this" suggests his boastful and belligerent attitude • Sven's reply to Malcolm's offer of the tartan cloth: "We were going to take it in any case" suggests his determination to show Malcolm who is in charge, despite Malcolm's attempts to manipulate/be courteous

ANSWERS FOR HIGHER ENGLISH **225**

Question	Expected Answer(s)	Max Mark	Additional Guidance
20.	Candidates may choose to answer in bullet points in this final question, or write a number of linked statements. Possible answers are shown in the "Additional Guidance" column.	10	Up to 2 marks can be achieved for identifying elements of commonality as identified in the question, i.e. the relationship between the individual and the community. A further 2 marks can be achieved for reference to the extract given. 6 additional marks can be awarded for discussion of similar references to at least one other short story by Mackay Brown. In practice this means: Identification of commonality (2) e.g. Individuals will usually show loyalty and commitment to the community (1) though some will rebel against or betray the community values to achieve their own fulfilment/achieve their own ends (1) From the extract: 2 marks for detailed/insightful comment plus quotation/reference; 1 mark for more basic comment plus quotation/reference; 0 marks for quotation alone. e.g. Malcolm the weaver attempts to exploit the Viking raid for his own selfish aims to settle old scores within the community, such as the non-payment for cloth, to gain favour with the raiders (2) From at least one other text: as above for 6 marks Possible answers include: • *A Time to Keep* loyalty to the community can mean suspicion of 'outsiders' such as Inge (from just over the hill) and Bill (a whaler). Bill's sense of their 'separateness' contributes to the negative relationship he has with the other men in the community • *A Time to Keep* Bill is appalled by the community taking charge of his wife's death, represented by the women's show of grief expressed in "litany of the dead person's virtues...most of them lies", and the minister's comments. He rejects their sentimental clichés about going to "a better place" • *The Bright Spade* seven men show loyalty and heroism in setting off into the storm to look for food for the community- but the sacrifice of their lives in fact helps no one • *The Wireless Set* Howie feels he is bringing progress and development to the 'backward' community by bringing home the wireless set; his attitude contrasts with that of his parents, who uphold the traditional values of the community and view the outside world with suspicion • *The Eye of the Hurricane* Barclay's initial sense of superiority and objectification of the community ("simple uncomplicated people") gives way to genuine involvement in the face of Cpt. Stevens' suffering and flawed but heroic humanity

226 ANSWERS FOR HIGHER ENGLISH

Text 3 — *Prose — The Trick is to Keep Breathing* by Janice Galloway

Question	Expected Answer(s)	Max Mark	Additional Guidance
21.	2 marks awarded for detailed/insightful comment plus quotation/reference; 1 mark for more basic comment plus quotation/reference; 0 marks for quotation/reference alone. Possible answers are shown in the "Additional Guidance" column. (Marks may be awarded 2 + 2, 2 + 1 + 1, 1 + 1 + 1 + 1)	4	Possible answers include: • "protection against witches" suggests something evil/sinister about the place • "well outside the place...be part of" use of irony emphasises the sense of isolation/remoteness • "undesirables"/"difficult tenants"/"shunters"/"overspill" suggests the inhabitants are unwanted in the main town • Contrast between how it is meant to appear/idyllic setting eg "wild currant bushes"/"tiny, twisty roads" and what it is like in reality eg "pubs with plastic beer glasses"/"kids use the bends to play chicken" • "lying low"/"leaping out" suggests children are wild/out of control • "buses go slow"/"infrequent" emphasises remoteness/isolation • "graffiti" — vandalism indicates neglect • "It rains a lot." short sentence highlights the sense of misery emphasised by the weather
22.	2 marks awarded for detailed/insightful comment plus quotation/reference; 1 mark for more basic comment plus quotation/reference; 0 marks for quotation/reference alone. Possible answers are shown in the "Additional Guidance" column. (Marks may be awarded 2 + 2, 2 + 1 + 1, 1 + 1 + 1 + 1)	4	Possible answers include: • "never surrenders first time" personification suggests that the key refuses to be found easily • "rummage" suggests frantic search/desperation • "as though begging to be mugged" comparison suggests Joy's feelings of vulnerability • "Not mine." minor sentence emphasises her lack of belonging/ownership • "grit"/"litter" emphasises how Joy finds the place unwelcoming/unhomely • "withered leaves" suggests Joy's obsession with death/decay • "slaters run frantic"/"insects make me sick"/"disgust me" emphasises Joy's irrationality/neurotic nature • "fight my way inside" emphasises Joy's desperation to escape the outside world. • "gritty little packets"/"skeletons outside"/"too many eyes"/"unpredictable legs" suggests Joy's fear
23.	2 marks awarded for detailed/insightful comment plus quotation/reference; 1 mark for more basic comment plus quotation/reference; 0 marks for quotation/reference alone. Possible answers are shown in the "Additional Guidance" column. (Marks may be awarded 2, 1 + 1)	2	Possible answers include: • "Try to feel (the other continent)" suggests her desperation to escape • "I find the bottle...I put an envelope...sitting the bottle aside...reshape the cushions..." list of activities suggests she is trying to impose order/structure on her own situation • "But things have to be set in place." short sentence emphasises her desire for control • "Stillness helps..."/"It keeps me contained" short sentences emphasise her attempts at self-control/order

ANSWERS FOR HIGHER ENGLISH 227

Question	Expected Answer(s)	Max Mark	Additional Guidance
24.	Candidates may choose to answer in bullet points in this final question, or write a number of linked statements. Possible answers are shown in the "Additional Guidance" column.	10	Up to 2 marks can be achieved for identifying elements of commonality as identified in the question, i.e. how Galloway explores the impact of loneliness. A further 2 marks can be achieved for reference to the extract given. 6 additional marks can be awarded for discussion of similar references to at least one other part of the text. In practice this means: Identification of commonality (2) e.g. devastating life changing, destructive nature of loneliness (1) can affect mental health/ability to communicate/ability to form relationships (1) From the extract: 2 marks for detailed/insightful comment plus quotation/reference; 1 mark for more basic comment plus quotation/reference; 0 marks for quotation alone. e.g. Joy attempts to cope with loneliness by focusing on distracting herself and creating a sense of order in her surroundings: "A lot depends on stillness later and I have to get a lot of moving around out of my system now." (2) From at least one other part of the text: as above for up to 6 marks Possible answers include: • Joy tries to cope with her loneliness following Michael's death by engaging in a number of casual relationships with men • Joy distracts herself from her loneliness by engaging in a variety of mundane activities e.g. sewing, reading magazines, various rituals including bathing etc. • Joy forces herself to engage in the activities suggested by her friend Marianne, including visiting Marianne's mother, Ellen, regularly • In order to hide her loneliness from others, Joy attempts to appear upbeat and in control to others for example Tony, Myra etc. • Joy attempts to alleviate her loneliness after Michael's death by trying to re-create his physical presence e.g. spraying his aftershave

228 ANSWERS FOR HIGHER ENGLISH

Text 4 — *Prose — Sunset Song* by Lewis Grassic Gibbon

Question	Expected Answer(s)	Max Mark	Additional Guidance
25.	2 marks awarded for detailed/insightful comment plus quotation/reference; 1 mark for more basic comment plus quotation/reference; 0 marks for quotation/reference alone. Possible answers are shown in the "Additional Guidance" column. (Marks may be awarded 2 + 1, 1 + 1 + 1)	3	Possible answers include: • "strong on Rich and Poor being Equal" suggests firmly held socialist principles; a belief that all wealth should be shared out evenly • "Broke he might be but he wasn't mean" suggests that regardless of his own financial problems, Chae is a generous host • "there was broth..." suggests that he provides an abundance of food which clearly signifies his gratitude • "he could hold to the turnip-field" suggests Chae has a lively sense of humour which often reveals the ridiculous in his fellow man
26.	2 marks awarded for detailed/insightful comment plus quotation/reference; 1 mark for more basic comment plus quotation/reference; 0 marks for quotation/reference alone. Possible answers are shown in the "Additional Guidance" column. (Marks may be awarded 2 + 1, 1 + 1 + 1)	3	Possible answers include: • "his great lugs like red clouts hung out to dry" suggests comical physical appearance (his prominent ears compared to washing on a line) • "as though he hadn't seen food for a fortnight" gross exaggeration to convey his greedy consumption of the meal • "like a colie ta'en off its chain" overstated comparison to a ravenous dog just released • "a spree to the pair of them" sense that this is a bout of self-indulgence rather than part of a day's work • *"fair an expert getting"* condescending use of the word "expert" has the intention of belittling Chris • *"The kitchen's more her style than the College."* patronising judgement reveals his own prejudice
27.	2 marks awarded for detailed/insightful comment plus quotation/reference; 1 mark for more basic comment plus quotation/reference; 0 marks for quotation/reference alone. Possible answers are shown in the "Additional Guidance" column. (Marks may be awarded 2 + 2, 2 + 1 + 1, 1 + 1 + 1 + 1)	4	Possible answers include: • "the yokels and clowns everlasting" suggests Chris resents the total disregard for learning displayed by those she perceives as country bumpkins and forever stupid • "dull-brained and crude" suggests Chris rejects those who have laughed as slow-witted and vulgar • "a coarse thing, learning" suggests many see no refining qualities in knowledge • "a lot of damn nonsense that put them above themselves" suggests many perceive education as valueless and will lead to a false sense of superiority in their offspring • "give you their lip" suggests many think that education leads to impudence • "to put him up level with the Rich" suggests Chae contradicts the views of others by declaring that education provides social equality • "the more of sense and the less of kirks and ministers" suggests Long Rob agrees with Chae and states that education improves a person's ability to think clearly and reject organised religion • "was shamed as she thought" suggests Chris revises her view of Chae and Long Rob whose kindness she recognises, despite their lack of possessions

ANSWERS FOR HIGHER ENGLISH **229**

Question	Expected Answer(s)	Max Mark	Additional Guidance
28.	Candidates may choose to answer in bullet points in this final question, or write a number of linked statements. Possible answers are shown in the "Additional Guidance" column.	10	Up to 2 marks can be achieved for identifying elements of commonality as identified in the question, i.e. Chris's conflicting emotions towards the community in Kinraddie. A further 2 marks can be achieved for reference to the extract given. 6 additional marks can be awarded for discussion of similar references to at least one other part of the text. <u>In practice this means:</u> Identification of commonality (2) e.g. Chris is appalled by the small-mindedness of the Speak (1), but she values the innate kindness of her neighbours in times of need (1) From the extract: 2 marks for detailed/insightful comment plus quotation/reference; 1 mark for more basic comment plus quotation/reference; 0 marks for quotation alone. e.g. Chris is angered by Munro's patronising comments, aimed to reduce her to his servant, but she also acknowledges the considerate nature of Chae and Long Rob (2) From at least one other part of the text: as above for up to 6 marks Possible answers include: • The two Chrisses are torn between love of school and learning ("you hated the land and the coarse speak of the folk") and her love of the land and its people • Chris is angered by the rumours about Will and Mollie Douglas, but she begins to learn about relationships after meeting Mollie on the road • Chris is aware of gossip about the Strachans, their financial problems and insurance money from the fire, but she also knows that she, her family and the community do all they can to assist at Peesie's Knapp • Chris is initially untroubled by the community's view of her seemingly heartless lack of sorrow at the death of her father, but she is comforted by their neighbourly concern at the graveside • Chris disregards the community's sense of outrage that she should marry Ewan so soon after her father's death, but she is delighted that so many locals should celebrate her wedding and wish both of them well

230 ANSWERS FOR HIGHER ENGLISH

Text 5 — *Prose — The Cone-Gatherers* by Robin Jenkins

Question	Expected Answer(s)	Max Mark	Additional Guidance
29.	2 marks awarded for detailed/insightful comment plus quotation/reference; 1 mark for more basic comment plus quotation/reference; 0 marks for quotation/reference alone. Possible answers are shown in the "Additional Guidance" column. (Marks may be awarded 2, 1 + 1)	2	Possible answers include: • "indigo clouds" dark colour suggests the darkening, angry sky • "mustering" suggests soldiers gathering, and reflects the literal and metaphorical storm • "rumbles (of thunder)" onomatopoeia reflects the ominous sound of thunder • "whisked away" suggests the panic of the birds before the storm • "ominous" suggests something powerful/dangerous/frightening • "river of radiance" alliteration/metaphor emphasises the long thin streak of light, shining like water
30.	2 marks awarded for detailed/insightful comment plus quotation/reference; 1 mark for more basic comment plus quotation/reference; 0 marks for quotation/reference alone. Possible answers are shown in the "Additional Guidance" column. (Marks may be awarded 2 + 2, 2 + 1 + 1, 1 + 1 + 1 + 1)	4	Possible answers include: • "frightened and exhilarated" combination suggests tumult of emotions • "frightened" suggests scared/terrified • "exhilarated" suggests a rush of energy/his identification with natural forces • "chattered...sense" suggests he is so overcome with excitement that it affects him physically • "dribble out" suggests he is so overwhelmed he loses control of his actions • "he raised his hand" suggests a need to join with the elements/wants physical contact with them • "meaningless chatters" suggests incoherence due to excitement • "screamed" suggests extreme/heightened reaction
31.	2 marks awarded for detailed/insightful comment plus quotation/reference; 1 mark for more basic comment plus quotation/reference; 0 marks for quotation/reference alone. Possible answers are shown in the "Additional Guidance" column. (Marks may be awarded 2 + 2, 2 + 1 + 1, 1 + 1 + 1 + 1)	4	Possible answers include: • "We'd better get down" indicates that Neil takes responsibility for their safety/makes important decisions • "But up here...dangerous" indicates that Neil is aware of Calum's lack of understanding/takes on role of parent • "I don't like..."/"Did you see..."/"Was it from..." simplicity of language shows Calum's childlike dependence on Neil • Repeated use of Neil's name suggests Calum seeks reassurance/comfort from his big brother • "Was it from heaven...?" suggests Calum's naivety and his reliance on Neil's wisdom • Repeated questions ("In the shed...horse?/"What shed... horse?") indicates Neil's frustration with Calum's childlike ways

ANSWERS FOR HIGHER ENGLISH **231**

Question	Expected Answer(s)	Max Mark	Additional Guidance
32.	Candidates may choose to answer in bullet points in this final question, or write a number of linked statements. Possible answers are shown in the "Additional Guidance" column.	10	Up to 2 marks can be achieved for identifying elements of commonality as identified in the question, i.e. how the writer uses symbolism to develop the central concerns of the text. A further 2 marks can be achieved for reference to the extract given. 6 additional marks can be awarded for discussion of similar references to at least one other part of the text. In practice this means: Identification of commonality (2) e.g. Jenkins uses characters, incidents and setting as representative of wider issues (1) such as the conflict between good and evil/devastation of war/sacrifice of innocence due to cruelty of mankind (1) From the extract: 2 marks for detailed/insightful comment plus quotation/reference; 1 mark for more basic comment plus quotation/reference; 0 marks for quotation alone. e.g. Calum's childlike interpretation of the light on the trees as coming from heaven, despite the danger of the storm, symbolises his innocence/innate goodness (2) From the rest of the text: as above for up to 6 marks Possible answers include: • The deer drive is a small version of what is happening in the outside world and represents the violence humanity is capable of • The presence of the destroyer/planes in this natural setting represent the inescapable conflict between good vs. evil • Calum's death in the tree represents the crucifixion with his blood purifying the world corrupted by Duror • Duror is often associated with a decaying tree representing the evil spreading within him • The cones represent hope for the future/re-birth as after destruction/war new life will grow

232 ANSWERS FOR HIGHER ENGLISH

SCOTTISH TEXT (POETRY)

Text 1 – *Address to the Deil* by Robert Burns

Question	Expected Answer(s)	Max Mark	Additional Guidance
33.	2 marks awarded for detailed/insightful comment plus quotation/reference; 1 mark for more basic comment plus quotation/reference; 0 marks for quotation/reference alone. Possible answers are shown in the "Additional Guidance" column. (Marks may be awarded 2 + 2, 2 + 1 + 1, 1 + 1 + 1 + 1)	4	Possible answers include: • "whatever title suit thee" rather dismissive comment creates an informal/comic tone (especially when contrasted with the introductory quotation from Milton used by Burns) • List of epithets for the Deil (in particular, "Auld Hornie" and "Clootie") convey a slightly affectionate camaraderie between the Deil and the speaker • "cavern grim and sootie" stereotypical view of the Deil's abode is somewhat mocking of the Calvinistic view of Hell • "spairges about...wretches!" ridiculous depiction of Satan torturing damned souls makes the concept of the Deil's actions seem quite comical • "cootie" use of homely term for the Deil's cauldron makes Satan seem domesticated rather than a great force for evil • "Hear me..." use of imperative makes the speaker seem more powerful than Satan, so creating a tongue-in-cheek tone • "I'm sure...gie" the speaker's unlikely camaraderie and mock understanding of the Deil's tasks/ patronising attitude to the Deil creates a humorous tone • "skelp...scaud...squeel" – alliteration highlights the ridiculousness of Satan's supposed tasks • "poor dogs like me...us squeel" the speaker's readiness to admit his sins and accept the stereotypical punishment conveys a child-like impression of small misdemeanours and punishments rather than grave sins
34.	2 marks awarded for detailed/insightful comment plus quotation/reference; 1 mark for more basic comment plus quotation/reference; 0 marks for quotation/reference alone. Possible answers are shown in the "Additional Guidance" column. (Marks may be awarded 2, 1 + 1)	2	Possible answers include: • Repetition/positioning of "great" stresses the immense power and fame of the Deil • "Far kenm'd an' noted"/"travels far" suggests that the Deil is an omnipresent being, known everywhere • "thou's neither lag...nor scaur" listing of the negative qualities which are absent from the Deil makes him seem a supremely confident being • "roarin' lion" use of the metaphor creates impression of bravery/strength/nobility • "a' holes and corners tryin'" suggests once again the Deil's omnipresence/ability to invade all places • "on the strong wind'd tempest flyin'" suggests that the Deil has the power to control/overcome the strongest forces of nature • Parallel structure of "Whyles, on...Whyles, in..." highlights the ability of the Deil to move effortlessly between the greatest and smallest places • "Unseen thou lurks" connotations of menace and threat suggest the Deil is a powerful predator

ANSWERS FOR HIGHER ENGLISH **233**

Question	Expected Answer(s)	Max Mark	Additional Guidance
35.	2 marks awarded for detailed/insightful comment plus quotation/reference; 1 mark for more basic comment plus quotation/reference; 0 marks for quotation/reference alone. Possible answers are shown in the "Additional Guidance" column. (Marks may be awarded 2 + 2, 2 + 1 + 1, 1 + 1 + 1 + 1)	4	Possible answers include: • "I've heard my rev'rend graunie say" the speaker's introduction to this anecdotal section of the poem suggest an old wife's tale, not to be taken seriously • Burns' use of a clichéd description ("lanely glens… auld ruin'd castles…the moon…eldritch croon… dreary, windy, winter night") emphasises that these anecdotes are the stuff of folklore/unbelievable tales • "graunie…douse, honest woman" the tongue-in-cheek description of the speaker's grannie suggests he is aware of the silly nature of these stories but is determined to defend them thus making them seem even less reliable • "bummin'" use of comic vocabulary undermines the seriousness of grannie's tale • Series of anecdotes becomes progressively less believable, with the speaker suggesting a natural reason for the supposed presence of the Deil (an owl's screech, the wind in the trees, the rushes waving, a startled drake) yet still continuing with his assertions of the Deil's presence • "quaick, quaick" use of onomatopoeia adds a comic note when the speaker continues to insist that he has heard/seen the Deil

234 ANSWERS FOR HIGHER ENGLISH

Question	Expected Answer(s)	Max Mark	Additional Guidance
36.	Candidates may choose to answer in bullet points in this final question, or write a number of linked statements. Possible answers are shown in the "Additional Guidance" column.	10	Up to 2 marks can be achieved for identifying elements of commonality as identified in the question, i.e. Burns' use of humour to explore serious issues. A further 2 marks can be achieved for the reference to the extract given. 6 additional marks can be awarded for discussion of similar references to at least one other poem by Burns. In practice this means: Identification of commonality (2), e.g. Burns' satirical/comical observations of characters/religious beliefs/social classes (1) lend power to his, often scathing, condemnation of injustices/Calvinist doctrines/hypocritical moralising (1) From the extract: 2 marks for detailed/insightful comment plus quotation/reference; 1 mark for more basic comment plus quotation/ reference; 0 marks for reference alone. e.g. "Spairges about the brunstane cootie/To scaud poor wretches!" - the exaggerated depiction of Satan personally undertaking the stereotypical tortures of Hell is effective in ridiculing the Calvinistic views of eternal damnation and the punishment of sins. (2) From at least one other poem: as above for up to 6 marks. Possible references include: • *A Man's A Man for A' That* Burns' humorous depictions of the aristocracy are juxtaposed with his admiration for the common man, thereby strengthening his appeal for social equality • *A Poet's Welcome* Burns' satirical comments concerning the gossiping critics of his daughter's social position show the lack of compassion and humanity within the Kirk • *Holy Willie's Prayer* the hypocrisy and bigotry revealed by Willie in his "prayer" allow Burns to satirise the Calvinist doctrine of predestination • *Tam O' Shanter* the humour created by the speaker's po-faced moralising on Tam's foolish behaviour at various points in the poem allows Burns to criticise those who take pleasure in judging others too readily • *Tam O' Shanter* comical anti-climax of final line, reference to horse losing tail serves as a reminder of human frailties

ANSWERS FOR HIGHER ENGLISH 235

Text 2 — *Poetry* — *Valentine* by Carol Ann Duffy

Question	Expected Answer(s)	Max Mark	Additional Guidance
37.	2 marks awarded for detailed/insightful comment plus quotation/reference; 1 mark for more basic comment plus quotation/reference; 0 marks for quotation/reference alone. Possible answers are shown in the "Additional Guidance" column. (Marks may be awarded 2 + 2, 2 + 1 + 1, 1 + 1 + 1 + 1)	4	Possible answers include: Challenges • Isolation/bluntness of the opening line emphasises the strength of the speaker's rejection of traditional gifts • Positioning of "Not" at the start of the line intensifies the speaker's rejection of traditional symbols of love • Given the mundane connotations of "an onion" the incongruity of it as a symbol of love • Subversion of "moon" as a traditional romantic image as it is mundanely described as "wrapped in brown paper" Reinforces • "moon" traditionally associated with romantic evenings • "promises" suggests devotion/commitment/fidelity • "light" suggests something pure and life-enhancing • "undressing" suggests something seductive and sensual
38.	2 marks awarded for detailed/insightful comment plus quotation/reference; 1 mark for more basic comment plus quotation/reference; 0 marks for quotation/reference alone. Possible answers are shown in the "Additional Guidance" column. (Marks may be awarded 2 + 2, 2 + 1 + 1, 1 + 1 + 1 + 1)	4	Possible answers include: • Development of the extended image in "blind you with tears/Like a lover" highlights the pain and suffering that love brings • Imagery of "wobbling photo of grief" suggests the pain/distress caused by a failed/complex relationship • Single line stanza abrupt dismissal of more stereotypical love tokens/straightforward no nonsense approach • Alliteration of "Not a cute card or a kissogram" suggests contempt for predictable/insincere/unthinking view of love • Image of "fierce kiss" to suggest the lingering taste of the onion suggests the difficulty of escaping the relationship/an underlying threat or danger in the relationship • word choice of "possessive" suggests the constricting/controlling nature of the relationship • juxtaposition of "possessive" and "faithful" undermines the notion of commitment in a relationship • bluntness/positioning of "for as long as we are" at end of verse suggests impermanence of love
39.	2 marks awarded for detailed/insightful comment plus quotation/reference; 1 mark for more basic comment plus quotation/reference; 0 marks for quotation/reference alone. Possible answers are shown in the "Additional Guidance" column. (Marks may be awarded 2, 1 + 1)	2	Possible answers include: • "Take it." Moving to an acceptance of a 'real' rather than a superficial view of love • "platinum loops...wedding-ring" the onion (mentioned earlier) becomes associated with the restrictive aspects of marriage/love • "Lethal" suggests movement towards a dark conclusion/dark view of love • "cling to your fingers" echoes earlier ideas of the negative long term effects of a broken relationship/possessiveness within a relationship • "knife" leaves the reader with final thought of love's potential to wound

ANSWERS FOR HIGHER ENGLISH

Question	Expected Answer(s)	Max Mark	Additional Guidance
40.	Candidates may choose to answer in bullet points in this final question, or write a number of linked statements. Possible answers are shown in the "Additional Guidance" column.	10	Up to 2 marks can be achieved for identifying elements of commonality as identified in the question, i.e. how emotional conflict within an individual is explored. A further 2 marks can be achieved for reference to the text given. 6 additional marks can be awarded for discussion of similar references to at least one other poem by Duffy. In practice this means: Identification of commonality (2) e.g. the complexities of human experience can create emotional conflict in an individual's life (1), which can change significantly the individual's personality/ outlook on life (1) From the poem: 2 marks for detailed/insightful comment plus quotation/reference; 1 mark for more basic comment plus quotation/ reference; 0 marks for quotation/reference alone. e.g. the speaker is attracted to other, more positive aspects of love such as intimacy and tenderness but adopts a more realistic/cynical attitude towards love "Not a red rose...onion" (2) From at least one other text: as above for up to 6 marks Possible comments include: • *Anne Hathaway* the speaker is left bereft by the death of her husband, but by remembering the passionate nature of her relationship, she has become more resigned to her loss • *Havisham* the unresolved tension between love and hate that the speaker's rejection provokes, leads to an on-going deterioration in her mental state • *War Photographer* the emotional impact of the horrors the photographer has witnessed in his assignments abroad conflicts with the pride he feels in doing a professional job • *Originally* the unresolved emotional conflict of maintaining identity: where is home and all the emotional baggage the question entails • *Mrs Midas* the unresolved conflicting emotions she feels for her husband: the contempt she feels for his desires which brought about their separation conflicts with the physical intimacy she now misses.

ANSWERS FOR HIGHER ENGLISH   **237**

Text 3 — *Poetry — For my Grandmother Knitting* by Liz Lochhead

Question	Expected Answer(s)	Max Mark	Additional Guidance
41.	For full marks both the past and the present must be dealt with, but not necessarily in equal measure. 2 marks awarded for detailed/insightful comment plus quotation/reference; 1 mark for more basic comment plus quotation/reference; 0 marks for quotation/reference alone. Possible answers are shown in the "Additional Guidance" column. (Marks may be awarded 2 + 2, 2 + 1 + 1, 1 + 1 + 1 + 1)	4	Possible answers include: Past • "sure and skilful hands of the fisher-girl" word choice emphasises sense of control and confidence, despite her youth • "master of your moments" — alliteration/slogan effect conveys sense that she was in charge/on top of the task • "deft and swift" monosyllables and consonance emphasise her skill and speed when gutting the fish • "slit the still-ticking quick silver fish" fast-paced rhythm and repetition of short "I" vowel sound conveys the efficiency and ease with which she tackled the task • "Hard work...of necessity" positioning and choice of words emphasises how much her efforts were needed Present • "There is no need they say" — opening, blunt statement and dismissive tone convey her lack of perceived usefulness • "the needles still move/their rhythms" sense of her passivity/lack of agency emphasised by description of the needles as the active ones, rather than the grandmother • "You are old now": blunt statement positioned at start of Stanza 2, emphasises the definite nature of her plight • "grasp...not so good" — sense of her diminishing alertness/control in the literal and metaphorical use of "grasp"
42.	1 mark for comment plus quotation/reference (x2) 0 marks for quotation/reference alone. Possible answers are shown in the "Additional Guidance" column.	2	Possible answers include: • "hands of the bride" connotations of special/romantic time when hand receives ring/holds hands • "hand-span waist" suggests that she was cherished by her husband/physically dainty and exquisite • "hands...scrubbed his back" suggests devotion/physical closeness with her husband as they worked together in difficult circumstances • "hands...six" suggests the multiple challenges of her life • "scraped...necessary" list of verbs suggests her energy and ability to cope in down-to-earth way
43.	2 marks awarded for detailed/insightful comment plus quotation/reference; 1 mark for more basic comment plus quotation/reference; 0 marks for quotation/reference alone. Possible answers are shown in the "Additional Guidance" column. (Marks may be awarded 2 + 1, 1 + 1 + 1)	4	Possible answers include: • "the kids they say grandma...already" reported speech without punctuation suggests an often-repeated 'lecture' conveying sense of isolation/lack of compassion/lack of communication • Repetition of "too much/too many" emphasises their perception of her uselessness/sense that they repeatedly remind her that her contribution is not needed • "At your window you wave...Sunday" poignant picture of the grandmother waving goodbye conveys sense of her loneliness • "painful hands...shrunken wrists" physical incongruity of hands on tiny wrists suggests how frail and clumsy she now is • "Swollen-jointed...Old" list of adjectives in minor sentences building to the climax of "Old" emphasises the pitiful nature of her physical condition • "as if...how to stop" climactic final line suggests her lack of control over her life

238 ANSWERS FOR HIGHER ENGLISH

Question	Expected Answer(s)	Max Mark	Additional Guidance
44.	Candidates may choose to answer in bullet points in this final question, or write a number of linked statements. Possible answers are shown in the "Additional Guidance" column.	10	Up to 2 marks can be achieved by identifying elements of commonality as identified in the question, i.e. Lochhead's exploration of the theme of personal and/or social change. A further 2 marks can be achieved for reference to the poem given. 6 additional marks can be awarded for discussion of similar references to at least one other poem by Lochhead. In practice this means: Identification of commonality (2) e.g. Lochhead uses characters to represent aspects of life past/present, encouraging us to respond to their experience (1) showing that change can be either positive or negative — destroying valuable aspects of past or looking forward to a more positive future (1) From this poem: 2 marks for detailed/insightful comment plus quotation/reference; 1 mark for more basic comment plus quotation/reference; 0 marks for quotation/reference alone. e.g. the grandmother represents an older Scotland where traditional ways of life e.g. fishing or mining provided security and continuity, which is lacking in the modern world (2) From at least one other text: as above for up to 6 marks Possible comments include: • *Some Old Photographs* sense that Scotland of the past had social cohesion and predictability, e.g. 'all the dads in hats', though this certainty is undermined in "what was/never really" • *View of Scotland/Love Poem* the traditional Hogmanay, with its rituals which everyone followed, has been replaced by a more spontaneous celebration of life — "There is no time like the/present for a kiss" • *Last Supper* change reflected in membership of the 'revenge group' and/or dramatic reaction to partner's betrayal • *My Rival's House* the mother is hostile to change in the relationship with her son and fights against the necessity of his growing up and forming a new relationship • *The Bargain* the speaker's relationship, which thrived in the past but now faces an uncertain future, reflected by their inconclusive visit to the stalls

ANSWERS FOR HIGHER ENGLISH 239

Text 4 — *Poetry — Basking Shark* by Norman MacCaig

Question	Expected Answer(s)	Max Mark	Additional Guidance
45.	2 marks awarded for detailed/insightful comment plus quotation/reference; 1 mark for more basic comment plus quotation/reference; 0 marks for quotation/reference alone. Possible answers are shown in the "Additional Guidance" column. (Marks may be awarded 2, 1 + 1)	2	Possible answers include: • "stub" onomatopoeia suggests sudden/unexpected contact • "where none should be" conveys the idea of things being out of the ordinary/out of place • "To have it (rise)" emphasises disbelief at the action • "rise" apparent action by 'rock' suggests surprise/incredulity • parenthetical aside implying the speaker does not want to repeat the experience "(too often)" • "slounge" onomatopoeic qualities suggest slow, relaxed movement of shark in its own element where he is the intruder
46.	2 marks awarded for detailed/insightful comment plus quotation/reference; 1 mark for more basic comment plus quotation/reference; 0 marks for quotation/reference alone. Possible answers are shown in the "Additional Guidance" column. (Marks may be awarded 2 + 2, 2 + 1 + 1, 1 + 1 + 1 + 1)	4	Possible answers include: • "But not (too often) — though enough." evaluative comment suggests that the speaker continues to dwell upon the experience • "I count as gain" suggests that despite initial unease, he has come to recognise the value of the experience • "displaced" word choice suggests the shift in his thinking • "shoggled" suggests shaken out of a comfortable mind-set • "decadent townee" self-derogatory comment suggests his sudden recognition of his superficiality/alienation from nature • "shook" suggests that the speaker was literally and metaphorically disturbed by the experience • "wrong branch...family tree" suggests that he is now less sure of his place in the evolutionary framework
47.	2 marks awarded for detailed/insightful comment plus quotation/reference; 1 mark for more basic comment plus quotation/reference; 0 marks for quotation/reference alone. Possible answers are shown in the "Additional Guidance" column. (Marks may be awarded 2 + 2, 2 + 1 + 1, 1 + 1 + 1 + 1)	4	Possible answers include: • metaphor of "Swish up...clearer" suggests the initial confusion as a result of the encounter has led to greater clarity • "I saw me...emerging" suggests rebirth of his sense of himself/humanity • "in one fling" parenthesis emphasises the sudden epiphany • "emerging from the slime of everything" suggests a realisation of humanity's primeval origins • "So who's the monster?" question emphasises that the speaker has been forced to rethink humanity's superiority to apparently primitive beings • "made me grow pale" suggests physical shock at realisation of humanity's insignificance/depravity • "sail after sail" repetition suggests realisation of grandeur/majesty/timelessness of the shark

240 ANSWERS FOR HIGHER ENGLISH

Question	Expected Answer(s)	Max Mark	Additional Guidance
48.	Candidates may choose to answer in bullet points in this final question, or write a number of linked statements. Possible answers are shown in the "Additional Guidance" column.	10	Up to 2 marks can be achieved for identifying elements of commonality as identified in the question, i.e. how MacCaig uses symbolism to develop central ideas in his poetry. A further 2 marks can be achieved for reference to the text given. 6 additional marks can be awarded for discussion of similar references to at least one other poem MacCaig. <u>In practice this means:</u> Identification of commonality (2) e.g. MacCaig uses people/objects/places as symbols to explore important human issues/relationships (1) and in doing so makes us re-evaluate/consider our own views (1) From the poem: 2 marks for detailed/insightful comment plus quotation/reference; 1 mark for more basic comment plus quotation/reference; 0 marks for quotation alone. e.g. the shark represents the apparently primitive aspect of nature, however MacCaig's reflections challenge our perception of our superiority (2) From at least one other text: as above for up to 6 marks. Possible answers include: • *Visiting Hour* "withered hand trembles on its stalk" symbolises the fragility of human life and makes us consider our own mortality • *Assisi* the contrast between the inner spiritual beauty and the outer physical appearance of the beggar makes us reflect on appearance against reality • *Aunt Julia* she represents a lost heritage which makes us consider the importance of valuing and preserving the past • *Memorial* "the carousel of language" represents the vitality of relationships and communication he can't recapture provoking thoughts on finality/loss • *Sounds of the Day* "the bangle of ice...numb" represents the pain and deadening effect of loss which makes us consider love as a destructive force

ANSWERS FOR HIGHER ENGLISH **241**

Text 5 — *Poetry — Heroes* by Sorley MacLean

Question	Expected Answer(s)	Max Mark	Additional Guidance
49.	2 marks awarded for detailed/insightful comment plus quotation/reference; 1 mark for more basic comment plus quotation/reference; 0 marks for quotation/reference alone. Possible answers are shown in the "Additional Guidance" column. (Marks may be awarded 2, 1 + 1)	2	• Repeated use of "not" and "nor" emphasises the point that the soldier is not one of the Gaelic/Scottish heroes listed/mentioned • "Englishman" general term sounds insignificant when set against Scottish/Gaelic heroes mentioned/listed • "poor little chap" diminutive word choice/description makes the soldier seem unheroic • "chubby cheeks" suggests soldier is young/baby-like and therefore unheroic • "knees grinding" suggests fear/clumsiness and is therefore unheroic • "pimply unattractive face" youthful, immature, unappealing, unheroic appearance
50.	2 marks awarded for detailed/insightful comment plus quotation/reference; 1 mark for more basic comment plus quotation/reference; 0 marks for quotation/reference alone. Possible answers are shown in the "Additional Guidance" column. (Marks may be awarded 2 + 2, 2 + 1 + 1, 1 + 1 + 1 + 1)	4	Possible answers include: • "notched iron splinters" extremely violent weaponry suggested by using the word "splinters" which are generally associated with wood and superficial injuries, here linked with iron and something more deadly is implied. Harsh consonant sounds underline this. • "the smoke and flame" description of hell-like environment • "the shaking and terror of the battlefield" 'shaking' here is ambiguous, could be the ground literally shaking with the force of explosions, or could refer to extreme fear felt by the soldiers • "bullet shower" bullets are 'raining down,' rapid, intense frequency • "hero briskly"/"wasn't much time he got" (soldier) has to respond to events without time to think/has to respond with unnatural speed/sense of life cut short • "bucking with tearing crashing screech" harsh violent word choice, participles suggest violent events happening simultaneously • "biff" ironically colloquial rendering of blow to his body • "put him to the ground" in battle soldier is victim of forces outwith his control • "mouth down in sand and gravel" the use of the word "mouth" here, rather than the more usual "face", suggests more brutality, perhaps conveying almost the "taste" of the battlefield and the indignity of his fall

242 ANSWERS FOR HIGHER ENGLISH

Question	Expected Answer(s)	Max Mark	Additional Guidance
51.	2 marks awarded for detailed/insightful comment plus quotation/reference; 1 mark for more basic comment plus quotation/reference; 0 marks for quotation/reference alone. Possible answers are shown in the "Additional Guidance" column. (Marks may be awarded 2 + 2, 2 + 1 + 1, 1 + 1 + 1 + 1)	4	Possible answers include: • The "no"…"or"…"or" construct/structure highlights the lack of recognition afforded to the soldier and his memory and therefore creates pity • "not many of his troop alive" prevalence/victory of death among soldier's companions creates pity • "their word would not be strong" soldiers' voices seen as weak/would be ignored in terms of their accounts of the battle • image of "the mouth of the field of slaughter" pity created through awareness of the soldiers' susceptibility to the (metaphorically) greedy appetite that war has for death • "great warrior" pity created by the ironic tone created in this expression, and also genuine sense of sympathy conveyed for the soldier's fate • "poor manikin" pity created by the use of diminutive term, and this is emphasised by addition of the word 'poor' • "he took a little weeping to my eyes" reference to the traditional Gaelic expression creates genuine sense of pity for the soldier
52.	Candidates may choose to answer in bullet points in this final question, or write a number of linked statements. Possible answers are shown in the "Additional Guidance" column.	10	Up to 2 marks can be achieved by identifying elements of commonality as identified in the question, ie how the theme of destruction is explored. A further 2 marks can be achieved for reference to the text given. 6 additional marks can be awarded for discussion of similar references to at least one other poem by MacLean. In practice this means: Identification of commonality (2) e.g. MacLean explores the destruction of community, relationships and individuals (1) challenging the readers to consider the negative impact of war, change in community, careless treatment of others in relationships (1) From the poem: 2 marks for detailed/insightful comment plus quotation/reference; 1 mark for more basic comment plus quotation/reference; 0 marks for quotation/reference alone. e.g. the ironic description of the "soldier"/"warrior" highlights his ordinary nature and encourages the reader to reflect on the impact of war on us all (2) From at least one other poem: as above for up to 6 marks Possible answers include: • *An Autumn Day* seemingly random death of six companions highlights the futility, chaos, destruction of war • *Hallaig* the destruction of Highland communities caused by the Clearances, and the sense of loss engendered by this • *Screapadal* destruction caused by the forced Clearances, and by the modern world's intrusive impact on traditional ways of life • *I Gave You Immortality* potentially destructive power of love and the pain it can cause • *Shores* the destructive force and power of the sea and time

ANSWERS FOR HIGHER ENGLISH **243**

Text 6 — *Poetry — Nil Nil* by Don Paterson

Question	Expected Answer(s)	Max Mark	Additional Guidance
53.	2 marks awarded for detailed/insightful comment plus quotation/reference; 1 mark for more basic comment plus quotation/reference; 0 marks for quotation/reference alone. Possible answers are shown in the "Additional Guidance" column. (Marks may be awarded 2, 1 + 1)	2	Possible answers include: • "zenith" suggests that this moment is the pinnacle of the club's history • "majestic" suggests stately and magnificent, McGrandle is a grandiose figure • "golden (hair)" suggests something of great value • "sprinting the length" suggests an athletic prowess worthy of celebration • "balletic (toe-poke)" suggests great grace/poise/ artfulness • "nearly bursting the roof of the net" hyperbolic statement emphasises the speaker's appreciation and effusiveness about this moment in the history of the club
54.	2 marks awarded for detailed/insightful comment plus quotation/reference; 1 mark for more basic comment plus quotation/reference; 0 marks for quotation/reference alone. Possible answers are shown in the "Additional Guidance" column. (Marks may be awarded 2 + 2, 2 + 1 + 1, 1 + 1 + 1 + 1)	4	Possible answers include: • "from here/it's all down" the phrase 'all down' suggests that there is no respite/decline is inevitable and complete • "pitch-sharing, pay-cuts, pawned silver" the list of worsening downturns emphasises the progression of the decline • "absolute sitters ballooned over open goals"/"dismal nutmegs" suggests decline in quality of the players • "(scores so) obscene" suggests defeats were becoming more humiliating/unacceptable • "nothing inhibits the fifty-year slide" suggests inevitability of long term decline • "then nobody" climax emphasises total absence of support • "stud-harrowed pitches" suggests neglect/ disrepair/lack of care
55.	For full marks both the community and the pilot need to be dealt with but not necessarily in equal measure. 2 marks awarded for detailed/insightful comment plus quotation/reference; 1 mark for more basic comment plus quotation/reference; 0 marks for quotation/reference alone. Possible answers are shown in the "Additional Guidance" column. (Marks may be awarded 2 + 2, 2 + 1 + 1, 1 + 1 + 1 + 1)	4	Possible answers include: Community • "stopped swings" suggests all vibrancy has gone from the community/lack of youth • "dead shanty-town" suggests desolation/temporary nature of things • "cul-de-sac" suggests total dead end/lack of direction/aimless Pilot • "all that remains" suggests that every other physical part of the pilot is gone from existence and the stone is all that is left • "lone fighter-pilot" suggests isolation and vulnerability which contributes to the tragedy • "burn … melt … igniting" the combination of these words — all indicating heat and possible explosion — suggests danger/death • "no one around to admire …" suggests lonely nature of death

244 ANSWERS FOR HIGHER ENGLISH

Question	Expected Answer(s)	Max Mark	Additional Guidance
56.	Candidates may choose to answer in bullet points in this final question, or write a number of linked statements. Possible answers are shown in the "Additional Guidance" column.	10	Up to 2 marks can be achieved by identifying elements of commonality as identified in the question, i.e. how poet explores the impact of loss. A further 2 marks can be achieved for reference to the extract given. 6 additional marks can be awarded for discussion of similar references to at least one other poem by Paterson. <u>In practice this means:</u> Identification of commonality (2) e.g. Loss can be profound and life changing (1) and is a fundamental part of human experience, e.g. love, innocence, community, identity (1) From this extract: 2 marks for detailed/insightful comment plus quotation/reference; 1 mark for more basic comment plus quotation/reference; 0 marks for quotation/reference alone. e.g. "black shell" describes the Skelly Dry Cleaners as a husk devoid of life which emphasises this once flourishing business has now failed, adding to the hopelessness of the community (2) From at least one other poem: as above for up to 6 marks Possible comments include: • *The Ferryman's Arms* inevitability of death causes speaker to lose sense of identity ("my losing opponent … left him there") leading to feelings of hopelessness/lack of control • *11:00 Baldovan* loss of innocence leads to uncertainty/insecurity about our place in the future ("I cannot know the little good it will do me") • *Waking with Russell* the speaker has lost his old self through the birth of his son and has now gained a brighter, richer future • *The Thread* the difficult circumstances around the son's birth led to a fear of loss and recognition that life is fragile • *Two Trees* separation of the trees represents a loss of security, however their continued growth/survival suggests the resilience of the human spirit

SECTION 2 — Critical Essay

Please see the assessment criteria for the Critical Essay on page 79.

Acknowledgements

Permission has been sought from all relevant copyright holders and Hodder Gibson is grateful for the use of the following:

An extract adapted from the article 'Goodbye birds. Goodbye butterflies. Hello… farmageddon' by Isabel Oakeshott © The Times/News Syndication, 19 January 2014 (2015 Reading for Understanding, Analysis and Evaluation pages 2 & 3);

The article 'Pasture to the Plate' by Audrey Ayton, taken from 'The Observer Supplement', 10 July 1994. Copyright Guardian News & Media Ltd 2017 (2015 Reading for Understanding, Analysis and Evaluation pages 3 & 4);

An extract from 'The Slab Boys' © 1982 John Byrne. 'The Slab Boys' was first performed at the Traverse Theatre, Edinburgh, on 6 April 1978. All rights whatsoever in this play are strictly reserved and application for performance etc. should be made to the Author's agent: Casarotto Ramsay & Associates Limited, Waverley House, 7-12 Noel Street, London W1F 8G (rights@casarotto.co.uk). No performance may be given unless a licence has been obtained (2015 Critical Reading pages 2 & 3);

An extract from 'The Cheviot, the Stag and the Black, Black Oil,' by John McGrath. © John McGrath, 1981. Published by Bloomsbury Methuen Drama, an imprint of Bloomsbury Publishing Plc. (2015 Critical Reading page 6);

An extract from 'Men Should Weep' © Ena Lamont Stewart, 1947. Reproduced by permission of Alan Brodie Representation Ltd (www.alanbrodie.com) (2015 Critical Reading pages 8 & 9);

An extract from 'Mother and Son' by Iain Crichton Smith, taken from 'The Red Door: The Complete English Stories 1949-76', published by Birlinn. Reproduced with permission of Birlinn Limited via PLSclear (2015 Critical Reading pages 12 & 13);

An extract from 'The Wireless Set' by George Mackay Brown, taken from 'A Time To Keep', published by Polygon. Reproduced with permission of Birlinn Limited via PLSclear (2015 Critical Reading pages 14 & 15);

An extract from 'The Trick is to Keep Breathing' by Janice Galloway, published by Vintage, reprinted by permission of The Random House Group Limited. © Janice Galloway 1989 (2015 Critical Reading page 16);

An extract from 'Sunset Song' by Lewis Grassic Gibbon, published by Jarrold Publishing, 1932. Public domain (2015 Critical Reading pages 18 & 19);

An extract from 'The Cone-Gatherers' by Robin Jenkins, published by Canongate Books Ltd. (2015 Critical Reading pages 20 & 21);

The poem 'To a mouse' by Robert Burns. Public domain (2015 Critical Reading pages 22 & 23);

The poem 'War Photographer' from 'Standing Female Nude' by Carol Ann Duffy. Published by Anvil Press Poetry, 1985. Copyright © Carol Ann Duffy. Reproduced by permission of the author c/o Rogers, Coleridge & White Ltd., 20 Powis Mews, London W11 1JN (2015 Critical Reading page 24);

The poem 'My Rival's House' by Liz Lochhead, taken from 'A Choosing: Selected Poems', published by Polygon. Reproduced with permission of Birlinn Limited via PLSclear (2015 Critical Reading page 26);

The poem 'Visiting Hour' by Norman MacCaig, taken from 'The Poems of Norman MacCaig', published by Polygon. Reproduced with permission of Birlinn Limited via PLSclear (2015 Critical Reading page 28);

An extract from 'An Autumn Day' by Sorley MacLean, taken from 'Caoir Gheal Leumraich/White Leaping Flame: collected poems in Gaelic with English translations', edited by Christopher Whyte and Emma Dymock 2011. Reproduced by permission of Carcanet Press Ltd (2015 Critical Reading page 30);

The poem 'Two Trees' from 'Rain' by Don Paterson. Published by Faber, 2004. Copyright © Don Paterson. Reproduced by permission of the author c/o Rogers, Coleridge & White Ltd., 20 Powis Mews, London W11 1JN (2015 Critical Reading page 32);

The article 'Rude, impulsive, sulky . . . still, let our 16-year-olds vote' by Catherine Bennett, taken from 'The Guardian', 14 October 2012. Copyright Guardian News & Media Ltd 2017 (2016 Reading for Understanding, Analysis and Evaluation pages 2 & 3);

The article 'Letting 16 year-olds vote in the EU referendum would be a car crash' by Julia Hartley-Brewer, taken from 'The Telegraph', 19 November 2015 © Telegraph Media Group Limited 2017 (2016 Reading for Understanding, Analysis and Evaluation pages 3 & 4);

An extract from 'The Slab Boys' © 1982 John Byrne. 'The Slab Boys' was first performed at the Traverse Theatre, Edinburgh, on 6 April 1978. All rights whatsoever in this play are strictly reserved and application for performance etc. should be made to the Author's agent: Casarotto Ramsay & Associates Limited, Waverley House, 7-12 Noel Street, London W1F 8G (rights@casarotto.co.uk). No performance may be given unless a licence has been obtained (2016 Critical Reading pages 2 & 3);

An extract from 'The Cheviot, the Stag and the Black, Black Oil,' by John McGrath. © John McGrath, 1981. Published by Bloomsbury Methuen Drama, an imprint of Bloomsbury Publishing Plc. (2016 Critical Reading pages 4 & 5);

An extract from 'Men Should Weep' © Ena Lamont Stewart, 1947. Reproduced by permission of Alan Brodie Representation Ltd (www.alanbrodie.com) (2016 Critical Reading pages 6 & 7);

An extract from 'The Crater' by Iain Crichton Smith, taken from 'The Red Door: The Complete English Stories 1949-76', published by Birlinn. Reproduced with permission of Birlinn Limited via PLSclear (2016 Critical Reading pages 8 & 9);

An extract from 'The Whaler's Return' by George Mackay Brown, taken from 'A Time To Keep', published by Polygon. Reproduced with permission of Birlinn Limited via PLSclear (2016 Critical Reading pages 10 & 11);

An extract from 'The Trick is to Keep Breathing' by Janice Galloway, published by Vintage, reprinted by permission of The Random House Group Limited. © Janice Galloway 1989 (2016 Critical Reading pages 12 & 13);

An extract from 'Sunset Song' by Lewis Grassic Gibbon, published by Jarrold Publishing, 1932. Public domain (2016 Critical Reading pages 14 & 15);

An extract from 'The Cone-Gatherers' by Robin Jenkins, published by Canongate Books Ltd. (2016 Critical Reading pages 16 & 17);

The poem 'A Poet's Welcome to His Love-Begotten Daughter' by Robert Burns. Public domain (2016 Critical Reading pages 18 & 19);

The poem 'Mrs Midas' from 'The Other Country' by Carol Ann Duffy. Published by Anvil Press Poetry, 1990. Copyright © Carol Ann Duffy. Reproduced by permission of the author c/o Rogers, Coleridge & White Ltd., 20 Powis Mews, London W11 1JN (2016 Critical Reading page 20);

The poem 'The Bargain' by Liz Lochhead, taken from 'A Choosing: Selected Poems', published by Polygon. Reproduced with permission of Birlinn Limited via PLSclear (2016 Critical Reading page 22);

The poem 'Memorial' by Norman MacCaig, taken from 'The Poems of Norman MacCaig', published by Polygon. Reproduced with permission of Birlinn Limited via PLSclear (2016 Critical Reading page 24);

The poem 'Shores' by Sorley MacLean, taken from 'Caoir Gheal Leumraich/White Leaping Flame: collected poems in Gaelic with English translations', edited by Christopher Whyte and Emma Dymock 2011. Reproduced by permission of Carcanet Press Ltd (2016 Critical Reading page 26);

The poem 'The Thread' from 'Landing Light' by Don Paterson. Published by Faber, 1993. Copyright © Don Paterson. Reproduced by permission of the author c/o Rogers, Coleridge & White Ltd., 20 Powis Mews, London W11 1JN (2016 Critical Reading page 28);

An extract from the article 'Want to exercise your mind? Try playstation' by Steven Johnson © The Times/News Syndication, 13 May 2005 (2017 Reading for Understanding, Analysis and Evaluation pages 2 & 3);

An extract from the article 'The Writing Is On The Wall' by Boris Johnson, taken from 'The Telegraph', 28 December 2006 © Boris Johnson/Telegraph Media Group Limited 2006 (2017 Reading for Understanding, Analysis and Evaluation pages 3 & 4);

An extract from 'The Slab Boys' © 1982 John Byrne. 'The Slab Boys' was first performed at the Traverse Theatre, Edinburgh, on 6 April 1978. All rights whatsoever in this play are strictly reserved and application for performance etc. should be made to the Author's agent: Casarotto Ramsay & Associates Limited, Waverley House, 7–12 Noel Street, London W1F 8G (rights@casarotto.co.uk). No performance may be given unless a licence has been obtained (2017 Critical Reading pages 2 & 3);

An extract from 'The Cheviot, the Stag and the Black, Black Oil,' by John McGrath. © John McGrath, 1981. Published by Bloomsbury Methuen Drama, an imprint of Bloomsbury Publishing Plc. (2017 Critical Reading pages 6 & 7);

An extract from 'Men Should Weep' © Ena Lamont Stewart, 1947. Reproduced by permission of Alan Brodie Representation Ltd (www.alanbrodie.com) (2017 Critical Reading pages 10 & 11);

An extract from 'The Red Door' by Iain Crichton Smith, taken from 'The Red Door: The Complete English Stories 1949–76', published by Birlinn. Reproduced with permission of Birlinn Limited via PLSclear (2017 Critical Reading pages 14 & 15);

An extract from 'Tartan' by George Mackay Brown, taken from the book 'A Time To Keep', published by Polygon. Reproduced with permission of Birlinn Limited via PLSclear (2017 Critical Reading pages 16 & 17);

An extract from 'The Trick is to Keep Breathing' by Janice Galloway, published by Vintage, reprinted by permission of The Random House Group Limited. © Janice Galloway 1989 (2017 Critical Reading pages 18 & 19);

An extract from 'Sunset Song' by Lewis Grassic Gibbon, published by Jarrold Publishing, 1932. Public domain (2017 Critical Reading page 20);

An extract from 'The Cone-Gatherers' by Robin Jenkins, published by Canongate Books Ltd. (2017 Critical Reading pages 22 & 23);

The poem 'Address To The Deil' by Robert Burns. Public domain (2017 Critical Reading pages 24 & 25);

The poem 'Valentine' from 'Mean Time' by Carol Ann Duffy. Published by Anvil Press Poetry, 1993. Copyright © Carol Ann Duffy. Reproduced by permission of the author c/o Rogers, Coleridge & White Ltd., 20 Powis Mews, London W11 1JN (2017 Critical Reading page 26);

The poem 'For my Grandmother Knitting' by Liz Lochhead, taken from 'A Choosing: Selected Poems', published by Polygon. Reproduced with permission of Birlinn Limited via PLSclear (2017 Critical Reading pages 28 & 29);

The poem 'Basking Shark' by Norman MacCaig, taken from 'The Many Days: Selected Poems of Norman MacCaig', published by Polygon. Reproduced with permission of Birlinn Limited via PLSclear (2017 Critical Reading page 30);

The poem 'Heroes' by Sorley MacLean, taken from 'Caoir Gheal Leumraich/White Leaping Flame: collected poems in Gaelic with English translations', edited by Christopher Whyte and Emma Dymock 2011. Reproduced by permission of Carcanet Press Ltd (2017 Critical Reading page 32);

The poem 'Nil Nil' from 'Nil Nil' by Don Paterson. Published by Faber, 1993. Copyright © Don Paterson. Reproduced by permission of the author c/o Rogers, Coleridge & White Ltd., 20 Powis Mews, London W11 1JN (2017 Critical Reading pages 34 & 35).